Keeping Goats

A PRACTICAL GUIDE

Debbie Kingsley

Keeping Goats

A PRACTICAL GUIDE

THE CROWOOD PRESS

First published in 2022 by
The Crowood Press Ltd
Ramsbury, Marlborough
Wiltshire SN8 2HR

enquiries@crowood.com

www.crowood.com

British Library Cataloguing-in-Publication Data
A catalogue record for this book is available from the British Library.

ISBN 978 0 7198 4001 2

Cover image credits
Front cover: left, author; top and bottom right, Gert van den Bosch; middle right, Liz Turner. Back cover: top, Gert van den Bosch; middle left, Tereza Fairbairn; middle right, Carolyn McAllister; bottom left, Carolyn McAllister; bottom right, Dunlop Dairy.

Typeset by Simon and Sons

Cover design by Sergey Tsvetkov

Printed and bound in India by Parksons Graphics

CONTENTS

CHAPTER 1

INTRODUCTION

Millhams, Dolton, December 1977. (Documentary photograph by James Ravilious for the Beaford Archive © Beaford Arts)

My introduction to the antics of goats was in my twenties while renting a cottage on a farm. One night I heard a rhythmic drumming coming from the stableyard, and went to investigate. The two young goats bought earlier that week were circling the walls of their brick stable at top speed, like a pair of motorcyclists on the wall of death. I approached just as the first one was about to fly out through the top half of the stable door, which I promptly shut. I had never seen anything like it, and it taught me to never underestimate goats.

In complete contrast, I found hand-milking a couple of goats wonderfully calming.

OPPOSITE: Golden Guernsey buck.

Sitting with my head tucked against the doe's flank, eyes closed, day dreaming quietly as I squirted the milk into the pail, was balm in a very busy life. The kitchen had soft goats' curds in muslin hanging from hooks, draining into bowls, and tasted delicious spread on oatcakes or homemade bread. This simple making of nutritious food from goats' milk has kept people fed for thousands of years, and in times of dizzying modernity continues to provide many with a sense of reassurance ('I can make my own food...') and calm ('...and I have to do it in a relaxed manner').

There are an absolutely stonking one billion goats in the world give or take one or two, with more than half of them in Asia (China, India, Pakistan and Bangladesh); not enough for each person in the world, but every group of eight people could have a goat to share.

Goats reflect the earliest of livestock farming and domestication, and the continued existence of wild herds found from England to the Himalayas show in contrast just how adaptable our domestic goats are, thriving on the lives we keepers give them. It's believed that goats were domesticated over 10,500 years ago: they originated from the Bezoar ibex in the Middle East, and spread from there across the globe. It's not surprising that goats were targeted for domestication as providers of milk, meat, skins, fibre, fuel (dried dung), parchment, food and liquid carriers (horns, stomach, bladder and intestines) and musical instruments, and as agile, sure-footed beasts of burden.

Lynton feral goat on the cliffs.

Goats appear in the Bible, in mythology, astrology, in folk tales and fables, in art (Chagall has them playing violins), and as satanic priapic mischievous creatures, half man, half goat. In modern times we recognize a straggle of nimble, skipping goats with tinkling bells around their necks as a charming troupe in opening film sequences taking us to a pastoral past and a hand-to-mouth, simpler and harsher existence than our own. But goats give comfort too, their presence telling us that hunger, thirst and lack of clothing are not pressing concerns for their keepers.

Goats are full of contradictions. They thrive on harsh, rocky terrain, yet in domesticity are needy in their desire for shelter. They browse with abandon, making the most of wild herbs, plants and trees, but in our care are both picky and wasteful with their food. They relish drinking from a mountain stream, yet turn their noses up at a clump of leaves in the drinking bowl. They are independent explorers into every possible mischief, but love routine. They are free spirits, yet will follow their owner like a pet dog. They are anything but boring, and will constantly keep you on your toes.

Take a deep breath as you take on board the crucial information about the legal stuff and potential ailments, as both can tax the brain, and consider them pragmatically as part of your goat-keeping life, which will have many joys. This book is a beginner's guide to keeping goats, full of information that will enable you to put in place what is required for having happy, healthy, productive goats. It's not possible to guarantee anyone a problem-free goat experience, but with guidance, plus your own watchfulness and intelligent observation, you will build the knowledge for successful and enjoyable goat-keeping.

CHAPTER 2

WHY KEEP GOATS?

It's a tricky thing, determining whether livestock is something you want in your life, and if so, which species will best suit. There comes a point when all the reading, the watching of videos and television programmes, and visiting agricultural shows turns into a decision – that goats are (or are not) for you, and that it's time to do something about it. Keeping animals is not something to enter into lightly, as goats will have a significant impact on your life and how you spend your time.

It's worth expending some effort asking yourself why you want to keep goats. If you are after healthy, low-cholesterol meat with

zero food miles and absolute provenance, goat meat is a fantastic option. If the idea of making goat-milk ice cream, clotted cream, butter and cheeses appeals, you're on to a winner. If you love spending your time out of doors and have no worries about dealing with muck, urine-soaked straw, birth fluids, mud, farmyard smells both rich and fairly ghastly, then goats won't faze you.

If you have the funds or DIY ability to put up excellent stock fencing, a goat shelter, possibly a milking parlour and more, having goats will keep you occupied and entertained for years on end. If you are happy to create and stick with a routine, you'll be temperamentally suited to meeting the demands of goats. And if

OPPOSITE: Capra Grigia goats.

Boer kids on a hayrack.

the idea of demanding, potentially noisy, always energetic, inquisitive and amusing additions to your patch of land appeals, you're sorted.

With over three hundred goat breeds worldwide, goats are kept for their milk, meat, horns, fibre and skins; they are the ultimate smallholder animal.

THE PROS AND CONS OF GOAT KEEPING

There are many positives to keeping goats, and with more than 100,000 of them in the UK, lots of people clearly agree. There are many local goat clubs, which translates into a multitude of human advice sources available to the new keeper. Goats are happy to browse where other livestock would be confounded, and they can access the most difficult-to-reach places – which does, of course, have negative implications, as you, their keeper, need to be able to access those areas too. But they (mostly) seem to like people, which makes handling them a pleasure.

Goats may be a better option for clearing brushy areas than pigs – they will certainly be less destructive of the soil. Dairy breeds will provide plenty of milk for the home and be less daunting to keep than cows, and are the ideal choice if members of the family are intolerant to cows' milk. They don't need vast tracts of land to thrive, but this does mean you will need to bring their food to them – so forget the gym, as goat keeping has a fitness regime built in!

Goats browsing.

The challenges should not be ignored. Fencing has to be of the very best if you want anything to survive being explored and destroyed, and access to shelter is needed at all times, unless the weather is guaranteed to stay fair. The expense of providing forage (hay) year round has to be taken into consideration, and you may need to spend time collecting browse, whether tree hay, brash or other plants. Most veterinary medications are not licensed for goats so you will have to find a good goat vet (not always easy), and create and implement a tailor-made health plan with them. Whereas cows and sheep tend to avoid most toxic plants if given alternatives, goats will eat things that can make them very ill, so you need to be vigilant. And if you are milking your goats, there is no time off.

THE DIFFERENCES BETWEEN GOATS AND SHEEP

The phrase 'shepherds protect sheep from getting injured by their environment, while goatherds protect the environment from their goats' is marvellously apt, if somewhat sweeping. I've always found that individual sheep can get themselves into all sorts of trouble given the opportunity, whereas goats actively seek out those opportunities. But it does warn the prospective keeper that preparedness is all. The environment in which you keep your goats needs careful consideration so that their curiosity doesn't get the better of you, or at least not too often. If you are pondering on whether to keep sheep or goats, this table might help you to think things through. You can always keep both, of course.

The Differences between Goats and Sheep

	Goats	*Sheep*
Agility	Off the scale agile – supreme athletes from limbo dancing under narrow gaps to scaling walls.	Agile, in particular hill and mountain breeds.
Vocality	Can be very conversational, or fairly quiet; when a doe is in heat they are very noisy. Anglo Nubians are known for being particularly vocal. Bleating in otherwise quiet goats can indicate a problem. Not feeding treats can help avoid goats screaming every time you pass by.	Mainly quiet unless under stress or calling to young. When a sheep is bleating you investigate in order to resolve a problem (either that, or you're late with their feed, which is normally only required around lambing time).
Odour	Bucks in the breeding season stink. A few people don't mind the smell – most find it vile.	Rams in the breeding season have a fairly pungent smell, which you can detect as you approach their area, but it's not overpowering.
Behaviour	Goats can be very pet-like in their behaviour, keen to be with, and to follow their keeper. Can be destructive, and are extremely inquisitive about everything in their environment, which has both pros and cons. Head butting is normal behaviour between goats – but don't allow them to butt you.	Apart from those that are bottle fed as lambs and petted, sheep look to their flock for companionship. Individuals can be friendly, but the natural sheep prey instinct to flee is strong.
Social organization	The herd has a natural hierarchy and structure – goats are social creatures and shouldn't be kept alone.	The flock has a natural hierarchy and structure – sheep are social creatures and shouldn't be kept alone.
Feeding habits	Browsers rather than grazers, with browse making up approximately 60 per cent of their diet. Access to hay and mineral supplements is required year round.	Grazers rather than browsers. What they browse is approximately 10-15 per cent of their diet. Hay should only be provided in the winter months.
Cost	Tend to be more expensive to purchase and keep.	Less expensive to purchase and keep (there are exceptions for highly desirable individuals).
Commercial potential	There is a growing and developing market for goats, their meat and their dairy produce. Lack of availability keeps prices high, with just 105,000 goats in the UK.	Existing, well-developed market. Prices fluctuate nationally and globally. There are 23 million sheep in the UK.
Milk yield	Dairy doe: 3-5ltr per day.	Milking ewe: 2ltr per day.
Gestation period	Approximately 150 days (143-157).	Approximately 147 days (144-152).
Season	Goats come into season every 21 days in the autumn until bred.	Sheep come into season every 17 days in the autumn until bred.

	Goats	**Sheep**
Foot care	Goats may need their feet trimmed regularly, but only when necessary.	Best practice advice is to only trim sheep's feet when absolutely necessary/genuinely overgrown. Inappropriate trimming increases the risk of bacterial spread and long-term hoof injury.
Prolificacy	Goats regularly have multiple births, with triplets and quadruplets not uncommon.	It has been known for ewes to give birth to up to six lambs, but this is most uncommon. The usual number of lambs is two, with frequent singles and triplets.
Fencing needs	Excellent fencing is required (*see* Chapter 4).	Good stock fencing is required.
Horns	There are no polled (hornless) goat breeds, although a few individuals are born without horns. Do not confuse polled with disbudded: many kids are disbudded in the first week of life (by the vet) so that their horns don't develop. Angoras and Boers are often kept horned, while dairy breeds are mostly disbudded.	Many sheep breeds are naturally polled, in some breeds the males are horned and the females polled, and others have horned males and females, sometimes with multiple horns (four or six). In horned breeds, the males have larger, thicker horns than the females.
Fibre	Cashmere and Angora from fibre breeds.	Wool from most breeds apart from hair sheep and self-shedding sheep.
Meat	Delicious, low in fat.	Delicious. Nearly twice the calories of goat.
Tails	Naturally short-tailed.	Apart from the northern European short-tailed breeds, sheep have naturally long tails (often docked shortly after birth).
Shelter	Goats have little insulating fat (and unless a fibre breed, a thin coat), so must be provided with a built shelter against wind and rain.	In all but the most severe weather sheep manage well with the shelter of trees and hedges because of their good wool and fat insulation.
Water	Goats will not drink water that is in any way contaminated – clean water must be provided at all times.	Sheep prefer (and should be given) clean water, but are less fussy than goats if leaves or other natural detritus collect in their drinking trough.
Parasites	Goats do not build resistance to intestinal parasites.	Healthy adults build significant resistance to intestinal worms.
Lifespan	8-12 years. Bucks 8-10, does 11-12 and longer if not bred after 10 years (up to 16-18 years). The record is 22 years.	10-12 years. The record is an astonishing 28 years.
Space requirements	2-3 goats plus their kids per acre. Lower numbers of 1-2 goats per acre on areas of brush.	3-5 ewes plus their lambs per acre.
Entertainment value	If you have a GSOH, high.	They have their moments!

CHAPTER 3

LEGAL MATTERS

Let's start with a few quick words of reassurance that implementing the legal aspects of keeping goats should be neither time-consuming nor complex. There are things to learn about and requirements that you must not shirk, and it can all feel quite new for the first-time livestock keeper – but the reality is that this will take minutes of your time over a year, not days of sweat and toil. The part that is difficult and time-consuming is building

OPPOSITE: Rhubarb the goat and hens.

your knowledge of the rules; once grasped, your goats, not the paperwork, can have your full attention.

The first concept to get your head round is that whether you keep a couple of goats as pets or have a herd of hundreds, the rules apply equally to all. Goats are categorized as livestock (food-producing animals), and there is no distinction with regard to your legal obligations between commercial and hobby keepers, and no exemptions for the most pocket-sized of smallholdings.

The rules do change, and it is the responsibility of each livestock keeper to keep up to date with any new requirements; check for new regulations at www.gov.uk. The contact details for the various bodies given in this chapter are all in the further information sources in the appendices.

STEP ONE: REGISTER YOUR HOLDING

Registering your land (even if it's a large back garden suitable for hosting a couple of goats) means acquiring a County Parish Holding (CPH) number for the land where the livestock will be kept; there is no charge for this. The main purpose of the CPH number is to identify and trace the location of livestock; it's a unique nine-digit number, the first two digits relating to the county, the next three to the parish, and the last four digits are unique to the keeper: for example 12/345/6789. To apply for your CPH number, contact the Rural Payments Agency in England, Rural Payments Wales in Wales, and Rural Payments and Services in Scotland (there are no CPH numbers required in Ireland or Northern Ireland). If you intend to keep your goats on someone else's land you will need a CPH number if you are responsible for them.

Once you have your CPH number you can move livestock to your holding under a general licence (usually known as a movement licence; more on that below). You must register land within a month of starting to keep animals, but in practice, because you need the CPH number to complete the movement licence in order to bring your animals home, it makes sense to get this sorted as soon as you decide it's time to have some livestock.

SECOND STEP: REGISTER AS A GOAT KEEPER

The next requirement is to register as a goat keeper with the Animal and Plant Health Agency (APHA), which is also free. You will be asked for your CPH number as a reference, and can register over the phone. The APHA will give you a unique herd mark – UK, followed by a six-digit number. You must do this within thirty days of livestock moving on to the land, but you can get it beforehand, which will save hassle at a time when you are getting busily acquainted with your new goats. The herd mark is the information you will need when ordering ear tags or other identifiers for your goats.

THIRD STEP: IDENTIFYING INDIVIDUAL GOATS

The majority of goats are identified using double ear tags (one tag in each ear), but you can use one ear tag plus other options (*see* the table below). Goat identifying tags have the herd-mark number of the holding on which they were born, plus a unique number for that animal. Goats keep the same tags in for life, so the first goats brought on to your holding will have tags from their place of birth; you do not change these tags. The first kids born on your holding will be the first to be identified with your own herd mark, plus their individual number, starting with '1'. Goats must be identified within six months of birth for intensively reared stock (defined as animals housed overnight, which is the most likely scenario for goats), or within nine months for extensively reared stock (those not housed overnight), or when they leave your holding, whichever is first.

Goats for breeding and those to be kept beyond twelve months of age must have two tags (with identical information on both). You can choose whether or not one of these identifiers is an electronic identification (EID) tag, which contains an electronic chip that holds the same information as is written visibly on the tag. If a goat is intended for export then one of its tags must be an EID. All goat EID ear tags are yellow. A non-EID tag is called a visual tag and can be any colour that your chosen ear tag manufacturer produces (apart from yellow, black or red), and both tags must bear the same individual number.

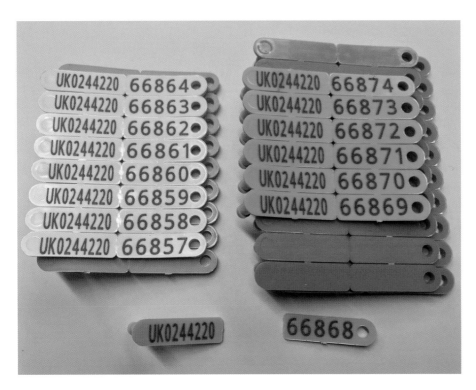

Two-part visual ear tags.

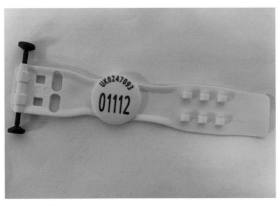

Pastern band.

Pastern band closed.

ALTERNATIVES TO DOUBLE EAR-TAGGING

For keepers preferring to use a single tag there are alternatives for the second identifier: a pastern (leg) band, a scannable bolus EID, which is ingested by the animal, or a scannable injectable EID. Ear tags or pasterns on animals with bolus EIDs must be black and have a 'B' printed on them, and ear tags on goats with injectable EIDs must be black and have an 'I' printed on them. EID ear tags and EID pasterns must be yellow (unless they are replacements applied on a holding other than the one where the animal was born, in which case they are red), and EID ear tags should, where possible, be attached to the left ear. Replacement ear tags applied on a holding other than the one where the animal was born must be red, unless they are replicas (an exact replacement of the original tag).

IDENTIFICATION OPTIONS

First identifier	Second identifier	Can be exported
Yellow EID ear tag	Visual ear tag	Yes
Yellow EID ear tag	Tattoo	No
Yellow EID ear tag	Pastern (leg) band	Yes
EID bolus	Black ear tag or pastern	Yes
Yellow EID pastern (leg) band	Visual ear tag	No
Visual ear tag	Visual ear tag	No
Visual ear tag	Tattoo	No
Visual ear tag	Pastern (leg) band	No
EID injectable chip (in groin)	Black ear tag	No

Two-part and one-piece ear tags.

Ear-tag applicators.

For goats intended for slaughter before twelve months of age a single identifier is fine, and it need not be an EID. The single ear tag, also known as a slaughter tag, only needs to display your herd mark and doesn't need to include an individual identity number for the animal. If you later decide to keep a kid with a single slaughter tag beyond a year old, you must replace the single tag with a pair of identifiers before its first birthday.

On a practical note, goat ears are less robust than those of a sheep, and a combination of delicate ears, a desire to stick their heads in the most inconvenient of places, and with some breeds having ears of distinctive length, it's important to use tags that minimize the risk of getting caught and so tearing the ear. Two-part tags can be purchased, or if you use single-piece tags, do cut the hinge part with a pair of snips so that the two parts swing and don't form a trap hazard.

The pastern band is a tamperproof ankle bracelet and is ideal for animals with damaged or sensitive ears, and it doesn't require an applicator to put it on. Note that each make and type of ear tag requires a specific applicator, and these are not generic. Even if you always purchase ear tags from the same manufacturer, check if their design has been updated when you buy new ones, as you might need a new applicator too.

MOVEMENT LICENCES

You need to complete a licence form every time you move livestock on or off your premises – whether to slaughter, buying in or selling stock, taking them to a show, or taking your goats to a holding with a different CPH; this is a free service. Increasingly these forms are completed online, and in time the system is likely to become entirely digital, although at the time of writing a paper-based option is still available. A new Livestock Information Service using electronic identification for all livestock (cattle, sheep, pigs, goats and deer) is being launched in England, with similar services in development by the Scottish, Welsh and Northern Ireland devolved administrations. The England service will be completing its transition during 2022, and goat keepers can access this either through the Animal Reporting and Movement Service (ARAMS) site www.arams.co.uk or by checking out the Livestock Information website www.livestockinformation.org.uk.

You don't need a movement licence if the movement is to or from the following:

- A vet (for emergency treatment).
- Land with the same CPH number.
- Land bordering your holding with a different CPH number, where you send or receive animals from frequently, on foot and without contact with other livestock.
- Common land bordering your holding that you've registered as linked to your holding.

Food Chain Information

When you take goats to the abattoir, you will need to complete the relevant food chain information included on the movement licence. This confirms (or otherwise) that the animals being taken to slaughter have passed the withdrawal period of any administered medication, so that the carcase is fit to enter the human food chain.

Movement Standstill

Movement standstill is a disease-damping measure designed to slow down the rate of spread of disease. Whenever cattle, sheep, goats or pigs are moved on to a holding, no cattle, sheep or goats may move off for a period of six days. For example, if you move a goat on to your holding, no goat (including the one just brought on), nor any cow, sheep or pig, can move off your holding until the six-day standstill has elapsed. The six-day standstill means that animals can be moved on the seventh day.

There are some exemptions to movement standstill. You can move livestock off your land during the standstill period if you are moving them direct to the abattoir. If you are lucky enough to have commoner grazing rights, animals may move between common grazing and its associated in-bye land without triggering a standstill period. Breeding goats of either gender do not trigger a six-day standstill on premises to which they are moved for breeding, provided that

they are isolated for six days in an APHA-approved isolation facility before they leave the premises of origin.

Goats may attend shows without having to observe a movement standstill period on the premises of departure, provided that they have been isolated from all other non-show animals on their premises of departure in an APHA-approved isolation facility for six days before attending the show. On return to the premises of departure, the show goats must be kept in an APHA-approved isolation facility for six days or the standstill will be imposed. You will still need to complete a movement licence for all standstill-exempt movements.

APHA-APPROVED ISOLATION FACILITY

If you plan to show your goats or take them to another holding for breeding, you may find it helpful, if you have regular on and off movements, to set up an isolation unit. The forms for doing so are available from APHA, and the facility will need to be approved by a veterinary inspector confirming that the required criteria have been satisfied. An isolation unit, whether pasture or building, must be dedicated for livestock isolation purposes and be physically separate (a minimum of 3m (10ft)) from any other livestock buildings or pastures. Goats using the isolation facility must either have been at an approved agricultural show(s) or be about to go to a show(s); be breeding goats of either gender moving to premises for breeding; or be moving to or from an artificial insemination centre. Manure and effluent from isolation facilities must not come into contact with other livestock, and dedicated protective clothing and footbaths must be used in the isolation facility.

HOLDING REGISTER

To protect the health of your livestock and to make it easier for APHA and other relevant bodies to trace your animals, you must keep a register of the animals on your holding. This will need to include information about your holding, tags and replacement tags in use, and the goat movements on and off your holding.

Electronic versions are freely available to download from www.gov.uk (search for 'sample sheep and goat holding register'). In addition to movements, the register should include births, deaths and details of any replacement identifiers if identical replica tags are not used. The holding register has to be kept for ten years from the end of the calendar year in which the last entry was made.

Holding register.

VETERINARY MEDICINE RECORD

It's a legal requirement to keep a record of all veterinary medicines administered to food-producing animals, including those administered by your vet or given in feed, even if you never intend to eat your goats or use their milk. The record must show the name of the medicine used, the supplier, the date of purchase, the date of administering the medicine (and end date if it is over a period), the quantity of medicine used, the identity and number of the goat(s) treated, and the withdrawal period for meat and milk as appropriate, the batch number of the medicine, and the expiry dates.

The batch number will be written on the packaging, and the withdrawal period will either be written on the packaging or included in the datasheet inside. If you lose the accompanying datasheet from any medicine you can find them all online at www.noahcompendium.co.uk.

There are livestock medicine record books for recording all the necessary detail available from most agricultural merchants, and electronic versions are freely available to download. Do complete your medicine records immediately after any treatment when the information is fresh in your mind and the details on the packaging are still legible. You must keep records of treatment given to animals, and of animal mortality, for at least three years.

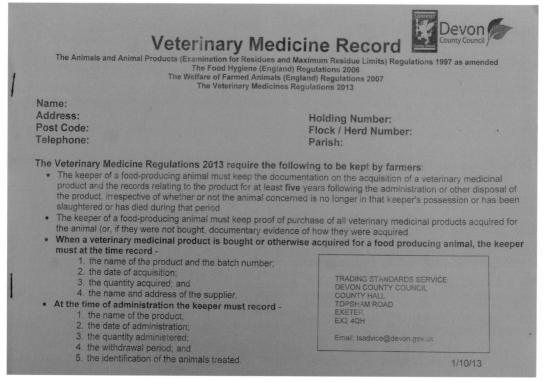

Veterinary medicine record.

TRANSPORT CERTIFICATE

You must have your competence independently assessed if you transport goats by road on journeys over 65km (40 miles) in connection with an economic activity. If your goats are kept purely as a hobby and there is no commercial element to your goat keeping (you don't sell goats, meat, milk or dairy products), then this will not be relevant. The assessment will be:

- a theory test for journeys over 65km and up to eight hours
- a practical assessment of competence including animal handling, and if required, driving skills for journeys over eight hours.

If assessed as competent, you will receive a certificate of competence. The certificate will be specific to your role of either transporter or attendant, the length of journeys you take,

and the species you transport. Certificates of competence are valid for life. You also need to ensure you have access to a suitable trailer to transport your livestock.

TOWING TRAILERS

Do check whether your car is suitable for towing a livestock trailer, and take account of the additional weight when loaded. A full car licence allows you to tow trailers weighing no more than 750kg, and you can tow heavier trailers with a car as long as the total weight of the vehicle and trailer isn't more than 3,500kg.

DISPOSAL OF FALLEN STOCK

Fallen (dead) stock cannot be buried or burned because of the risk of disease spread through groundwater or air pollution.

Instead, animals must be taken to, or collected by, an approved knacker, hunt kennel, incinerator or renderer, either by private arrangement or through the National Fallen Stock Scheme. There is a charge for removing deadstock. Place your deadstock as close as possible to the entry of your property (contained and covered), so that the removal vehicle doesn't have to drive through your holding to collect, as they are something of a bio-hazard.

FARM HEALTH AND SAFETY GUIDANCE

If you are running your holding as a business, your activities come within the Health and Safety legislation and you must acquaint yourself with the requirements. There are a number of courses run by the Health and Safety Executive for farmers, and they also publish free online guides to health and safety in agriculture.

FEEDING RESTRICTIONS

It may be all too tempting to take your lunchtime leftovers and give them to your goats, but the general rule in the UK is that once any food has been in a kitchen (domestic, professional or industrial) it is illegal for it to be fed to livestock, and this extends to pet goats and those not intended for meat. This doesn't just refer to foods of animal origin, but includes the vegetable portion too, due to the risk of cross contamination. As with human food poisoning, work surfaces, hands, utensils, taps, chopping boards and more become contaminated with micro-organisms, which are then transferred to other foodstuffs. Bacteria such as salmonella or campylobacter transfer easily, for example,

from raw poultry to salad or hunks of bread, causing potentially serious human illness, and the risk is the same for your livestock.

Due to the risk of cross contamination the ban on feeding kitchen waste to livestock includes vegetarian kitchens, where products of animal origin such as milk are used in food preparation. Only if you live in a fully vegan household may you feed your kitchen scraps to pet livestock.

However, if you have a vegetable garden there may be veggie treats that your goats will enjoy, plus any suitable weeds you've patiently hoed. All you need do is take these straight from the garden to your goats without going through the kitchen first.

PLANNING PERMISSION FOR GOAT HOUSING

Planning permission for small-scale goat housing is not usually necessary, and Permitted Development Rights exist for erecting structures in certain situations. Simple structures such as temporary, mobile or other structures used for the purposes of agriculture will not require permission. However, regulations will differ between commercial and hobby keepers related to the scale of the operation, so check with your local planning authority before you start any building work.

FURTHER LEGAL REQUIREMENTS

For information on the legal requirements for home slaughter, the abattoir, using skins and horns and selling your meat, *see* Chapter 10. For the legal requirements for selling milk and dairy products, *see* Chapter 11; and for those related to selling skincare products made from goat milk, and driving or walking your goats beyond your premises, *see* Chapter 14.

CHAPTER 4

LAND AND ACCOMMODATION

Cuppers Piece, Beaford, February 1983. (Documentary photograph by James Ravilious for the Beaford Archive © Beaford Arts)

HOW MANY GOATS CAN I KEEP ON MY LAND?

Being herd animals, you need to have more than one goat, but beyond a pair, how many have you actually got room for? There are huge variables as to what an acreage can cope with, depending on the size and breed of your goat, the quality of the land and the forage it produces, how much hay you are buying in, the wilfulness of the weather in any particular year, how much of the year your goats are

OPPOSITE: Pygmy goat.

goats and their kids. Scrubby land with a lot of brush is more difficult to benchmark, so depending on the desirability of what's growing, you might find an acre of scrub can sustain just one to two goats, or significantly more. Another approach to estimate stocking rates is by weight: this amounts to a total of 225–350kg (500–770lb) of goat per acre on quality goat pasture.

It's all very well having a mathematical benchmark, but as with any livestock, start with low numbers in order to assess how the land responds across the seasons. It is much easier to add to the herd if you've initially underestimated suitable stocking rates than having to dispose of excess goats you've now named and to which you've become attached. Nor do you need to fill your land with the maximum possible number of goats! If you are breeding, you'll be increasing your flock exponentially and will need room to cope with growing kids. Your particular regime for managing goats may differ considerably from that of your neighbours, even on similar ground, so the final stocking rate you come up with after a year or two of trial and error could be significantly higher than the given benchmark.

English goats on their climbing frame.

housed, and what supplementary feed you are offering (*see* Chapter 8). A practical guideline to get you started is that an acre of good, productive pasture can sustain two to three

Anglo Nubians at grass.

HOUSING AND SHELTER

There are many choices when it comes to providing shelter for your goats, depending on your preference and budget, and how you see your goat-keeping life. A simple three-sided open barn with permanent access to a field might suit your purposes, large enough to house an undercover hay rack and be closed off with hurdles when you wish to contain the goats for kidding or handling. You may have existing stables, a garage or a cattle shed, or some other building that you intend to convert for goats, or you may be planning to build something new for your lucky herd.

For the most part, goats can be turned out during the day unless the weather is vicious (*see* Chapter 11 for information on grazing and dairy goats). Regarding housing, whether a conversion, a make-do-and-mend or purpose-built arrangement, bigger (and higher) is always better, and there are some important considerations to take into account.

![Boer doelings in an open-fronted shed.]

Boer doelings in an open-fronted shed.

English goats in their shelter.

A roundhouse for goats.

HOUSING REQUIREMENTS

Communal goat housing is common, where goats are managed in a way similar to housed cattle, with shared areas; this suits the herd structure, rather than goats being housed in individual 'stables', like horses. Even in communal spaces there will need to be some separation: a separate area for weaned kids, a separate place for bucklings, and so on. Goat housing with individual pens does have the benefit of requiring no additional space for kidding; in communal housing individual bonding pens will need creating, and hurdles are perfect for this. Individual pens also allow for specific treatment or feeding of particular goats. Unless being used for quarantine or isolation purposes, individual pens benefit from mesh panels so that goats can see each other and still feel part of the herd.

Communal goat barn.

Goat pen for males.

Space: Indoor space allowances depend on whether goats are individually penned or live in a communal barn area. For the former, allow 4sq m (4.80sq yd) of floor space per goat, and for communal housing a minimum of 2sq m (2.4sq yd) per goat. A more generous allowance is needed if you perceive bullying issues. In communal housing any horned goats need to be housed separately from those without horns.

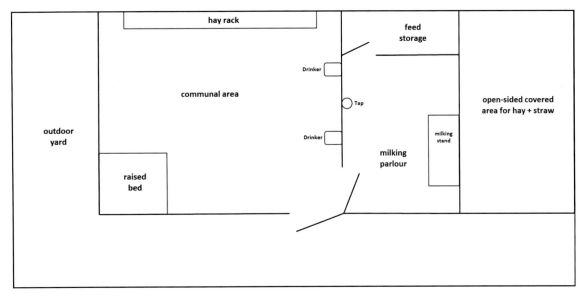

Simple communal barn layout.

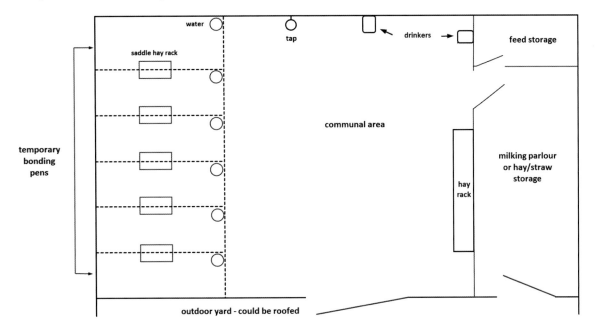

Communal barn with temporary kidding area.

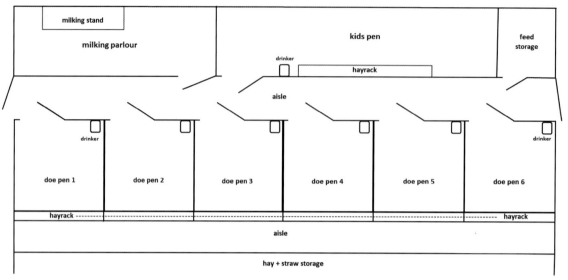

Housing with individual pens layout.

Ventilation: Your building must be well ventilated to ensure a flow of fresh air and the natural removal of stale and moist air, while being free of draughts. Position doors/openings away from prevailing winds, and install a vented ridge at the apex of the roof.

Materials: The materials of your housing should ensure there is no moisture condensation on roofs, walls and other surfaces, as moist air brings a high risk of pneumonia to your goats. Avoid corrugated tin unless it is of the anti-condensation type. Fibre cement roofing is ideal. Make sure your housing is free of anything on which a goat could hurt itself, including loops of baler twine, protruding nails, empty feed sacks, a

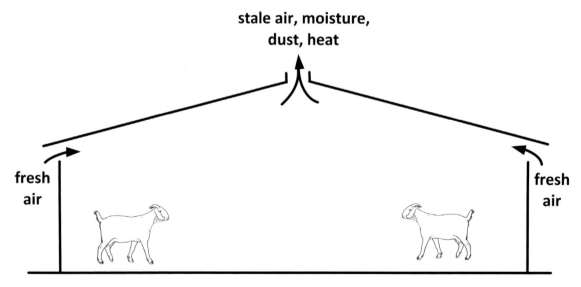

Goat housing ventilation.

mislaid pair of foot trimmers, and so on (the list is endless).

Size does count: Larger and taller buildings offer better air space for your goats, which supports good respiratory health, and make your life as chief goat housekeeper and waiter a whole lot easier. The absolute minimum height has to allow you good standing access for cleaning and tending to your goats and for them to stand upright on their hind legs at full stretch. If you can, allow a minimum 2–3m (6.6–9.8ft) at the ridge, and taller is better. If you live in a very cold climate, large spaces can be too chilly for your goats, so make the housing fit for your region and ensure that additional bedding is provided at the coldest times of year.

Floor surfaces: Preferences for floor surfaces vary. Earth floors have their place as they allow urine to drain and can be kept hygienic with a regular covering of hydrated lime. Concrete floors are easier to muck out, are less attractive to rats, can be made slightly ridged to avoid slipping, and floors can be installed with a slight slope to allow draining. Straw bedding will be needed whatever the floor surface.

Dividing the space: The design of internal partitions and gates will vary depending on how you wish to split things up, but a minimum height of 1.3m (4.3ft) is recommended. Meshed gates rather than solid partitions are useful, as they allow individually penned goats to see each other. If you are separating does and kids overnight for kid-at-foot milking, they can be in neighbouring secure spaces and still in full view of each other. If you keep a buck you will need separate housing for him.

Raised beds: Because goats are so agile and draughts are often at ground level, you can create raised bed areas on which goats can loaf and sleep.

Water: Fresh water must be available to all your goats at all times, so access to a piped water supply is essential. If using individual pens you can attach ring holders outside the pen to take feed and water buckets, and provide a gap for the goat to put its head through; this prevents the goat defecating in its water. Alternatively put automatic bowl drinkers in each pen at 60cm (24in) high (plus step) for adults, and 40cm (16in) high for young animals. For communal housing

Raised goat bed.

Drinker with step access.

Feeding arrangements.

Hayrack with step access.

provide enough drinkers to avoid pushing and queues, with one drinker for up to ten lactating goats or fifteen dry goats.

Feeding arrangements: Feed buckets in individual pens should be in ring holders either outside the pen, or if inside, positioned too high for the goats to defecate in. For communal housing, consider using a feed barrier that goats put their heads through to eat, with enough space for every goat to eat simultaneously. Salt licks or lumps of rock salt should be available to all goats.

Hay mangers or racks should be positioned so that goats cannot climb on to them and spoil the hay with their feet, pee or poo. Use mangers or racks that they can't pull too much out of at one time, as anything dropped on the floor will be wasted, and smaller mesh minimizes the risk of a goat or kid getting any part of itself stuck. Lidded racks are particularly useful for minimizing spillage. Avoid haynets of the type used for horses, as goats can get tangled in them and kids can strangle themselves.

Play area: For kids and young goats an inside play area is much appreciated; this might be a sturdy table that they can lie on or under, a tree trunk, or something more imaginative with steps, ramps and different heights.

Gutters and drains: Guttering and drainage are essential for ensuring that rainwater doesn't simply soak into the wall and rot your building.

Electrics: Electrical wiring, switches, lights and sockets must all be kept well out of reach of the most agile goat. Protect wiring with conduit, and use metal-clad sockets that are waterproof and rated for outdoor use.

Milking parlour: If you are milking, a place dedicated as a milking parlour can be created in a discrete area of your housing. This should be walled and have a concrete floor, and any materials used should be of a type that can be kept scrupulously clean.

Hygiene and access: Ensure that all gates and passageways are wide enough to accommodate whatever mucking out and cleaning equipment you intend to use, whether that be a large wheelbarrow, a dumpy sack for hauling fresh straw, and for people to manoeuvre through.

Storage: Include space to store straw, hay and other goat feed. Make sure these cannot be accessed by your goats – devouring large quantities of concentrated feed can have fatal consequences.

MUCK MANAGEMENT

Housed goats need to be mucked out daily to maintain hygiene and good health, so design housing to make this a quick and easy task by making gates and passageways wide enough to accommodate whatever equipment you intend to use. Manure should be stored in a dedicated muck-heap area that cannot create run-off into water courses. This should be composted down for spreading as desirable natural farmyard manure on the land.

OUTDOOR FACILITIES

There may be times when your goats need to be confined to barracks. Having a well-fenced concreted yard attached to your barn means the goats can still exercise securely outside. The yard is also somewhere you can place unwieldy armfuls of browse for them to enjoy.

The concept of play areas for livestock may seem a little strange, but goats being gymnasts, explorers and perpetually curious, some solid climbing opportunities will help keep them out of mischief. Large rocks, chunks of tree trunk, big cable-reel drums, or much fancier climbing ramps and platforms are all much appreciated and create hours of fun for your goats. A play area could be incorporated into a yard or out at pasture, or both.

Trio of Golden Guernseys playing.

Skidsteer to aid mucking out.

Goats under cover.

If your goats are out at pasture during the day with, if they are lucky, access to woodland and scrub too, a field shelter is still needed so they can get out of the rain as necessary. Mobile field shelters built on skids that can be pulled behind a four-wheel-drive vehicle or tractor are particularly useful as they can be moved to different pastures if the gradient of your land allows this. You can use any sort of structure that gives the goats shelter from the elements.

FENCING

Making your fences goat-proof takes thought, care and expense, so take a deep breath and budget for it. Goats will climb on fences, jump over them, and try to wriggle under too, so additional considerations are required beyond standard sheep stock fencing.

Standard stock fencing is 80cm (32in) tall with eight horizontal strands and has vertical gaps of 15 or 30cm (6 or 12in); choose

Goat fencing.

Meshed gate.

Goat with its head stuck in an 8/80/15 stock fence.

8/80/30 stock fencing rather than 8/80/15, as heads and horns are much less likely to get stuck in the wider openings.

If using standard stock fencing, use long fencing stakes (1.8m/6ft) so that you can add a couple of strands of plain or barbed wire to give additional height to the fence, to a total above-ground height of 1.3m (4.3ft) – even for pygmies who are inveterate jumpers notwithstanding their miniature stature. For those top strands you could use electrified wire or tape, powered with solar panels on sunny days, or an energizer and battery year round.

Although more costly, you can buy 1.2m (4ft) stock fencing, and much higher stock fencing is available such as that used for deer, including 1.5m, 1.8m and 2m (5ft, 6ft and 6.5ft) heights. If you have a fast road or other worrying hazard beyond the proposed fence, it makes sense to opt for a total fence height of 1.5m (6ft).

If using timber (metal posts are also available), buy fencing stakes and rails that are guaranteed for fifteen years if you are in any but the driest of environments; the additional cost will be insignificant in comparison to the effort and cost of replacing every post within a decade. Be aware that the essential bracing of fences using diagonal struts at field corners can offer a convenient jumping-out point for goats, so use a box strainer design, or ensure that conventional strainers are behind, and not in front of the fencing.

Fencing stakes should be much closer together than for other livestock to ensure that fencing cannot be lifted by a persistent nose, ideally no more than 1.75m (5.7ft) apart, rather than the 3.5m (11.5ft) spacing commonly used for sheep. If you have existing sheep stock fencing, adding an additional fence stake mid-way between each stake will make it nicely robust for goats.

Box strainer.

Box strainer with a goat ladder created inadvertently alongside (not a good idea).

Conventional strainer behind fencing.

Conventional strainer in front of fencing (not advisable).

Don't even contemplate using half-round stakes for fencing as these are barely fit for poultry, never mind goats: use 75-100mm diameter stakes.

Rather than the usual approach for stock fencing of banging in fencing staples on the bottom, top, plus three of the interim horizontal wires, plan on banging in staples on every one of the eight strands on each stake. Put the stock fencing on the inside, not the outside of the stakes, so that if goats push against it, it won't be pulled free of the fencing staples. You can help stop them rummaging underneath the fence by ensuring the stock fence is twangy tight and not in any way slack, with the bottom wire at ground level; this is not an easy ask on hillocky ground, and bits of rail or other goat-proof obstacles may need to be put in place at ground level to fill any tempting gaps.

Unlike sheep fencing, a line of rails should be attached to the stakes along the top line of the stock fencing on the inside to accommodate the inevitable front hooves that will stand on the fence; this stops the fencing from being pushed groundwards over time and also strengthens the whole structure.

Constant offenders that get their horns stuck in fencing will benefit (they may

Goat with pipe taped to its horns.

disagree) from having a section of plastic waterpipe taped to their horns to keep them out of trouble.

For all gates, outdoors and in, you are advised to use two sorts of latch, belt and braces fashion, to make them truly goat proof. Goats have all the time in the world to work their mouths around gate closers, so plan to outwit them from the start.

Electric Fencing

Electric fencing can be a very satisfactory and quickly erected method of fencing, in particular when you want to move the

Goat secured behind permanent electric wire fencing.

goats around various parts of your holding, although some goats do sneer at it. Use the tallest netting you can find, around 1.2m (4ft) high, and be prepared to strim the grass by the base of the fence regularly to stop it shorting out. To do this, move the posts inwards a pace, strim, then put the fence back – you don't want your strimmer, shears or mower to cut through the fence.

Remember to check the fence is on and working each day – and you don't need to shock yourself to find out: pocket-sized electric fence testers are readily available, and hang a sign on the fence that explains to any visitors that it's electrified. Electric netting comes in 25m, 50m and 100m (82ft, 164ft and 328ft) lengths, but should not be used for horned goats or for kids, which could get entangled.

In addition to the electric fencing (preferably netting or tape, as wire has the potential to be dangerous as it can wrap round livestock and cut into them) you will need an energizer, an earth rod and a power source: a leisure battery, solar panels or mains. Solar is a useful back-up for keeping the battery charged, but may not be reliable

Goat secured behind electric fence netting.

enough on its own in extended cloudy weather.

A line of electrified tape or wire is a helpful addition with permanent fencing, placed on the inside as the top wire, using insulators to distance the electrified line 15cm (6in) from the main structure.

Tree Protection

If you have goats in an orchard or in areas where vulnerable trees are growing you will need to build tree guards around each tree. If the guard you use is impenetrable by the goat's head the guard should be 1.8m (6ft) high and can be set close to the trunk; if the guard is of a design that allows the goat to get its head through, it needs to be at least 50cm (20in) away from the trunk, and a minimum height of 1.5m (5t), using three or four fencing stakes to make a triangular or square guard.

TETHERING

Basically, don't do it. It makes the goat vulnerable to attack, to getting itself all caught up, or at worst even to strangulation.

HANDLING AND HANDLING EQUIPMENT

Goats have to be contained for handling for their own safety and yours, and definitely for your sanity: chasing animals around in order to check or treat them is stressful for all. For those who use a milking stand, these can be used for carrying out health and foot checks and administering medication, unless you are concerned about there being any mental connection for the goat with (what should be only mildly) stressful activities.

If you have even a handful of goats you'll need to contain them, which means hurdles. Apart from milking stands there's not much commercial handling equipment available specifically for goats, but sheep-handling equipment is readily available at all agricultural merchants and will do equally well for goats, although for committed jumpers you might find the taller alpaca hurdles more useful. Once gathered inside a hurdle corral it's helpful to reduce the

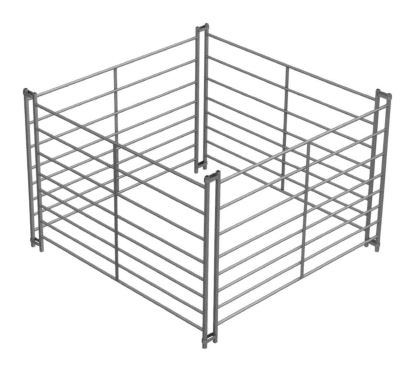

Alpaca hurdles - useful for containing agile goats.

number of hurdles to confine the space as much as possible so that animals can't rush about.

Although not commonly used for goats, you can buy a sheep turnover crate that will turn the goat so its feet point upwards or towards you, depending on design, making inspection, treatment and hoof trimming easy on your back – and you can also check a buck's pizzle.

Once corralled, catch and restrain goats by putting your arm round their neck (or for kids, round the whole body, or simply pick them up), and don't be tempted to use their horns as handles. If working on your own, goats can be haltered and tied short to a hurdle; if you are giving them an oral drench make sure they are not tied too tightly so that you can still tilt the head up to administer the drench correctly (*see* Chapter 9).

Turnover crate.

CHAPTER 5

TOOLS AND EQUIPMENT

Millhams, Dolton, September 1976. (Documentary photograph by James Ravilious for the Beaford Archive © Beaford Arts)

There's no getting away from it: if you keep goats you need certain items of kit. I doubt any goat keeper could do without buckets, hoof trimmers, a muck fork and a wheelbarrow, but other items will depend on what you are using your goats for. If you are dairying and making cheese, there's a whole raft of delights that will need to go on your shopping list, and if you have cashmere or angora plans and intend to shear yourself, that has purchasing consequences too. Some items are much better bought new (who wants to start off with blunt, not expensive anyway, hoof shears?), but dairying

OPPOSITE: Anglo Nubian.

equipment such as milking machines and cheese moulds seem to be available second-hand fairly regularly.

This short chapter covers the essential equipment, the things that will make your life easier if you have them, and those items of kit that are worth asking for on your birthday. Of course, what is essential to some will be entirely unnecessary to others. If you intend to breed your goats there will be all sorts of associated items that you'll need to sort beforehand, but if that's not part of your plan you can dispense with budgeting for up-to-your-armpit disposable gloves and obstetric lubricant gel. I hope this information will stop you for the most part having to scour each chapter in order to make a shopping or DIY materials list. For a full list of kidding items, *see* Chapter 13.

ESSENTIAL EVERYDAY ITEMS

You may not think the items described below are essential. All I can say is that we would be lost without them. If buying second- or third-hand, do your homework first on prices for new kit, as some used things may be a false economy, costing almost as much as new and having a much shorter useful life. Items such as galvanized metal water-bowl

Goats in a trailer.

drinkers corrode and leak with age, which makes them entirely unfit for purpose no matter how cheaply you bought them at the local car boot sale. All pre-owned housing or equipment should be given a very thorough disinfecting before allowing your goats anywhere near it.

Home-made hay manger.

Essential Everyday Items

Handling and transporting your goats	
Trailer or large dog crate	When bringing home kids they will fit happily in a large dog crate in the back of a car; for transporting adults or numbers of goats safely and appropriately you'll need access to a livestock trailer.
Hurdles	For containing your goats for handling, treatments, to create kidding pens etc. You might find alpaca hurdles at 1.3m (4ft) high are more helpful than 1m (3ft) sheep hurdles for containing goats, although more challenging for you to climb over.
Halters, headcollars, collars and leads	For securing or moving your goat.
Housing, feeding and drinking	
Housing	Shelter is essential for goats. Anything from a three-sided shelter to a fancy barn. *See* Chapter 4 for options.
Hayrack	Built inside the shelter, and mobile versions as required.
Drinkers	Goats need constant access to clean water, and automatic bowl drinkers or ones with push tubes are less likely to be contaminated (and easier to clean out) than low-level sheep water troughs.
Buckets	Plastic, rubber, stainless steel depending on their purpose, for carrying anything and everything: milk, water, feed, tools, medicines, etc. Calf buckets make ideal food buckets for individual goats.
Feed troughs	For feeding several goats together.
Goat- and rodent-proof feed bins	Make sure these cannot be accessed by your goats. Metal dustbins can easily have their lids knocked off. Use feedbins or old chest freezers with the locks removed as cheap effective options.
Feed scoops	Purpose made, or any container that you know holds the right amount of feed will do (large yogurt tubs, empty fencing staple buckets, etc).
Bedding material	Straw or shavings. You might like rubber stable matting underneath if you want luxury accommodation, particularly in cold climates.
Mucking out	
Wheelbarrow	Plastic or metal.
Muck fork	For cleaning out your goat sheds.
Shovel	As above.
Milking equipment	
Milking stand	*See* Chapter 11.
Milk pail(s)	At least one with a lid for carrying milk.
Strainer and straining filters	To maintain milk hygiene.
Churn/milk container and/or bottles/jars	For storing milk, preferably with plastic reusable lids.
Teat dip cup and strip cup	Milk hygiene and goat welfare.
Consumables	Dairy wipes, dairy cleaners/teat dip/disinfectants/sterilizer solutions.
Udder balm/cream	Goat welfare.

(Continued)

Cheese and dairying equipment	
Consumables	Cheesecloths, starter, rennet, cultures.
Cream separator	Old-fashioned ceramic or nifty electric version.
Hand churn or electric mixer	For butter making.
Stainless-steel items	Pans, buckets, double boiler, colanders.
Curd cutter	A palette knife works well for small-scale cheese making.
Electronic thermometer and timer	Timings and temperatures are critical in dairying.
Cheese moulds, trays, draining mats	Shapes and sizes to suit.
Cheese press	Can be simple and homemade.
Wide-necked vacuum flask	Or fancy electric yogurt maker.
Measuring jugs	Designed for ease of cleaning.
Ladle and spoons	To ladle and spoon.
Other useful tools	
Penknife	A penknife in every jacket pocket saves time and tempers (for opening feed sacks, cutting straw- and hay-bale twine etc).
Loppers and secateurs	For cutting browse to take to your goats.
Fencing tools and consumables: iron bar, post bumper, wire fencing tools (fencing pliers, strainers etc), graft, staples	Even if you pay someone to do your fencing there will inevitably be repairs, but hopefully not for a decade or so.
Cordless tools	Not just drills, but cordless anything for working anywhere where running electric extension leads is difficult or impossible. An extra battery is useful so you won't have to wait hours for a recharge while you're in the middle of repairing a shelter.
Torch	Head torches in particular are brilliant on the hopefully rare occasions when you need to tend to your goats at night and during kidding.
Animal care and first-aid essentials	
Dedicated storage cupboard for medicines and associated kit	So that you can find what you need immediately.
Digital thermometer	For taking a goat's temperature rectally.
Foot shears	For foot trimming. A hoof file or rasp is also useful.
Faecal worm count packs (FEC packs)	To send away poo samples to check worm burdens, coccidiosis, fluke etc.
Wormer and dose gun	To administer treatment according to FEC results.
Antiseptic spray	Use like a liquid plaster on minor wounds and foot problems.
Antibiotic spray	For foot infections and wounds where you are concerned about secondary infection (vet prescribed).
Syringes and needles	For administering injections.
Strong farm detergent	Many makes available. Use to clean sheds, bedding areas and equipment, and as foot dips for biosecurity.

Sharps and Doop (destruction of old pharmaceuticals) containers	For the safe disposal of used needles and unused/out-of-date medication.
Stock marker spray	To mark animals that have been treated, to avoid double or missed dosing.
Other essentials	
Somewhere dry to store straw/hay/bedding	You don't want soggy forage or bedding.
A good vet	Ask around to find someone with goat experience.
Veterinary medicine record book	This is a legal requirement.
Holding register	This is a legal requirement.
Ear tags and applicator	For kids born on your holding or to replace missing tags on adults.

Muck scoop and rake.

CLOTHES AND FOOTWEAR

Clothes aren't tools, but count as essential equipment in my book. As a year-round welly wearer, neoprene-lined ones for winter are key to warm feet and good moods, while unlined ones are cooler and much more bearable in hot weather. You may prefer sturdy work boots in all but the wettest weather, and comfortable socks are critical to avoid blisters when you are likely to be wearing wellies or heavy boots for extended periods. And for winter keep a handful of beanie hats by the front door to keep head and ears out of rain and sharp winds.

Gloves of many kinds, from rubber-palmed builders' gloves to thick leather when handling fencing materials, are other essential items, and I particularly like disposable vinyl ones for any messy jobs, such as dealing with a wound when you don't want to introduce bacteria, and for kidding. A decent pair (or two) of waterproof jackets and trousers will keep you dry on those days when there are no gaps in the rain, and for particularly mucky jobs and protection against poo, farm boilersuits can't be beaten.

Old English goats on a scaffold climbing frame.

Goats wearing a collar and lead.

Other Useful Pieces of Kit

Reference books	*See* booklist in Appendix.
Electric fencing kit (and batteries, energizer, tester, warning sign)	*See* Chapter 4.
Heat lamps and bulbs	For kidding time.
Weigh crate	For managing goat health, medicine quantities, and assessing meat return.
Freezer	For storing your home-reared goat meat and colostrum.
Pasteurizer	If you prefer to pasteurize your milk.
Ice-cream maker	If you really love making lots of ice cream!
Shearing equipment	For fibre breeds.
Heat tape	To stop water pipes freezing.

DRINKING OPTIONS

Automatic drinking bowl

Water trough

On-demand drinker with push function

Compact non-spill drinker

Goat with electric netting.

CHAPTER 6

STARTING YOUR HERD

Cuppers Piece, Beaford, June 1983. (Documentary photograph by James Ravilious for the Beaford Archive © Beaford Arts)

With over 300 goat breeds worldwide, a prospective keeper could be forgiven for being dazzled by choice. In the UK there's a more manageable core range of options, with seven primarily dairy breeds (the Golden Guernsey and British Guernsey are usually considered as one breed), two

fibre types, one meat breed, rare breeds, native goats and pygmies, plus an endless variety of crosses. However, things never stand still, and breeds new to the UK (such as the Valais Blackneck and Kalahari Red) are being imported by pioneering breeders, which adds variety. The guide to the breeds

OPPOSITE: **Newborn Saanen kid.**

Angora goats.

in Chapter 15 gives you over eighty breeds to contemplate.

WHAT TO CHOOSE

A long time ago a friend of mine went shopping for a table and came home instead with some goats. Luckily that inspired outing ended rather well, but before doing anything as rash as bringing home a posse of goats purely because they appealed in the moment, your first task is to decide why you want to keep goats and for what purpose. Are you keen to make your own dairy produce: milk, butter, cheese, kefir, ice cream, yogurt or fudge? Perhaps the idea of creating skin-friendly goat-milk soap, cleanser or moisturizer appeals. Producing low fat, high quality meat may be the deciding factor for you, and crafters might be excited about the potential of mohair and cashmere production. Maybe you want to sell breeding stock to other goat keepers? Are your goat intentions commercial or purely hobby related?

Whatever drives you, your choice of goat needs to meet your requirements, even if you just want some energetic and enlivening pets. If you've enthusiastically bounced

straight to this chapter, do get to grips with the earlier chapters first as there are crucial requirements to put in place before exchanging cash for real live animals.

Not All Goats are the Same

Goat may be the most widely consumed meat worldwide, but the UK goat population is a mere 105,000 compared to 23 million sheep, 3.4 million cows and 4.5 million pigs. If you are commercially inclined this suggests market possibilities, and although every goat has the potential to become meat, they are not all equal in this regard. A Pygmy weighing 11-25kg (24-55lb) is not going to produce a carcase of note, whereas the stocky Boer approaching 100kg (220lb) has the conformation and size appropriate for what is acknowledged to be the best meat goat in the world. Equally, if it's milk you're after, a pure Boer doe could theoretically be milked, but their yield would compare poorly with the superbly milky Saanen's annual 2,000ltr (440gal).

Pygmy and Golden Guernsey.

Mixed breed goats Rhubarb and Custard.

Anglo Nubians at Surrey Docks.

Decide what you want from your goats – whether for conservation grazing, milk, meat, fibre, show stock, companionship, entertainment, time-consumer, education tool, or a mix of these – and choose accordingly.

Terrain and Location

Goats being an extraordinarily agile species, you probably don't have to concern yourself too much about the suitability of your terrain, as long as you can fence it securely and have somewhere flat to set up the essential shelter or barn (*see* Chapter 4). Don't forget that the

human in charge of the goats' care (that'll probably be you) will need to reach them easily at least twice a day, every day. No livestock thrives on a bog, but woodland and scrubby ground as well as native grassland will keep your goats happy.

The location where you intend to keep your goats may still have an impact on breed choice. The charmingly Roman-nosed, dangly-eared and thin-skinned Anglo Nubian is best suited to warm and hot climates so may not be ideal for keeping in frost pockets or areas known for extended periods of cold and wet.

Goats that Gladden Your Heart

There's no doubt that spending time observing your animals improves your

Kids on a climbing frame.

husbandry skills: knowing and beginning to understand normal healthy behaviour will help you to start identifying problems even if your diagnostic skills are as yet undeveloped. If you choose goats that gladden your heart and appeal to your eye you will spend more time with them, even if this mostly means gazing lovingly over the gate watching them simply be. If one type of goat doesn't make you smile, choose ones that will. Even so, be practical too – a very large breed may feel overwhelming to handle, or goats with huge horns make you fearful.

Build your confidence with goats by visiting experienced keepers and spending time with their goats; you may be surprised at what you decide is appropriate once you've been a little hands-on and gained some assurance around a herd.

WHERE AND HOW TO BUY

Once your homework is done and preparations made, it's time to go goat shopping. Goats are herd animals, so you will need to buy a minimum of two to ensure their health and happiness. If you are nervous of making a poor choice, overwhelmed by the options or the excitement of actual purchase, ask for guidance from an experienced keeper. Your best choice of seller is a reputable breeder, all of whom are keen to maintain their reputation and will be available to offer advice in those early months. There are plenty of ways to find and meet breeders.

Goat Societies and Agricultural Shows
There are a number of local goat societies in the UK and Ireland, and these are a sound choice for sourcing goats using local groups and their networks, particularly as many good goats are never advertised for sale. Have a few days out visiting agricultural shows – take the opportunity to discover more detail about the various breeds, and talk to the people showing their stock (but be sure not to interrupt them as they don their white coats and head for the show ring). Take a note of their contact details for later conversations: most have banners with this information alongside their goat pens.

Websites
Many breeders have websites giving information about their herd, and sometimes list what is available for sale. The various goat breed societies have websites, and a secretary who can signpost you to a local breeder. Be aware that many breeders are busy, and society officers work on a voluntary basis and aren't necessarily updating 'for sale' web pages regularly, so don't be put off making contact if the most recent advert is dated two years ago.

Classified Adverts
Farming and smallholding publications and websites will have classified adverts, as do online livestock 'for sale' and goat forums, and agricultural merchants still have the ubiquitous sign boards with postcards of 'for sale' advertisements. Once you have a shortlist of options visit as many breeders as you can; you will get a good feeling about the ones you would like to buy from.

Livestock Auctions
These can be great fun to attend, and are informative places for getting your eye in. Those goats that you thought were desirable may go for a lower amount than you anticipated because more experienced eyes can tell they are, for example, geriatric, have poor conformation, or show signs of lameness, and that's helpful in building your knowledge. Do be wary of purchasing from an auction as the animals you are interested in may be prime examples that arrive in the best of health, but if penned next to some less

healthy animals they might be the recipient of offloaded disease or parasites. Nor can you ring up the auctioneer later to ask advice about the best worming practices, or how to improve ventilation in your goat shed.

Dispersal Sales

That being said, do consider buying from dispersal sales. Rather than excising any below par livestock that the keeper wants to remove from their herd, everything is for sale – all the animals that they would be keeping if ill health, down-sizing, retirement, divorce, emigration or other meaty life moments hadn't intervened.

Breed Sales

Unlike sheep breed society shows and sales where animals are judged and given rosettes, cups and kudos prior to being sold at the society auction, the goat world doesn't currently engage in these breed sales because of concerns about the risk of CAE (caprine arthritis encephalitis) transmission. But this is being looked into, and breed sales might be a future possibility for buying quality goats.

BUYER BEWARE!

Don't buy any livestock that you feel sorry for, as it's a sure road to misery and expense. To start you on your goat-keeping journey you want healthy, sound animals that will give pleasure, and buying poor examples in a dubious state of health only encourages unscrupulous sellers. Don't buy sight unseen, either; avoid collecting your new goats from a motorway service station car park, or having them delivered to your property without having had the opportunity to see them at the seller's site first.

Visit the seller and assess if what you see is something you aspire to – not the glory of their house or garden, but how they are keeping their goats. Don't expect pristine surroundings (there will be poo, probably baler twine and signs of pragmatic 'make do and mend', and in wet weather there will be mud), but do check out the goat accommodation and its general cleanliness, look at the whole herd, and note the facilities for handling or milking the goats. As well as getting to grips with how well cared for the herd is, you may pick up some very helpful ideas for your own set-up.

If you are moving on to a farm or smallholding you might find that the vendor is keen to include their livestock in the sale. If you have any doubts about the goats' age, health or general fitness, or even if they simply aren't what you want, make sure that they are sold on before you take possession of the property. Disinfect any existing goat accommodation and equipment with a farming and livestock-approved disinfectant before bringing your own goats on site.

Purchase Costs

The price of goats varies hugely depending on breed, desirability, pedigree status, excellence of conformation, championships won, rarity, beauty, age, health, milkiness, change in seller circumstances and more.

If you are interested in showing your goats you need to be buying goats of show quality, so be prepared to pay accordingly. The cost of the average goat can easily be at least double, and more likely treble that of the average sheep of similar age and breeding potential,

Goats on fresh bedding.

so if you are more familiar with sheep prices, don't plan your budget expecting a similar outlay. There is something ironic in this, considering that historically goats were seen as the poor man's choice of livestock, when sheep or cattle were beyond the reach of the peasant pocket.

In 2021 the average female dairy kid was around £200–£250 at three months, although young (under a year) cross-breed does can cost as little as £60. Female meat goats ranged from £300 to £700, with cross breeds £200–£500. Boer breeding bucks ranged from £300 to £1,000. You can pay less or more than these indicative prices, and choosing meat wethers (castrated males) to finish for your freezer will cost you from £75.

There are far more costs than the purchase price involved when taking on any livestock; you need to have the financial resources to keep goats well.

GOLDEN RULES FOR SELECTING HEALTHY GOATS

As noted, do check out the seller's herd on site, and be sure that you like what you see.

If possible, buy from a closed herd where they breed rather than buy in replacement stock, raising a percentage of their best young females to take the place of older goats that are no longer productive. A closed source herd is desirable because every time new animals enter a holding they bring with them a disease risk. However, if home-bred females are being kept, unrelated males will have to be brought in, so be realistic about the source herd's closed status. Be aware that if they loan out their bucks for stud purposes this will increase disease risk. Related to this is the best practice of buying livestock from as few sources as possible – the more places you buy from, the higher the risk of bringing in disease with your newly acquired animals.

What to look for:

- Are the animals structurally sound with no signs of lameness? Are the legs straight and even, not cow hocked or pigeon-toed? Are the feet free of foot rot and other foot problems such as scald or CODD?
- Is the mouth well shaped without an undershot or overshot jaw?
- Do the goats have good body conformation? Are they overfat, too thin, just right? (For more information on body condition scoring, *see* Chapter 8.)
- Is the coat in good condition? Are there any sores or itchy patches? Are there any visible signs of external parasites such as lice or mange?
- Are the goats nice and clean around their bottoms with no loose dung or scouring?
- Are they coughing or breathing fast? Are there any swellings/cysts on the goat?
- Are they behaving as you'd expect for the species: lively, active, not hiding in corners? Do they exhibit good temperament? Challenging animals are not for the inexperienced (possibly not for anyone).

- Is the breeder forthcoming and informative about their animals? Are they happy to share their goats' treatment history – for example, do they have any test results for worms or fluke, or records of any medication that's been used in the last six to twelve months? Is there a history of CLA (*caseous lymphadenitis*) in the herd?
- When were blood tests last carried out to test for CAE (*caprine arthritis encephalitis virus*) status, and what is the herd's CAE history?
- Do they have any particular health problems on their holding? Do they vaccinate against clostridial diseases and/or any specific issues? Does their stock have contact with other people's livestock (through showing, or neighbouring livestock)? Do they share equipment with other smallholders/farmers?
- Does the herd belong to a health accreditation scheme?
- Have the goats you are interested in given birth before, and was that successful? Are they pregnant? If so, when are they expected to give birth? If you want to breed, ask them about the herd's normal kidding percentage (the number of kids born from their does, worked out as follows: if you have ten does that have twenty-two live kids, 22 is divided by $10 \times 100 = 220$ per cent kidding percentage across the herd).
- What age are they? Are they the right age range for your needs?
- Ask if you can see the parents of the goats you are interested in. Check why they are for sale.

Although not related to health status, if you want registered pedigree stock make sure this will be in place before you buy. Only the breeder can register their animals,

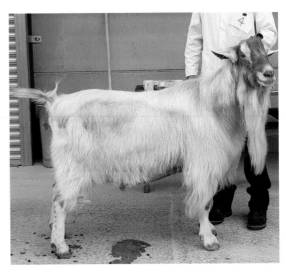

British Toggenburg male.

so this is not something you can do yourself later.

If you are buying a buck and want to improve the meatiness of your kids or the quality of their fibre, focus on those traits in the male. The commonly offered advice is that males should be 'masculine', but what that actually means is harder to define, although size and head and body shape are part of this, as well as the obvious focus on genitalia. Make sure the buck you are interested in has really great feet and moves well, and don't consider anything lame or that is low on its pasterns (you want their legs to be upright, not low or sloping over the goat equivalent of ankles).

Check that his teeth are in good order, with no staining round the mouth; the teeth will also enable you to check his stated age. The testicles should be firm and should contain two testes, with a scrotal circumference of at least 25cm (10in) depending on the breed (*see* below). Ideally, check the penis to make sure it has no sores. The buck should be in good body condition as he will be working hard and will lose weight once he starts mating.

JANE ROSS'S TIPS FOR NEW GOAT KEEPERS

Jane Ross has kept goats for over forty-five years and feels that she now knows her subject 75 per cent. Here are her tips if you are thinking about venturing into keeping goats.

- Researching before you buy is very important as to appropriate breeds, and in order to appreciate the significant commitment involved. That commitment is not just in the summer but also in the muddy winter, and goat emergencies can arise at any time.
- Find yourself a goat-friendly vet, which may not be as easy as for sheep or cattle, and be aware that having goats will cost you money, and be prepared for potentially significant vet bills.
- Make sure you have your CPH and herd numbers before bringing goats home.
- Make sure housing is adequate for the number of goats. For two goats a 3.5 × 3.5m (12 × 12ft) stable will suit if they have to be shut in all day over the winter or whenever it's raining.
- Contact the British Goat Society (BGS) for details of your nearest goat club for ongoing support from other local goat keepers. Don't be afraid to ask questions of local goat keepers; there's a lot of goat experience out there. Visit agricultural shows to talk to other goat keepers; pick their brains to give you a better idea of what breed will suit.
- Buy stock from reputable breeders, and do not buy from a market – they may be cheaper but they are there for a reason. See the rest of the herd when buying goats: are you happy with the way the goats look, are they on clean bedding, has the herd been tested annually for CAE? Ideally, look for three consecutively clear years from CAE because you can get false negatives, and ask for the results for the whole herd, not just for the goat that's for sale.
- Tests for Johne's are only important if you're selling milk, and CLA is mostly an issue for commercial herds, so not as critical as CAE. Don't buy kids from commercial herds unless they do blood testing and have the relevant certificates.
- If you have any doubts about provenance, take the goat's ear-tag number and check with BGS if it's registered before purchasing. A reputable breeder will give the new owner the CAE certificate, a copy of the registration certificate, and any milk records of the dam.
- British Alpines are truly not suitable for novices as they are challenging to manage, and Anglo Nubians can be noisy. For dairy goat novices, the pure Saanen takes a lot of beating: they are the backbone of a lot of breeds, inclined to be helpful and less likely to escape. Think about supporting rare breeds (*see* Farm Animal Genetic Resources Committee figures showing how many kids have been registered, and how many bucks are available).
- Feed best quality horse hay, and for dairy breeds either coarse calf feed or adult cattle dairy food: it's cheaper than goat feed, but more importantly contains a better level of minerals, so you don't have to hope the goats help themselves to free choice minerals.
- For preventative care regarding coccidiosis, consider giving all adult females Baycox if they are dry, otherwise use Vecoxan at double the recommended sheep dose once a year, ideally before mating. Treat kids at 2.5 weeks, 6 weeks, 12 weeks and 6 months. Lambivac vaccinations for clostridial diseases should be given twice a year (in preference to Heptavac). To manage worm burdens, do an FEC count every three months for any goat you suspect has worms, then take advice from your vet.

Buck with young companion.

You don't want any sign of mites or lice, so check for a good clean coat with no sores or rubbed patches.

Ask the owner for the buck's vaccination and treatment history, and how he has been fed, as this helps you plan your own ongoing husbandry. And in the excitement of the moment, don't just pop your new chap in with your does: a minimum twenty-one days' quarantine is recommended to enable you to monitor any ailments that might arise, and twenty-eight days is better. Don't forget that your buck will need company when not running with the does; a wether (castrated male) companion is ideal.

QUARANTINE

It's impossible to overstate the importance of quarantine to avoid bringing disease on to your holding. Even if the vendor has wormed the goats recently, talk to your vet about using one of the new generation, vet-prescribed worm products to avoid wormer-resistant parasites contaminating

your holding and creating future problems. They may, as an alternative, suggest worming with two different products, and you may also be advised to use a product to deal with any lice.

Quarantine facilities should ideally be somewhere that can be disinfected afterwards, or a small paddock that can be rested for several months after the quarantine has been completed. Don't quarantine a goat in isolation; at the very least ensure it can see other goats while making sure they can't physically contact each other. If you're bringing home your first goats you shouldn't have this issue as there will be at least two keeping each other company. And don't forget that any future goats joining your herd should also undergo a quarantine period. If CAE tests have not been carried out in recent months ask your vet to do that while the goats are in quarantine.

MOUTH AND TEETH

Teeth tell a goat's age, so it pays to understand what's going on inside their mouth; you won't want to buy animals at the end of their lifespan if you are hoping to keep and/or breed from them for many years to come. If you want to try your hand at breeding with an experienced goat or two, older animals may do you well as long as they are in good health and body condition, and don't have a history of difficult kiddings or barrenness.

At the front of its mouth a goat only has teeth (incisors) on its bottom jaw, which meets the gum pad on the upper jaw. A goat has molars top and bottom at the side of its mouth; check these are in place as they are essential for dealing with their fibrous diet. Avoid goats with staining round

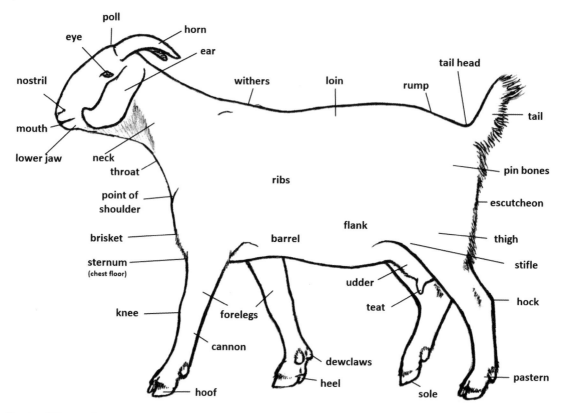

Parts of the goat.

their mouths as they are clearly having problems chewing – but don't confuse this with molasses stains or other temporary discoloration if a goat has had its head in a mineral bucket or been enjoying its coarse-mix breakfast.

Goat's teeth.

Goat Teeth Development

Age	Goat teeth development as goat ages	
At birth	One or two temporary incisors.	
Six weeks (kid)	Eight milk incisors.	
One year old/in their second year (goatling)	Two central milk incisors are replaced with larger permanent teeth.	
Two years old/in their third year	Four large incisors.	
Three years old/in their fourth year	Six large incisors.	
Four years old/in their fifth year	Eight large incisors – known as a full-mouthed.	
Aged	As a goat ages it may lose some of its teeth – when it is known as broken mouthed – which can make the intake of adequate nutrition more challenging.	

Check that the goat has a normally shaped jaw, neither undershot (parrot-mouthed) nor overshot (monkey-mouthed), as either can make chewing difficult. In both conditions the incisors on the lower jaw fail to meet the dental pad on the upper jaw, meaning the goat is unable to get all the nutrition it needs.

Animals with this defect should not be bred from as it is a genetic trait that gets passed on to offspring. In most goats, the bites are set by the time the newborn is a few months old and are unlikely to improve – the problem is more likely to become pronounced as they grow.

Jaw Type

Normal jaw. The incisors meet the dental pad exactly.	
Undershot jaw. The teeth close behind the dental pad because the lower jaw is too short.	
Overshot jaw. The incisors extend forward past the dental pad as the lower jaw is longer than the upper jaw.	

Very undershot jaw.

UDDER AND TEATS

The doe's udder and teats are of paramount importance, critically so if you are intending to breed from or milk her. For non-dairy breeds the udder should still be checked regularly to make sure there's enough/not too much milk for her kids. A goat with a single kid may need milking if she has an excess, and those with multiple kids and a small milk supply may need their kids' diet supplemented.

When checking an udder in anticipation of a purchase feel for lumps that might indicate mastitis (infection and inflammation of the udder) and a subsequent inability to produce milk. Unless you are intending to show or breed for showing an udder does not need to be a thing of beauty. However, it still needs to be functional, with two well-spaced teats that you can milk or a kid can suckle from, so avoid enlarged pendulous teats that a kid can't fit in its mouth at birth, or such tiny buttons that you can't hand milk it. The idea of ground clearance when associated with an udder, rather than a vehicle, may seem a little odd, but if you are planning to graze your goats on rough land they don't want to be

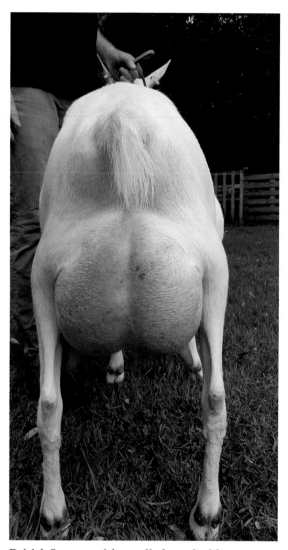

British Saanen with a well-shaped udder.

dragging low-slung udders over thistles and scrub that would cause damage, or be treading on their own teats; teats should be above the level of the goat's hocks.

Goats normally have two working teats (although some have been bred to have four), and all teats need to be functional. Supernumerary and split teats, sometimes called cluster and fishtail teats, or blind teats that don't actually produce milk, are to be avoided, as should blown teats that are too large for a kid to feed from.

Goat Udders

Desirable udder	
Sausage teats	
Fishtail teats	
Multiple teats	
Antler teats	
Blown teats	
Non-functioning teat	
Pendulous udder	

LEGS AND FEET

Legs will vary in width and length depending on breed, but should be straight from all angles, well spaced at the front, and not narrow at the chest. Feet should be upright and straight too, and above the feet the pasterns should not be low to the ground. Knees should be neat and not swollen, neither knock-kneed nor bow-legged. Watch the goat move to ensure there is no lameness, and pick up its feet and check there is no smell or sweatiness between the hoof claws. Feet should not be overgrown or over-trimmed. Unlike a sheep that you sit on its bottom to check or trim feet, with goats you lift their

Desirable and Non-Desirable Leg Shapes

Pasterns strong, short and upright, hocks wide apart and straight, feet sound and neat.	
Too much angle at the pastern; too closely set to the ground.	
Overly curved at the hock, with feet tucked too far under the body.	
Leg is too straight with inadequate angle at the hock.	

feet, bending each leg in turn at the knee so that the hoof floor is facing upwards, in much the same way that a farrier works on a horse.

TESTICLES

You may not be buying an entire (uncastrated) breeding male at the start, but when or if you do, his scrotum needs some scrutiny, which requires getting 'hands on'. Treat the scrotum gently as you would an udder, and feel to make sure there are two testicles, evenly sized, with no lumps or scarring, that feel firm and springy to the touch and are not too pendulous. Size does matter as sperm production is related to the circumference of the scrotum. Of course a Pygmy goat will differ from a Boer, but the average mature buck should have a scrotum circumference of at least 25cm (10in).

Avoid a buck whose scrotum is split - where the bottom of the scrotum is shaped like a 'W' rather than a neat 'U'. This is because of the genetic possibility of female offspring

having poor udders and the higher likelihood of trauma, the crevice providing a home for ticks and thistles and thorns. There is no evidence that a split scrotum causes reduction in fertility. The buck's teats also deserve a onceover as this is a trait that will be carried on to his daughters.

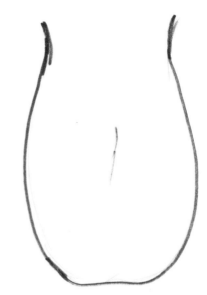

Buck scrotum - desirable.

Anglo Nubian male showing a well-shaped scrotum.

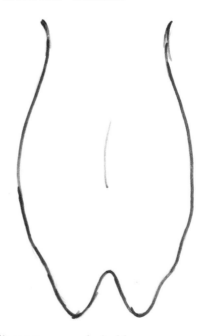

Split scrotum - undesirable.

Goat Categories

(*See* Chapter 15 for a full guide to goat breeds)

Types and Breeds	Description	Purpose	
Meat Boer	Originates from South Africa, introduced to the UK in 1987. Known as the world's best meat breed.	For meat. As a sire for dairy herds to produce kids with a viable meat carcase.	
Dairy Pure Breeds Golden Guernsey (also rare) Saanen Toggenburg	Golden Guernsey: a small goat with moderate milk yield. Saanen and Toggenburg: imported from Switzerland, high-yielding milk goats.	For milk production and associated dairy products.	
Native English (also rare) Old English (also rare) British Primitive	English: Utility smallholder breed. Old English: native without Swiss or Nubian ancestry. Primitive and feral goats found mostly on hilly mountain areas of the UK.	Dual purpose, suitable for milk and meat. British Primitive covers what was previously known as the Old English/Scottish/Welsh/Irish, British Landrace or Old British Goat.	
Native Dairy Anglo-Nubian British Alpine British Guernsey British Toggenburg British Saanen	These goats were created by crossing the British native goats with imported goats.	For milk production and associated dairy products.	

Types and Breeds	Description	Purpose	
Fibre Angora Cashmere	The Angora goat produces mohair (not to be confused with Angora wool, which comes from Angora rabbits). There is no specific cashmere breed; it is the name given to any goat with a soft downy undercoat, selectively bred to produce a yield of cashmere.	Mohair and cashmere production.	
Rare Breed Bagot English Golden Guernsey Old English	Bagot: a small, long-haired, hardy breed of nervous disposition, not keen on being handled. Categorized as an at-risk rare breed. English is a priority rare breed. Golden Guernsey is an at-risk rare breed. Old English is a priority rare breed.	Bagots are used as conservation grazers. English: multi-purpose utility. Golden Guernsey is raised for milk production. Old English: dual purpose.	
Pygmy Pygmy	Hardy, genetically small, compact goat originating from Africa.	No productive use – kept as pets.	

Goats in their new home.

THE QUESTION OF HORNS

The question of horns is particularly pertinent to considerations of purchase. If you are new to goat keeping, the prospect of horned animals may be a little alarming; however, you do have options. Although individual goats may be born polled (without horns), all goat breeds are horned.

Do not confuse polled with disbudded: many kids are disbudded in the first week of life with a local anaesthetic and the use of a disbudding iron (in the UK this must be done by a vet) so that their horns don't develop. Angoras and Boers are often kept horned, while dairy breeds are mostly disbudded, which is why you might incorrectly assume that the ubiquitous white

Dutch Landrace buck.

Toggenburg kids disbudded.

dairy goat never had horns, or the potential for them, in the first place.

In addition to being used in the same way as the antlers of a deer or an antelope in fighting for supremacy in the herd, horns have an important role in temperature regulation. This is why goats in hot climates and heavily fibred breeds tend to be left with their horns intact, rather than being disbudded. When kids are born you can feel the horn buds immediately, and they grow surprisingly quickly.

Although horn play and butting is entirely natural between goats, don't allow kids to butt you or other people, and don't push back if they try and butt you, as this will encourage them to continue what will become extremely problematic behaviour as they mature – ignore it and move away.

Avoid breeding polled males and females together if they have polled descendants as there is a risk of their offspring being intersex and of no use for breeding.

Organic Saanen doe complete with horns.

CHAPTER 7

HUSBANDRY TASKS FOR EACH TYPE OF HERD

Park Farm, Umberleigh, August 1985. (Documentary photograph by James Ravilious for the Beaford Archive © Beaford Arts)

The previous chapter outlined the importance of choosing the right goats for your needs, and how different breeds are suitable for different purposes. It's fair to say that there are probably as many livestock keepers who learned about the specifics of their chosen breed or species after purchasing as there are those who engage in thorough pre-purchase research. It's also possible that you may not be entirely sure what sort of herd you want, but fancy a few goats to grace your life, with a hope that perhaps you might get a bit of milk, fewer weeds, and some fun on the way.

OPPOSITE: Lynton feral goats.

It's true that the most committed meat eater, who will eagerly choose a goat dish if it's on the menu, may initially baulk at the concept of eating their own animals. This reluctance often (though not always) changes over time as the reality of breeding, resulting in surplus males in particular and overstocking of land, requires a pragmatic response for the continuing health and sustainability of the herd. What also dawns is an increasing appreciation that having absolute knowledge of what has gone into your meat and how it has been raised becomes ever more important.

As you become familiar with day-to-day husbandry and its complexities are revealed, awareness of good practice – and its opposite – builds, and so a shift to understanding the benefits of one's own meat source is made. If you are interested in supporting rare breeds, the best way to save them is to eat them. As the Rare Breed Survival Trust says: 'It sounds daft, but it's true. The more a breed is wanted, then the more popular it becomes, and numbers increase.'

This chapter provides a brief overview of the tasks and routine activities required depending on the type of goats you acquire. The list in the 'Goats as Pets' section is relevant to every type of goat, but additional activities come into play if you are keeping goats specifically for meat, milk or fibre.

Arapawa goats and kids in New Zealand.

GOATS AS PETS

If you have a few goats kept as pets, it's not a question of popping them in a paddock with some shelter, a bit of grub and water, and leaving them to get on with it. If you're not breeding from your pets they may be under less strain physically, but you can't relax your role as goat keeper. Their feet may need trimming just the same as any goat, they will need to be checked for ailments and disease and receive appropriate preventative treatments, and all fencing, shelter and other

Cross-breed pygmy goat.

infrastructure basics need to be in place (*see* chapters 4 and 9 for more detail). The core things that you'll need to deal with are listed below.

- Daily observation and regular handling
- Maintenance of fencing
- Maintenance and mucking out of housing and shelter year round
- Permanent clean water supply
- Grass/forage/browse supply
- Avoiding over-stocking, employing rotational grazing
- Avoiding obesity
- Providing mineral and salt supplements
- Controlling toxic plants
- Regular foot care
- Worm/fluke/lice analysis and treatment
- CAE (Caprine arthritis encephalitis virus) testing
- Prevention/treatment of fly strike for pet fibre breeds
- Shearing of pet fibre breeds
- Clostridial vaccinations
- Protecting from pain, suffering, injury and disease
- Paying vet bills
- Providing enrichment – logs or sturdy man-made structures for goats to play on
- Meeting all legal requirements (registering as a holding, tagging, completing movement licences, maintaining a holding register and veterinary medicines log, etc.)
- Dead stock removal.

It's worth mentioning straightaway that bucks do not make suitable pets; choose does or wethers for this role. Quite apart from the serious stink at breeding time, their buckish behaviour – including their love of coating themselves lavishly in their own urine, deciding that human females are fair game, and their size and strength – contributes to making the buck a formidable creature. That darling buckling that follows you about at three weeks of age is another matter entirely at maturity: don't be deceived.

GOATS FOR MEAT

Keeping goats for meat (*see* Chapter 10 for more detail) can be achieved by buying wethers or young males, or doelings not seen as suitable for breeding, and raising them to a decent meat weight – but in many cases rearing for meat means breeding, and with that comes significant additional input from the goat keeper. The core things that you'll need to deal with are listed below.

There will be the same maintenance and husbandry tasks as for pets, plus the following:

- Sourcing breeding males for purchase/ hire and their care
- Ability to separate groups of goats (not all should be put with the buck, and you need to have facilities to keep the buck separate from females at certain times and ages)
- Setting up your barn for kidding (isolation pens, heat lamps etc. – *see* Chapter 13)
- Getting does scanned to determine the number of kids being carried
- Managing the feed requirements for in-kid does
- Constant care over the kidding period, and acquiring knowledge to deal with dystocia (difficult births) and newborns requiring intervention
- Increased vet bills
- Care of young kids
- Castration if necessary
- Disbudding of goats if necessary (by the vet)
- Worming programme for kids
- Clostridial disease vaccination

Boer doelings at play.

- Ear tagging
- Determining which kids are suitable for future breeding, and those for meat
- Culling policy for breeding does
- Trailer for abattoir trips
- Finding a suitable butcher
- Having skins tanned for rugs, etc.
- Marketing and sales of surplus meat.

DAIRY GOATS

In order to provide a milk supply, does will need to be bred, so all the requirements listed above for pet and meat goats apply (if surplus males are used for meat), plus the need for milking and associated dairying. The list below gives an outline of these tasks. For more detail, *see* Chapter 11.

- Separating the kids from the does (either permanently, or as part of a 'kids at foot' system)
- Permanent housing facility for dairy goats
- Learning how to milk
- Building a milking stand for human convenience and avoiding bad backs
- Setting up a suitable, hygienic, easy-to-clean milking parlour

British Alpine goat.

Boer-cross dairy goats.

- Acquiring and keeping spotlessly clean the necessary milking and dairying equipment and chilling facilities (an extra fridge perhaps)
- Milking every day (possibly twice a day, twelve hours apart)
- Being prepared, if you have a very milky breed, for a great deal of milk to use/process on a daily basis
- Learning how to make butter and cheese, yogurt, cream, ice cream etc.
- Determining if your milk/cheese supply is for home use or for sale, in which case complying with the appropriate legislation
- Making time for milking and dairying.

CROSSES: GOATS FOR MILK AND MEAT

There's no need to keep top-of-the-line pedigree goats if you simply want a bit of meat for the table and freezer, and a modest milk supply. You might cross a dairy-breed doe with a Boer buck to produce chunky males that will make good eating, and females that

may not be quite as milky as their pure dairy breed mum, but are perfectly fit for purpose to grow on as future milkers. The requirements are as the three task lists above.

GOATS FOR FIBRE

All the same requirements regarding fencing, housing, feed, foot care and so on for pet and meat goats apply to the fibre goat. However, the Angora only produces enough milk to rear her kids so is unlikely to provide you with dairying opportunities. *See* Chapter 14 for more detail on keeping goats for their fibre. The following tasks will also be required in the care of fibre goats:

- Shearing twice a year
- Providing extra feed if shorn at a cool time of year (to keep the goats warm)
- Storing fibre effectively to avoid spoilage before spinning
- Treatment against lice and flystrike
- Marketing and selling of fibre to others for spinning and processing, or processing it oneself.

Angora goats grazing.

GOATS AS ANIMAL COMPANIONS

Goats are often kept in a secondary capacity as companions, not just for otherwise solitary males, but as friends for other species such as horses, donkeys, llamas and alpacas. They cost less than equines or camelids to buy and keep, and will certainly enjoy the top quality hay provided, although they will need to be kept firmly away from the bucket and

Horse with goat companions.

Donkey with goat companions.

bins containing their feed. Make sure any minerals you make available are suitable for all the species in question.

Take time over introductions, allowing them to be side by side with a fence between them or in neighbouring stables. You'll need to monitor them together over a period of time before being satisfied that neither will come to harm. Otherwise, the tasks are the same as for pet goats.

YEAR-ROUND MANAGEMENT PROGRAMME

The calendar below is based on March kidding; create your own version depending on your kidding dates and management programme. Year-round you should check feet, body condition, worm counts and parasite burdens, and deal these with accordingly (*see* Chapter 9).

Goat Calendar

Month	Activity
January	Scan does 80-100 days from their breeding date. Start feeding concentrates to those expecting multiple kids and any thin singles 50 days before kidding if body condition score warrants it. Check for lice, and treat if needed.
February	Trim hairy does around the back end. Lambivac vaccine to does 4 weeks before kidding (include doelings, wethers and bucks too if timing is appropriate).
March	Clean the kidding area and set up bonding pens and kidding kit. Keep a close eye on heavily pregnant does. Take FEC samples from does to see if worming or flukicide is required post kidding. Kidding starts. Ring bucklings within 7 days, and get the vet to disbud kids if required.
April	Kidding continues. Post-kidding treatments and checks: treat for lice, worms and fluke if required. Trim feet if needed. Keep an eye on does for mastitis. Ear-tag kids. Process year-old meat goats via the butcher when they are at their peak.
May	Lambivac kids at 10-12 weeks (first dose). Keep alert for pink eye and orf outbreaks. Wean entire bucklings at 6 weeks. Wean wethers and doelings at preferred time. Sell weaned kids if appropriate.
June	Lambivac kids at 14-16 weeks (second dose). FECs for kids, and worm as required. Protect fibre breeds against blowfly strike (this may be necessary earlier or later).
July	Haymaking – hopefully.
August	Haymaking continues. Ensure potential breeders have a good body-condition score in the lead-up to mating. Make sure doelings cannot be accessed by entire bucks. Adults get six-monthly Lambivac booster. Check buck condition, and fertility test if desired.
September	Annual CAE blood test before does are bred (also CL and Johne's if desired). Pre-mating treatments and checks: FECs, treat for fluke, worms and external parasites if required. Trim feet if necessary. Teeth, tits and toes check for does and bucks. Body-condition scoring. Keep breeders, the rest go for mutton.
October	Buck to does (if March kidding desired).
November	Remove bucks after two cycles (43 days).
December	Make a list of all fencing and housing to be fixed (a year-round task). Kids get their six-monthly Lambivac booster.

CHAPTER 8

FEEDING AND NUTRITION

Goat and washing line, near Dolton Beacon, June 1981. (Photograph by James Ravilious for the Beaford Archive © Beaford Arts)

THE DIGESTIVE SYSTEM

Goats, just like cows and sheep, are ruminants and have a stomach made up of four chambers: the rumen, the reticulum, the omasum and the abomasum. The rumen is the largest and first chamber, where feed is initially mixed with saliva. From here the food is regurgitated back into the mouth as cud, and as the goat sits and rests it chews the cud and then swallows it again. Once the food is nicely liquefied it moves into the reticulum, where it is fermented and methane is produced; then it travels onwards to the omasum. Here it is reduced into even

OPPOSITE: **Nubian goat.**

smaller particles and fluid is removed, and the food is then sent to the final chamber, the abomasum. Digestive enzymes and acid break down proteins, and the food then moves into the small intestine where starch is turned into glucose (energy), and complex fats into fatty acids; it then passes into the large intestine where bacteria complete the digestive process. The remains are delivered as faecal matter.

With their four stomach chambers, goats are perfectly designed to digest fibrous plant material rather than grain, which can create all sorts of digestive, foot and bladder problems. There is a huge amount of contradictory and confusing information available about the feeding of goats (and this is equally true of all livestock). I prefer keeping things as natural and as suitable to an animal's digestive system as possible, with concentrated feed supplements made available only at those times in a goat's life when its body has additional demands that need to be supported: for example when producing milk for a human household, in the late stages of pregnancy, for growing youngstock (but only if needed), and to any underweight bucks or does as they approach the breeding season. This is the nutritional pay-off for humans having domesticated goats, and requiring them to work harder for us.

In the same way that I want pasture-fed sheep and cattle to produce great lamb, hogget, mutton and beef, I want that when

Goat heaven.

eating goat meat, too. This doesn't mean simply turning a goat outside and letting it get on with it. Good quality hay is essential for goats and is made, of course, through human intervention, and there will be plenty of times when goats are housed when it is desirable that not only hay is on hand, but browse is provided too. Secateurs and loppers will be your new best friends.

A number of different factors determine the daily intake of a goat, the primary ones being goat weight, forage quality, and in does, the stage of production (whether they are gestating or lactating). Heavier goats will consume more on a daily basis compared to lighter ones, and does that are lactating will consume more feed than those that are not. You should manage feed according to the individual body condition (*see* below) because it is as problematic to have thin goats as it is to have goats that are too fat. If you intend to feed communally you may need to adjust this to meet individual goat requirements in order to put weight on thin goats and to ratchet back the calorie intake of the overweight. Goats are surprisingly fussy eaters, so make sure they find their feed palatable and that it is fresh and clean. Forage and browse, fresh or preserved, should form 60-100 per cent of a goat's diet.

GRAZING AND BROWSING

Goats will graze as well as browse, and taller pastures, with a sward height of around 7cm (3in) and more, will help in minimizing worm burdens by keeping the goats feeding above ground level. Grazing plants are likely to be mostly grasses, but broad-leaved plants are also valuable in the mix (docks, clovers, vetches, chicory, plantain). If you are reseeding a pasture, do include the last four in the grass mix; docks need little extra encouragement other than disturbed ground.

Browse includes the leaves, soft shoots, bark and the fruits of woody plants from trees and shrubs. Ash, elder, elm, hazel, hawthorn and willow are all safe choices and much enjoyed by goats, and as willow grows by the simple expedient of putting a piece in damp ground, you could profitably create a

British Alpines browsing on a hazel hedge.

Grazing Toggenburg.

Harvesting willow.

willow bed to cut from for your appreciative goats. Nettles are also enjoyed by goats; these can be cut and fed when dried, or just left to wilt slightly (do wear gloves when harvesting!).

DRY MATTER

Dry matter (DM) is an indicator of the amount of nutrients that is available to the animal in any particular foodstuff, and is what remains after all the water is evaporated out of a feed, whether grain, fresh or dried forages. Fresh pasture has a high water content so has a lower percentage of dry matter than an equivalent weight of dryer feed such as hay or grain: grass has 17 per cent DM, grass silage 26 per cent DM, hay 90 per cent DM. The daily amount of dry matter needed depends upon several factors including weight and the goat's stage of production - whether lactating, pregnant,

weaning, finishing. At least 60 per cent of the diet should consist of forage, and the daily feed intake of goats ranges from 3-5 per cent of bodyweight, or more for a prolific milker (*see* Chapter 11).

PRESERVED FORAGE

Preserved forage is the plant material that has been cut and stored by humans, and then given to livestock to eat. Preserved forage for goats will be mainly hay made from grass, but it might also include tree hay or dried nettles.

When grass is cut it contains 75-85 per cent water; after drying in the sun until it has around 16 per cent moisture it is gathered into bales; these need to be stored under

Eating hay.

Storing small hay bales.

cover to keep the hay dry and palatable. Silage and haylage are also grass crops, and are conserved before they reach the dryness of hay. Silage at 60–70 per cent moisture is harvested just twenty-four hours after cutting and stored in large clamps, the air excluded by covering the clamp with plastic. It is usually fed to cattle, but some larger goat dairy herds feed silage; however, it is not in common use on a domestic scale.

Haylage is mid-way between hay and silage, baled and wrapped when there is around 30–40 per cent moisture in the stems. Haylage is useful for goat keepers where there is inadequate barn space for the storage of hay, but if made in large bales, as is often the case, a tractor will be required to manoeuvre the bales where they are needed, and the herd will need to be large enough to eat a whole bale before it heats up. Hay does not need to be eaten in a hurry, but wrapped haylage bales once opened will last only five to seven days before starting to rot; the heat makes the haylage a perfect host for unwelcome

bacteria, and any warm haylage should not be fed but thrown on the muck heap. Mouldy hay, haylage or silage should not be fed; neither should lawn cuttings.

Tree hay is made by cutting branches from deciduous trees when they are in full leaf (in the summer), then bundling them up and hanging them in a dry place. This is a labour-intensive process, but it produces nutritious browse for your goats to eat. Alder, ash, aspen, beech, birch, hazel, hornbeam, rowan, sycamore, willow and wych elm all make quality tree hay. There is a whole agricultural system of silvopasture, which is the planting of trees in abundance to provide forage and shelter for livestock, and goat keepers could do this on a suitable scale.

Depending on how much pasture there is available, goat keepers will choose either to make their own hay, or buy it in. On our farm, which ranges from very heavy wet clay to better draining ground, we produce a varied fifty to a hundred small bales per acre depending on the quality of grass, the type of soil, the weather, and how the area

Tree hay.

is managed. If you are buying it in, get good quality horse hay, not rougher forage that might be more suitable for cattle. A small hay bale will average 20kg (44lb), but bales can vary considerably depending on who has made them.

Quantities of Hay Required

Goats will need 1–2kg (2–4.5lb) of hay daily, and more if other feedstuffs are not available, with milkers needing nearer to 3.5kg (8lb) of hay per day. This will help you calculate the amount of hay you will need to make or to buy and store; as mentioned above, be aware that small bales vary in size and weight, and if buying from a dealer in larger quantities it makes sense to buy it by weight rather than by number of bales.

Other Forage Feeds

Good quality straw is also enjoyed, whether wheat, barley or oat straw, and will provide low-calorie roughage that is of particular use for managing the weight of fat goats. Nice quality straw used for bedding will often be nibbled when freshly scattered, but it can also be put in mangers as part of the forage feed to bulk out the diet for those that need to avoid putting on more condition.

Feedstuffs such as lucerne or alfalfa pellets or cubes developed primarily for horses may have the same nutritional content as the unprocessed variety, but are not the equivalent of long-stem forage in terms of keeping the rumen healthy and ensuring that goats do not gorge; do not feed these as substitutes for forage.

CONCENTRATES AND GRAIN

Concentrates, hard feed, cake or compound feed are all generic names for proprietary feeds. The types of hard feed available specifically for goats include coarse mixes and pelleted feeds, plus straights (individual crops rather than combined feedstuffs) such as sugar-beet pulp, soya beans, wheat, peas, beans, barley, oats, flaked maize, bran, fodder beet. The quantities given below are averages, and the goat owner will need to keep an eye on the body condition of their goats to determine what suits individual animals best.

Apart from does in the last few weeks of pregnancy and early weeks of lactation, and for young growing goats, well-fleshed meat goats and pygmy goats should not require concentrates if they have plenty of quality hay and browse available.

Quantities of Concentrates

A maintenance ration of hard feed for an adult goat is usually between 0.5 and 1kg (1 and 2.2lb) per day when fed with hay, splitting the ration into at least two feeds if needed. Dairy goats being milked twice a day will be fed a daily ration of 1.5kg (3.3lb) of 18 per cent protein dairy nuts.

Goat Coarse Mixes

The composition of goat coarse mix depends on the manufacturer, and bagged rations will vary from 12 to 18 per cent protein; they will include barley flakes, rapeseed meal, maize flakes, molasses, locust bean seed, soya, beans, peas, sunflower seeds, oats, calcium carbonate, sodium chloride, distillers' dried grains, vegetable oils, plus a range of vitamins and trace elements (iodine, cobalt, manganese, selenium and zinc).

Although dairy goat pellets are available, do consider feeding dairy-cattle rather than goat-specific rations. Cattle feed is not only cheaper, it has a better mineral content, which suits goats well. Feed dairy-cattle nuts for the milkers and coarse calf feed or calf weaner pellets for kids.

Proprietary Goat Mixes

Coarse goat mix (15% protein, 6% fibre)

All-round goat mix.

Dry goat mix (14% protein, 5.5% fibre)

Dry goat mix.

Herbal goat mix (13.7% protein, 6% fibre)

Herbal goat mix.

Pygmy goat mix (13.5% protein, 12% fibre)

Pygmy goat mix.

Shelf Life

The industry standard for using bagged feed is three months from the date of manufacture and bagging; however, the vitamins, minerals and trace elements are good for at least four to five months, so there would be no performance issues if bags were to go out of date whilst on farm.

It's certainly possible to create home-mixed rations from straights if you are confident in meeting the protein and energy requirements of your goats; for the rest of us, proprietary feed takes the guesswork out of the equation.

Make Changes Gradually

When introducing hard feed or changing the type of hard feed, make these changes gradually to allow the microbes in the rumen to adjust. This is not being finickity; rumen acidosis, which can be fatal to your goats, can occur if this regime is not followed. Eating quantities of what is highly fermentable feed produces excess amounts of gas and acid in the rumen. Signs include depression, breathing hard, grinding of teeth, lying down, constipation or scours, seizures, bloating (on their left side), staggering and death, and you should call your vet if you see any of these signs or suspect acidosis. Introduce concentrate feed only if needed, and in small increments at the rate of 0.25kg (0.5lb) per day, and gradually build up to the levels required to maintain condition.

Storing Concentrated Feedstuffs Safely

You may or may not be feeding hard feed to your goats, but still have feed on your holding for poultry, horses, cattle or sheep, for example. Under no circumstances should the goats be able to access this or their own stores of concentrated feed. Keep feedstuffs in a place that the goats cannot get into, and in containers they cannot breach. The consequences of goats gaining access to large quantities of hard feed can be and often are fatal through rumen acidosis (also known as grain overload – *see* above). Any spilled feed should be cleared away before goats can eat it.

Feed bin.

BODY CONDITION SCORING

Body condition scoring (BCS) is a hands-on method for assessing the amount of fat and meat carried by an animal, and is used to assess the nutritional status of your goats at different critical points in your herd year. Typically you would score your goats a couple of months before mating to ensure that both males and females are fit for breeding; then check does again a couple of months before kidding (ideally at the same time as pregnancy scanning) in order to manage their nutrition; you would check the developing kids to ensure they are putting on weight and condition as desired; and when choosing animals to take to slaughter.

Scores are measured by feeling for fat cover with your hands over two parts of the animal's body: the loin and rib (the spinous and transverse processes) and the breast (sternum). The sternum is the bone running along under the goat, from the brisket between the two front legs.

A five-point scale is used, where a score of one is assigned to very thin animals, and a score of five to a very fat animal (*see* table). Healthy goats should have a BCS of between 2.5 to 4.0; those with a BCS of 1 to 2 indicate a management or health problem. At mating and again at kidding, does should have a BCS of 3–3.5; by weaning time it would be lower, but should be no less than 2.0, after the demands of feeding their young. At slaughter, goats should have a BCS of 2–3.

Five-Point Body Condition Score

Condition score	Loin and rib score	Sternum score
BCS1: Goat looks emaciated, backbone visible with continuous ridge, flank hollow, ribs visible, no fat cover. Spinous and transverse processes are prominent and sharp, and can be easily grasped with the fingers. Loin is thin with no fat cover. Sternal fat is easily grasped and moved from side to side, joints joining ribs and sternum are easily felt. Goat is much too thin.	Loin and rib score 1.	Sternum score 1.
BCS2: Thin, backbone visible with continuous ridge, some ribs can be seen, little fat cover. The spinous processes are prominent but smooth, individual processes felt only as corrugations. Transverse processes smooth and rounded, but possible to press fingers under. Loin muscle present with little fat cover. Sternal fat is wider and thicker but can still be grasped and lifted. Joints less evident. Goat is a little too thin.	Loin and rib score 2.	Sternum score 2.
BCS3: Backbone not prominent, ribs barely discernible, with even fat cover. Spinous processes smooth and rounded, and bone only felt with pressure. Transverse processes also smooth and well covered, and hard pressure needed to find the ends. Loin muscle is full and with moderate fat cover. Sternal fat wide and thick with very little movement when grasped. Joints barely felt. Goat is in good condition.	Loin and rib score 3.	Sternum score 3.
BCS4: Backbone and ribs can't be seen, sleek appearance. Spinous processes only detectable as a line. The ends of the transverse processes cannot be felt. Loin muscles full and rounded with a thick cover of fat. Sternal fat difficult to grasp because of width and depth, and cannot be moved from side to side. Goat is in fat condition.	Loin and rib score 4.	Sternum score 4.
BCS5: Backbone buried in fat, ribs not visible and covered with excessive fat. Spinous and transverse processes cannot be detected with pressure, and dimpling in fat layers. Loin muscles are full and covered with thick fat. Sternal fat extends and covers the sternum joining the fat over the ribs and cannot be grasped. Goat is much too fat.	Loin and rib score 5.	Sternum score 5.

FEEDING REQUIREMENTS

Feeding the Milking Dairy Doe
Commercial dairy goats being milked twice a day will be fed a daily ration of 1.5kg (3.3lb) of 18 per cent protein dairy nuts – which include the necessary vitamins and minerals including copper – in addition to their roughage. The nuts fed are frequently cattle dairy nuts, which contain a better level of minerals than many proprietary goat feeds, so you would hope that the goats don't feel the need to help themselves to free-choice minerals. As each doe is being milked, dairy nuts are given as a 0.25kg (0.55lb) feed (totalling 0.5kg (1lb) across their two milkings), with the remaining kilo being fed back in the barn alongside their hay. A milking goat should be fed from about four to six weeks before kidding, building up to at least 0.5kg (1.2lb) at kidding.

Be aware that certain foodstuffs such as brassicas will taint a goat's milk, which makes it less pleasant to drink or eat in the form of cheese, yogurt or butter.

Feeding Males
Males, both entire and wethers, should be given very limited amounts of grain (if any) at a maximum of 1.5 per cent of bodyweight to avoid urinary calculi – a build-up of calcium crystals or stones causing blockages in the urinary system, which can be fatal. Depending on his condition in the lead-up to the breeding season a buck may need between 0.5 and 0.8kg (1–1.8lb) of a 14 per cent protein concentrate in the two to six weeks before he is put in with the does – the more condition that is required, the earlier the concentrates should be given. If he has a body condition score (BCS) of 3.5–4, no hard feed is required. Adult males will eat approximately 2kg (4.4lb) of hay daily.

Feeding the Pregnant Doe
You are aiming for a body condition score (BCS) of 3–3.5 for a doe when she is being

Waiting to be fed.

mated, and this should be maintained throughout pregnancy, ensuring she does not drop below BCS 3. When her kids are weaned, she should be a minimum of BCS 2. Give her the best quality hay, particularly in the last third of her pregnancy in the lead-up to kidding, and ensure that she has constant access to minerals (her calcium requirements increase significantly in late pregnancy) and clean water. In order for her to meet her energy needs and maintain condition it is probable that some concentrates need to be fed in the last four to six weeks – but ensure she does not get over fat.

Providing hay outside on a sunny day.

TROUGH AND RACK SPACE IN COMMUNAL AREAS

Two-bale hay rack.

Feed trough for communal use.

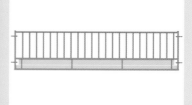

Vertical-railed feed barrier.

If communal hay racks are kept full enough to feed all goats throughout the day they will come and eat at will; like this there is minimal chance of bullying, and more nervous goats should be able to access as much hay as they need. If you do find any goats standing guard over a hay rack you will need to put another rack in place. If you are feeding concentrates communally, this is another matter, as these should not be made available ad lib, but at routine times split into one, two or three daily feeds.

Enough trough space is required so that goats can eat simultaneously: allow 0.4–0.5m (1.3–1.6ft) space for each adult goat, and less for pygmies and kids at 0.25–0.35m (0.8–1.2ft). If you find goats patrolling the length of a trough keeping shy feeders away, put another trough some distance away to allow everyone to feed at the same time.

Wherever possible, raise feeders off the floor to goat shoulder height to avoid contamination. All feeding containers and any feed scoops must be kept clean. Leftover food should be disposed of, and rations decreased, or altered to something more palatable so as to minimize waste.

Access to feed bowl.

Supplements and Minerals

Goats have a high mineral requirement, and mineral supplements should be offered ad lib. These will include calcium, cobalt, copper, iron, magnesium, phosphorus, selenium, sodium, zinc and others. Goats can be copper deficient, so this addition is particularly critical. If you have sheep, ensure they cannot access goat mineral supplements or feedstuffs, as copper is toxic to sheep. Added minerals will not be needed for those goats eating dairy nuts as they already contain enough, but they should be made available for all others, either in a lick bucket or as loose minerals.

To stop them being knocked about or pooed in, place mineral feeders and lick buckets above head height, providing a block for goats to stand on to reach inside. If minerals are fed outside, a lid or small roof will be needed to keep them dry (a 5ltr

Caprivite minerals.

Himalayan rock salt.

Salt lick.

Goat minerals.

plastic container with a head-sized hole cut in the side works well, and can be hung from a fence stake). Only offer small quantities at one time so the minerals remain fresh.

Goats should have access to a salt lick or to lump rock salt at all times, including during housing. They can also be given a small daily amount of seaweed meal, as it is full of minerals including iodine and phosphorus, which is critical for the in-kid/freshly kidded goat.

Baking soda (sodium bicarbonate) can be provided ad lib for goats if being fed concentrates or grain to aid digestion and guard against bloat, as it acts as an antacid, balancing the pH in the rumen. It is also commonly used as a treatment for bloat: it is mixed with water to make a baking soda liquid solution, which is administered orally.

WATER REQUIREMENTS

Water is the most important part of any mammal's diet, and if a goat is in milk the

Water trough.

Water-bowl drinker.

amount of water it will need to consume is considerably higher than at other times. Fresh, clean water must be available to all goats at all times, so use drinkers that minimize the risk of contamination: keep drinkers small where practicable, and put them at a height where all goats can drink easily, but which will frustrate their desire to drop their poo in it; and have enough drinkers so that a bullying goat can't stand guard over a single drinker. Goats can drink as much as an astounding 18ltr (4gal) of water per day, although the average for a lactating goat is 4–8ltr (0.9–1.8gal) and a dry goat 2–3ltr (0.4–0.7gal).

There are a number of variables to take into consideration regarding how much water a goat requires. For each kilo of dry matter that a goat consumes it will need around 2–2.5ltr (0.4–0.6gal) of water; the less moisture there is in its feed, the more it will drink. For every litre of milk that a goat produces it will need 1.5–2.2ltr (0.3–0.5gal) of water. The temperature and humidity in any particular day will have an impact on the amount of water consumed, as will the weight of the goat. If a goat is pregnant its water requirement will increase as it gets nearer to kidding, and the number of kids it is carrying is also a determinant. If it is eating salt (which should always be available), this will increase the need for water, just as you enjoying a packet of crisps will make you more thirsty for beer (insert your drink of choice).

80 per cent of water is drunk during the day, and there are peaks in consumption immediately after any concentrated feed is given, and when dairy goats have been milked. After kidding and the ensuing enthusiastic licking of kids, a doe will drink a considerable amount of water. Depending on circumstances, goats will drink between five to twenty times a day.

TOXIC PLANTS

There are a fair number of plants that are out-and-out toxic to goats, but there are also foods that are fine to feed in small quantities but should not be given in large amounts, or, for example, to pregnant does. Brassicas, those healthy vegetables that so many of us consume on a daily basis, include cabbage, kale, broccoli, cauliflower, Brussels sprouts, mustard greens, swede and turnips, and contain a compound that blocks iodine absorption. As iodine is crucial for the development of kids, brassicas should not be fed to pregnant does; however, small amounts fed from your vegetable patch can be enjoyed by your other goats, although letting them forage in a cabbage or rape field with brassicas in abundance would not be desirable.

Plants can be toxic in a number of ways, from causing sudden death (yew, rhododendron, foxglove, laurel, water dropwort, linseed), to those that cause scouring, haemorrhage, photosensitization, bloat, liver damage, anaemia, stillbirth, vomiting and so on. Some plants such as buttercup and sorrel that may grow naturally in your pastures shouldn't cause particular issues if there is plenty of alternative food available – however, ingesting large amounts causes kidney damage. They contain oxalic acid and therefore taste bitter to herbivores, which does not encourage consumption. Some parts of plants are toxic when other parts are not; ivy leaves are fine, but ivy berries are not, for example. When pruning ornamental shrubs keep all their trimmings away from goats.

If you have grown your own Christmas tree and have made sure it's entirely free of baubles, you can feed it at the end of the festive season to your goats; but if it's a bought tree it may well have been sprayed with weedkillers, insecticides, preservatives or flame retardants, so definitely don't give it to the goats. And don't feed your goats chocolate!

PLANTS TOXIC TO GOATS

aconite	gladiolus	pine
alder	ground elder	potato leaves
anemone	hellebore	privet
avocado	hemlock	prunus family (apricots,
azalea	honeysuckle	almonds, cherries,
black nightshade	hydrangeas	nectarines, peaches,
box	ivy (berries only)	plums, sloes)
bracken	laburnum	ragwort
brassicas	laurel	rape
broom	lesser celandine	rhododendron
bryony	lilac	rhubarb
buckthorn	linseed	spindle tree
buckwheat	lobelia	St John's wort
buttercup	lucerne	tomato (leaves only)
charlock (wild mustard)	mayweed	tormentil
clover	meadow saffron	tulip
common sorrel	mullein	Virginia creeper
daffodil	oak (acorns are fine in	walnut
deadly nightshade	moderation)	water dropwort
fool's parsley	old man's beard	woody nightshade
foxglove	pieris (forest flame)	yew

Signs that a goat has ingested something poisonous include salivation, lethargy, depression, vomiting, scours, muscle tremors, and a bloated/painful abdomen. When you first get goats, talk to your vet about what emergency medication you should have on hand, and ask what they recommend if plant poisoning is suspected, as treatment may need to be given by the keeper swiftly before a vet can be present. The vet may suggest activated charcoal, vegetable or mineral oil, Milk of Magnesia, or prescription-only medications.

CHAPTER 9

THE HEALTHY HERD

Outside toilet with goats, Millhams, Dolton, February 1979. (Photograph by James Ravilious © Beaford Arts digitally scanned from a Beaford Archive negative)

Keeping a healthy herd is best achieved through sourcing healthy stock to begin with and preventing disease wherever possible. The cornerstones are good hygiene, avoiding pitfalls (such as incorrect or inappropriate administering of medication), carrying out routine procedures, timely treatment when needed, quarantining as appropriate, being active in your own never-ending education, and the support of a good vet.

Signs of Good Health/Ill Health

Livestock in good health should be in good body condition, eating well and have a clean mouth, pink gums and inner eyelids; they should walk soundly, breathe evenly (fifteen to thirty breaths per minute for an adult, twenty to forty for kids), have a good coat, bright eyes, be alert and inquisitive, and delivering pelleted faeces. Signs of poor health include underweight condition, coughing, itching and rubbing, loss of coat, heavy, quick or raspy breathing, cloudy eyes, pale inner eyelids and gums, a stained mouth area, a stained anal area or scouring, a hunched stance, lameness, swellings, abscesses, and so on.

OPPOSITE: Vet taking blood samples to test for CAE.

Healthy goat dung.

The role of the goat keeper is to appreciate the signs of good health so that you spot anything untoward in its earliest possible stage so that it is easier to treat, and causes less stress and pain to the goat. A good farmer spends their life actively looking for things they don't want to see in their livestock.

If you are out of your depth with regard to diagnosis or treatment of ailments – which is likely for all but the most experienced keeper – please *do not* refer to the notoriously unreliable Dr Facebook (and other social media platforms are just as problematic), which will supply a mix of contradictory, illegal and sometimes downright dangerous disinformation. The trouble is that even the best information out there (and there's plenty of that, too, from excellent, experienced keepers) gets lost in the wash of nonsense on the internet. For everyday concerns talk to your local goat group, and for anything else please talk to your vet: it's what they are there for.

When starting out you will inevitably need the vet quite frequently; these occasions will decrease somewhat as you gain experience, at which point your vet will increasingly be working with you on prevention rather than cure. With your vet's help you will build expertise and be able to determine when treatment is suitable (effective and/ or economic), and potentially when humane dispatch is the best route either to save a goat from suffering or to maintain the health of the rest of the herd.

Your vet is also essential for prescribing any prescription-only medicines (POM). Few medications are licensed for goats – the dosage required is often higher than that indicated for sheep, and more frequent treatment may be needed; your vet will therefore have to advise and prescribe off-licence treatments. Whether you or your vet administers medication, you must record it in your veterinary medicine record book (*see* Chapter 3).

This chapter covers the primary ailments and preventative treatments of which goat keepers should be aware. There are many more diseases and conditions that hopefully you are less likely to come across.

Developing a Health Plan with your Vet

There really is no substitute for having a good vet when you have livestock. A good vet will be keen to work in partnership with you, taking time to understand the level of your expertise, so they can bring their own deep knowledge and experience most fruitfully to the relationship to the benefit of your animals. They will help ensure the best health of your livestock, and is calmly on hand to help you through emergencies. Not every vet is familiar with goats, so do ask around the local large (farm) animal practices and get recommendations from local goat keepers. Many vets will include a complimentary initial visit to your holding to meet you and find out about the livestock you have.

Being active in building your own knowledge (reading books, going on courses, accessing some of the excellent online resources, including the Moredun Research Institute, Goat Veterinary Society and National Animal Disease Information Service) means you won't be bombarding your vet with generic questions. Even so, most vets will be happy to answer phone and email queries when you have a question that you can't resolve but which doesn't require a visit. Increasing numbers of veterinary practices run training days for their clients, so do take advantage of these, even if they are targeted at other species (there's little currently available for goats). Training courses on offer include the safe use of medicines, nutrition, lameness, lambing and parasite control.

Preparing for a Vet Visit

It will save time if you are able to describe what problem you are facing when you call your vet. Think about the animal's history, age and condition – whether it is pregnant or lactating, or if there are observable symptoms such as a lack of appetite, or scouring – and any recent treatments; taking and relaying the goat's temperature is also helpful. Don't forget to let the vet know if the animal is new to your holding or has been in contact with new stock, and tell them if the problem is a one-off or recurring, and whether it is restricted to one animal or not.

Make sure the goat(s) in question is (are) in a secure area where the vet is able to handle it, preferably under cover and with light and water available; it is not the vet's job to hurtle round a field trying to catch the patient.

TAKING A GOAT'S TEMPERATURE

If you are concerned that your animal is slightly off colour but are not quite sure, taking a rectal temperature gives a swift and helpful indication if something is wrong. Using a digital thermometer is quick and easy, and you should keep one in your goat first-aid kit. Be aware that batteries in digital thermometers are not replaceable, so do check your thermometer is working from time to time (in particular pre-kidding), and when it is dud, get a new one. Put a small blob of obstetric lube on the business end of the thermometer, turn it on and insert it gently into the anus, then tilt it slightly left or right so that it takes the temperature of the rectal wall, not of the faeces. Wait for the beep, remove it, and take the reading. Clean it thoroughly before storing for future use.

Digital thermometer.

Temperature Guide

	Normal Fahrenheit	*Normal Centigrade*
Goats	101.3–103.5	38.5–39.7
Kids	101.8–104.5	38.7–40.2

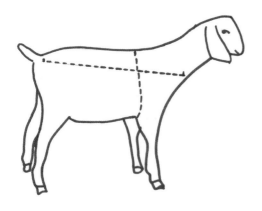

Measuring goats.

WEIGHING YOUR GOATS

A lot of medication is given according to the weight of an animal, so knowing what that weight is, rather than making a wild guess, is an important part of healthcare. Weigh scales are not cheap items but can be purchased second-hand at farm sales (ones for sheep or pigs will suit goats): in this case give them a really thorough clean, and treat with an appropriate farm disinfectant before use.

If you don't have livestock weigh scales and have kids or small goats to weigh, take your bathroom scales to the goat shed, put them on a flat surface, get on them (swear when you've read the result and resolve not to eat ice cream that week), pick up the kid, take another reading and subtract one weight from the other – and there you have it, the weight of said goat. Obviously this won't work for adults or hefty youngstock, in which case a tape measure can help you to make quite a good calculation of weight (*see* box).

USING MEASUREMENTS TO CALCULATE A GOAT'S WEIGHT

- Measure the circumference (known as 'heart girth') of the goat around the body and behind the shoulder in inches.
- Then measure the length of the body from the front of the shoulder to the pin bone at the rear in inches.
- Take the first measurement and multiply it by itself, then multiply that by the second measurement. Divide the whole by 300, which will give you the weight in pounds.
- Now you have the weight in pounds you can convert it to kilos by dividing the number of pounds by 2.2046.

For example:

If the circumference is 35in:
35 × 35 = 1,225in

If the length is 30in:
1,225 × 30 = 36,750in
36,750 ÷ 300 = 122.5lb
122.5 ÷ 2.2046 = 55.56kg

For the metric minded, measure in centimetres and divide by 10,838: for example, if the circumference is 90cm, and the length is 76cm:
90 × 90 × 76 = 615,600cm
615,600 ÷ 10,838 = 56.8kg

TESTING FOR GOAT DISEASES

Testing can be carried out for a number of key diseases to understand the health status of your herd, and any stock you wish to bring in.

CAE/CAEV (*Caprine Arthritis Encephalitis*)

CAE is a viral disease spread via colostrum or milk from infected does, through mating, and by shared equipment such as drenching guns and syringes. CAE can be relatively mild and easily missed in the early stages, but ultimately causes acute loss of condition, lameness, painful knee-joint arthritis, lung infections, and mastitis, which significantly hardens the udder. Individual goats may be infected yet stay healthy, but the effect on the herd is devastating; goats should therefore be blood tested annually for CAE, as apparently healthy individuals may be infected, and as they age they infect the rest of the herd. Even when risks are minimized, the maximum testing interval should be alternate years. Goats showing clinical signs should be culled.

CLA (*Caseous Lymphadenitis*)

CLA is a chronic contagious bacterial disease that causes abscesses in the lymph nodes in various parts of the body, notably in, but not restricted to, the base of the ear, below the jaw, and in front of and behind the hind leg and on the shoulder. Of course, not all abscesses are the result of CLA. Goats don't appear to be ill until the herd is heavily infected. CLA can be confirmed by lab tests of the contents of abscesses.

Infection is spread by the pus from burst abscesses, and any goat with abscesses should be isolated from other goats until there is a diagnosis, although the pus survives to be infectious on all manner of hard surfaces from walls and hurdles, to feed and drinking equipment. Control external parasites to minimize scratching and rubbing, which might break the skin, so making other goats vulnerable. There is no treatment and culling may be necessary.

Scrapie

Scrapie is a rare but notifiable infectious wasting disease affecting the nervous system of adults. It is very difficult to control. There is no cure, no vaccine, the condition is fatal, and animals pass on their susceptibility to their offspring. Testing is carried out post mortem, and mostly in herds that wish to export breeding animals. Scrapie gene testing can also be carried out to select breeding animals resistant to scrapie; these animals can be tested at any age using a blood or semen sample. Genotyping is not a test for the presence of scrapie, but if the animal were to be exposed to the disease, it reveals what chance it has of contracting it; this allows breeders to sell or breed from scrapie-resistant animals.

TB (Tuberculosis) Testing for Goats

There is no statutory programme of testing for TB in non-bovines in Great Britain, and the testing of goats is only carried out where infection has been confirmed in a herd, if there is suspicion of infection in a herd, or if private testing is requested by the herd owner. Confirmation of a positive test result will incur herd movement restrictions, the slaughter of goats that are reactors, and further compulsory testing.

Johne's Disease

Johne's (pronounced yo-knees) is a disease of adult cattle, sheep, goats, deer and rabbits caused by a bacterium. Goats can be blood tested to check for Johne's, and signs include gradual weight loss, a swelling under the jaw (which is why Johne's is often referred to as 'bottle-jaw'), with scours or soft faeces only seen in the final stages.

Affected goats may have roughness of the coat or loss of hair. Goats can be vaccinated with Gudair (which requires a prescription from your vet): this will reduce the number and severity of cases in an infected herd, but will not eliminate infection or prevent the spread to other animals. There is no cure or treatment.

Maedi Visna

Maedi Visna (MV) is an infectious, incurable viral disease that is very slow to develop and causes wasting and organ degeneration, and is ultimately fatal. It cannot be detected early in an animal's life. Some countries require MV-free accredited status for any animals to be imported, so this is important for those who wish to export their goats.

NOTIFIABLE DISEASES

Notifiable diseases are those that you are legally obliged to report to the Animal and Plant Health Agency, even if you only suspect that an animal may be affected; failure to report is an offence. Notifiable diseases can be endemic, which are those already present in the UK; or exotic, meaning those not normally present in the UK. Some endemic and exotic diseases are zoonotic, which means they can pass between animals and humans. For most notifiable diseases there are legal powers to cull animals to prevent the spread of disease during an outbreak. Goats are vulnerable to several notifiable diseases including anthrax, blue tongue, brucellosis, foot and mouth disease (FMD), goat pox, goat plague (which has never been found in Great Britain) and scrapie. Outbreaks of FMD are contained by the compulsory slaughter of infected animals.

ADMINISTERING MEDICATION

Injections

Depending on the product, injections are given subcutaneously (under the skin), intramuscularly (into the muscle), or intravenously (into the vein); the latter is a procedure to be undertaken by your vet, but a goat keeper will be expected to give subcutaneous and intramuscular injections as required. Most injections are given into the neck skin or neck muscle, unless the datasheet or vet indicates otherwise.

For a subcutaneous injection, pinch or 'tent' a fold of skin 10–15cm (4–6in) below the ear on the side of the neck where the skin is loose, and inject into the cushion of skin. For an intramuscular injection, inject slowly into the neck muscle 10–15cm (4–6in) in front of the shoulder, away from any area of bone and aiming upwards towards the head. For both injections gently massage the area afterwards to disperse the medication.

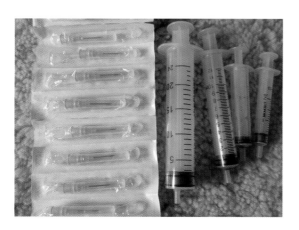

Needles and syringes.

NEEDLE SIZES FOR INJECTIONS

Hypodermic needles for goats	Gauge (the higher the number, the thinner the needle)	Length for subcutaneous injection	Length for intramuscular injection	Cap colour
Kids under 20kg (44lb)	21-gauge	13mm	13mm	Green
Kids 20 to 40kg (44 to 88lb) and adults	19-gauge	13mm	25mm	Yellow
Adults (for thicker solutions)	18-gauge	13–16mm	25mm	Pink

Injection sites.

Drenching and pour-on guns.

Drenching/Dosing Orally

When administering a wormer or flukicide as an oral drench, weigh your goats, check the drench gun is delivering the correct dose, and administer it correctly.

Underestimating weight: This is a common cause of under-dosing. Either weigh each goat individually and dose accordingly, or select and weigh the biggest in the group to determine the correct dose. The exception to the rule of dosing according to the heaviest animal is when using yellow wormer, which can be toxic at high levels.

Calibrate and maintain the drench gun: Also check its accuracy at regular intervals. Clean with warm soapy water after use, and use a little vegetable oil to keep it lubricated. Calibrate by squirting a single dose from the gun into a small container that you can then withdraw into a marked syringe to check that the correct dose is being delivered.

Make sure the goat is properly restrained: It is important that the goat can't leap about when you are drenching to be sure that it swallows the whole dose. Place a hand under the goat's head and tilt it slightly to the side. Slot the nozzle of the drenching gun into the gap between the molar and incisor teeth and then push it over the back of the tongue – do not push it in any further, and do not insert it just inside the front of the mouth. Pushing the gun down the goat's throat risks damaging the windpipe, and if the dose is administered just inside the mouth the goat may spit out much of it.

Antibiotic and antiseptic sprays.

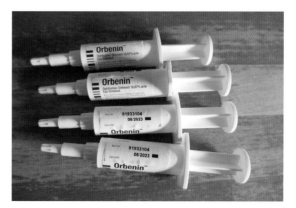

Antibiotic eye cream.

Pour-ons are applied along the back of an animal (sometimes in a line, sometimes as a spray, so you must check the datasheet for the correct mode and tool for application) using the appropriate dosing gun. Just like oral dosing guns, they should be calibrated and the goat weighed to ensure that the correct amount is applied.

Eye Creams

Antibiotic ointments are used for treating eye conditions such as conjunctivitis or pink eye. Both eyes will require medication as the condition is highly contagious. A tiny blob of cream dropped on each eyeball is needed, so the goat must be restrained; do not touch the eyeball with the dropper. This is something a goat keeper can apply.

FOOT CARE

The shepherds among you will probably be very aware that the old advice to trim your sheep's feet regularly is plain wrong. Current best practice guidance confirms that trimming is both overused and counter-productive, causing even more severe lameness and slower healing. Most lameness is caused by scald or footrot, and these require antibiotic treatment; trimming causes pain and further damages the foot. So why is

Topical Application of Medication or Treatments (Sprays and Pour-ons)

Antibiotic sprays are for the prevention of infections of superficial traumatic or surgical wounds and claw/hoof infections, in particular interdigital dermatitis (foot rot), scald, infected wounds and orf lesions. Antibiotic spray is often used unnecessarily in uninfected wounds where an antibacterial spray should be used (we all have a responsibility to minimize the use of antibiotics, focusing its use where it's really needed). Silver aluminium antibacterial spray is recommended for wounds from castrations, disbudding and dehorning, and surgical wounds. For minor wounds such as cuts and scrapes, use an off-the-shelf antiseptic spray, often known as violet or purple spray.

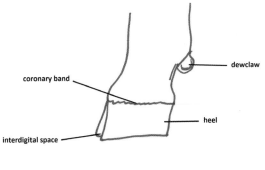

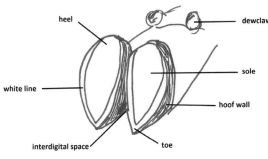

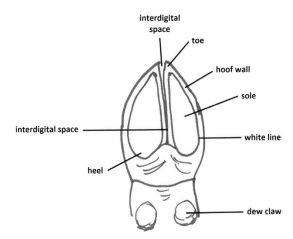

Foot anatomy.

place if hooves are genuinely overgrown, and once any infections have been treated and inflammation is under control. Goats that live on stony or hard ground may never need their feet trimmed, while those living on damp Devon pastures may need attention every six weeks. Even vets have widely divergent opinions on the desirable frequency for hoof trimming goats, varying from every six weeks to once a year; the best approach is to check for lameness daily, to look more closely at your goats' feet every month, and only trim if it is genuinely required.

When trimming, remove small amounts at a time to ensure you don't cause bleeding; your aim should be for the base of the foot to match the angle of the coronary band. Trim the feet of those that are sound first, and attend to any that are lame after that. Disinfect foot trimmers if you've used them on a lame goat or one with any of the issues described below so that you are not transmitting disease from one goat to another. To labour the point, there are many instances of lameness when trimming should not be done.

Overgrown foot.

this homily on sheep relevant to goats? The majority of information on goats still states that foot trimming should be undertaken regularly. However, although foot trimming is an important skill for goat keepers, what is even more important is appreciating when trimming is, and when it is not, appropriate.

Diagnosing the causes of lameness (with your vet if necessary) will enable you to treat accordingly; trimming should only take

Trimmed foot.

Picking up a goat's foot.

Diagnosing and Dealing with Lameness

Lameness can be a serious condition for goats; it causes pain, and may affect their appetite and long-term health. Check goats daily to make sure nothing is hopping, walking unevenly, or eating on its knees, and take action if you find lameness. Feet should be checked with the goat in a standing position, picking up each foot so that you can see the sole, as you would for a horse. If you have a milking stand this is ideal for checking and working on feet; if not, use a halter to tie up the goat while you attend to it. If the foot is overgrown and there is no infection requiring treatment, use sheep foot shears to trim. Do not foot trim a doe in her last two months of pregnancy.

Puncture Wounds

Hedge trimmings can be a particular hazard for goats, and as time-consuming as this may be, do remove them from the pasture – a spring-tine rake is a useful tool for this. Blackthorn and hawthorn are particularly pernicious, piercing a foot and causing infection, and small stones and twigs can get caught between the claws of the foot. When putting up or repairing fencing be sure to remove all pieces of wire and stray fencing staples – these are exactly the sort of foreign bodies that should not make contact with a goat's foot. Noticed quickly, removing a foreign

body from a foot can have instant rewards. Once removed, allow any pus to drain, clean the wound and squirt with antibiotic spray.

Scald (Interdigital Dermatitis)

Scald is caused by bacteria, it is infectious, and it is a common cause of lameness in kids when conditions are wet, often in late spring. The skin between the claws becomes pinker and swollen, and may be smelly, with a thin layer of white discharge. Individual cases should be treated using antibiotic aerosol sprays (POM). When several animals are affected, treating all goats in the group in a 10 per cent zinc sulphate solution or 3 per cent formalin in a footbath can provide effective control. After footbathing, goats must stand in a dry area (not muddy) so that the formalin or zinc sulphate can dry on the feet. It may be necessary to repeat the foot bathing at weekly or two-weekly intervals to prevent disease transmission and more lame goats. Foot trimming is not appropriate for scald.

Footrot

Footrot begins with scald and is extremely painful and contagious; goats with footrot are very lame. There is swelling and moistening of the skin between the claws, with infection spreading into the foot, which separates the horn tissue from the sole; where treatment is neglected this can extend up the hoof wall. There is a foul-smelling discharge, and

Footbath.

in severe cases the whole hoof horn might be shed.

Recommended treatment for mild cases is by antibiotic aerosol spray, but for more serious cases injection of long-acting antibiotics (POM) will also be needed. Affected goats should be isolated from the rest of the herd to stop the spread of infection. Any loose horn should only be trimmed once the footrot lesion is resolved.

Footbathing is not an effective way to treat footrot as the substances will cause pain and increase the risk of granulomas forming.

White Line Disease

Penetration of the white line – where the wall and the sole join – by stones or sharp objects can cause lameness and infection, progressing to a white line abscess, which may then burst out at the top of the foot. White line disease and abscesses require careful foot trimming to remove the foreign object and allow the pus to drain. Antibiotics will be necessary if the foot is hot and/ or swollen.

Laminitis

Laminitis is a painful condition normally connected with ponies on too rich a diet, but it is also known in goats. It can appear after kidding in association with a retained placenta, metritis (infection of the reproductive tract), mastitis and pneumonia, and in geriatric goats, or from acidosis after eating too much grain. Signs include an unwillingness to move or stand, shifting from one foot to another, walking on the knees and grinding the teeth (an indication of pain), and the feet are hot to the touch and tender. Anti-inflammatories will need to be prescribed, and grain should be removed from the diet. Goats with laminitis may develop deformed, hardened hooves, and will require regular hoof trimming to deal with the overgrowth of the horn.

Contagious Ovine Digital Dermatitis (CODD)

Goats with CODD are severely lame, typically from infection in one claw of a single foot. Ulcers develop at the coronary band (the junction of the hoof wall and haired skin of the pastern), and these can become severe. In the early stages not all affected goats will be lame, so careful examination of purchased animals for signs of CODD is essential. Treat by antibiotic injection and spray, and in all goats avoid over-trimming.

CAE

CAE (*see* above) can result in severe lameness.

Toe Granulomas

Toe granulomas (also known as strawberry footrot) are painful red swellings of tissue caused by over-zealous trimming, untreated lesions, or chemical irritation from overly frequent use of formalin footbaths. Treat with antibiotics if infected, and bandage the foot with copper sulphate; even with treatment they may not improve.

Shelly Hoof
This condition is frequently found when animals are pastured on wet ground: the outer wall of the claw becomes loosened and forms a pocket, providing an ideal home for unwanted soil and debris. Carefully trim away loose horn and remove any impacted material. If infected, use antibiotic spray.

Old Age and Osteoarthritis
In pet herds elderly goats are quite common and they can become arthritic, just like humans, which causes pain and lameness. Anti-inflammatories can be given as pain relief.

PREVENTATIVE AND ROUTINE TREATMENTS AND PROCEDURES

Clostridial Diseases
Clostridial diseases include enterotoxaemia, pulpy kidney, dysentery, braxy, black disease, blackleg, tetanus and botulism. They can strike without warning: the organisms responsible for these are widespread in the soil, the diseases are invariably fatal, and all goats are at risk. Vaccination is required and is a routine task for goat keepers; this does not need a vet visit. Do ask an experienced goat keeper (or a convenient shepherd will do!) to show you how it's done before you need to give your first injections.

The recommended vaccination for goats in the UK is Lambivac, available without prescription, which is administered under the skin (subcutaneous) in the neck. When you vaccinate your in-kid does do not forget to vaccinate bucks, wethers, youngsters, and any other goats that may not be in kid that year. The smallest bottle of Lambivac is 50ml, which is twenty-five doses, but do not store any leftovers because once the vial is breached, Lambivac has a very short shelf life of just ten hours. Therefore only buy the quantity you need, and inject all goats due for vaccination on the same day to ensure the medication remains viable.

Goats that have received their primary course (two doses of 2ml, four to six weeks apart) will then need a booster every six months. Time these so that pregnant does will receive a booster two to four weeks before kidding; this not only protects the doe but passes protection to the unborn kids. Kids will then need their primary vaccinations at ten to twelve weeks old, and must continue with boosters every six months. The Goat Veterinary Society recommends the following vaccination programme:

Vaccination Programme for Protection against Clostridial Diseases and Tetanus for Goats

Lambivic treatment	Administration frequency	Dose
Primary course	2 doses 4-6 weeks apart	2ml
Booster	Every 6 months	2ml
Kids from vaccinated does	Start at 10-12 weeks of age; second dose 4-6 weeks later	2ml
Kids from unvaccinated does	Start at 2-4 weeks of age; second dose 4-6 weeks later	2ml
Pregnant does	Booster 2-4 weeks before kidding	2ml

THE SAFE DISPOSAL OF SHARPS AND UNUSED MEDICATION

Use a proper sharps bin to dispose of used sharps (hypodermic needles, syringes with needles, scalpels, blades, disposable scissors, suture equipment). A sharps bin is a specially designed lidded box that you can buy from your vet: this will include the cost of disposal. For any unused/out-of-date medication you can buy a 'doop' ('destruction of old pharmaceuticals') bin from your vet; this will also include the cost of its disposal when full.

Sharps and doop bins.

TREATING INTERNAL PARASITES

Internal parasites are organisms that live in the body of the host, occupying the digestive tract or body cavities, body organs, blood, tissues or cells. Intestinal worms cause many of the problems that goats have, so goats should be tested regularly for these. Goats are very susceptible to worms and never build up an immunity, unlike sheep and cattle. The subject of wormers (*aka* anthelmintics) is complex, and veterinary advice has changed considerably over the years now that so many intestinal worms are resistant to wormers. Depending on the type of wormer purchased, it can be administered as an oral drench, a pour-on, or injected; do note, however, that the method of administration is specific to each product, and you cannot inject a pour-on, or use a pour-on as an oral dose, and so on. There is some concern that pour-on treatments may be poorly absorbed so do discuss this with your vet before purchase.

Testing faecal samples is critical in managing worm burdens and determining the use of anthelmintics. It is simple to send fresh poo samples (collected either from individuals or as a pooled, composite sample

Faecal sampling pack.

from the herd) to be checked for worm counts to identify if they are carrying a worm burden that needs treatment. Your vet can advise, or there are several laboratories and agricultural merchants that accept posted samples. Tests can check for a range of parasites including roundworm, stomach hairworm, nematodirus, tapeworm, ostertagia, coccidia, lungworm and fluke.

The Use of Wormers

The prolonged use of one wormer increases the production of resistant worms to that particular wormer, while too frequent changing of wormers can result in multiple resistance developing: wormers should therefore be changed no more frequently than annually, and your vet may advise that one family of wormer is used until it is no longer effective, and only then switched. Although there are many different wormers available, there are only five different families (white, yellow, clear, orange and purple), so when changing do make sure you move to a different family, not just a different make. Note that orange and purple wormers are vet-prescribed only.

As part of your goat health plan talk to your vet regarding the choice and switching of wormers, the frequency of faecal sampling, and correct dosing rates for goats. Don't mix wormers with any other product before administration, and no matter how often you use a product, always check the dose rates and withdrawal periods as they do change.

Goat Veterinary Society Wormer Recommendations

Goat Veterinary Society wormer recommendations	Current sheep dose rates	Recommended goat dose rates
Benzimidazole (white)	5mg/kg	10mg/kg
Levamisole (yellow)	7.5mg/kg	12mg/kg
Ivermectin (clear)	0.2mg/kg	0.3-0.4mg/kg
Doramectin (clear)	0.2mg/kg	0.2-0.4mg/kg
Moxidectin (clear)	0.2mg/kg	0.2-0.4mg/kg
Zolvix (orange)	2.5mg/kg	Under direction from your vet
Startect (purple)	0.2ml/kg	Under direction from your vet

FAMACHA Scoring

FAMACHA scoring is a test for barber pole worms (*Haemonchus contortus*) using the symptoms of anaemia to assess whether individual goats need treatment. Focusing on treating the animals that need medication instead of the whole herd reduces the potential for creating resistant worms, and the cost. The FAMACHA chart shows different colours of the membrane of the eye from a dark red (1) indicating no significant anaemia, to a white colour (5) that shows severe anaemia. Remember that just because your goat has nice pink eye membranes, this doesn't mean that it doesn't have other worm burdens; dung analysis is also needed.

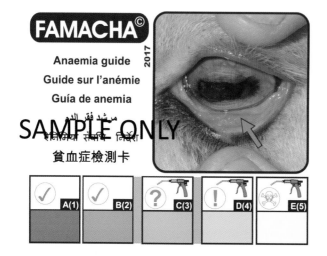

FAMACHA chart.

MINIMIZING WORMER USE

To minimize the use of wormers do not overstock your land, rotate the ground your goats have access to, while for some goat keepers a zero-grazing approach might appeal. This would mean supplying every mouthful of the goats' food and creating a purpose-made exercise space; however, not every keeper would want to see their goats without the opportunity to forage and simply just to be in natural surroundings. Always have dung samples analysed before worming so that you do not use any product unnecessarily. Grazing on certain plants such as chicory, bird's foot trefoil and sainfoin reduces the negative effects of worms, and these could be helpfully included in a pasture planting plan.

Liver Fluke

Fluke is a parasitic flatworm with a complex life cycle starting with the mud snail, and it's a serious issue for livestock on wet land as it compromises the liver and can be fatal if not treated. Fluke is incredibly hardy and built to survive; the good news is that you can ask the lab to include testing for fluke alongside worm analysis. Signs include anaemia, bottle jaw and weight loss. Goats can be treated with an oral dose of flukicide; talk to your vet about the size, timing and frequency of doses. You can help mitigate the risk somewhat by not allowing your goats on wet areas such as ponds, ditches and rivers, and putting hard standing under and around outdoor drinkers, but if you live in a wet region there is every chance that you will need to test and treat.

Coccidiosis

Coccidia are microscopic parasites found in the gut of all goats. Until immunity develops as the goat matures, kids up to three months are at particular risk, as coccidia damage the inside lining of their gut, causing bloody diarrhoea. There are a number of treatments for coccidiosis in sheep that the vet can prescribe for your goats off-licence, and kids may need several treatments from two to three weeks of age up to six months. Coccidia can also be tested for in dung samples, and test to see if adults require treatment prior to mating.

TREATING EXTERNAL PARASITES

Goats can suffer with all sorts of skin issues, and the cause of irritation, hair loss, scabbing or other conditions needs to be investigated to ensure that the appropriate treatment is given.

Lice, Ticks, Mites and Nasal Bots

Lice, ticks, mites and nasal bots can be treated with a topical product, applied to the skin or systemic (injectables), and if found in the herd all goats should be treated as these ectoparasites don't restrict their activity to one animal. Apart from itching, anaemia can be caused by sucking lice (lice charmingly come in two types – sucking and biting), and lice and ticks can be seen by the naked eye. Discussion with the vet is needed as products are licensed for sheep and cattle but not goats, and are not licensed at all for livestock producing milk for human consumption. Small numbers of individual ticks can be removed in the same way and using the same tick removers as used for dogs.

Flystrike

Flystrike is a risk when the weather is warm and wet, and fibre breeds with dirty back ends and goats with any wound are particularly at risk. Blowfly strike results from the larvae of greenbottle flies, blackbottle flies and bluebottle flies invading the living tissue of the host; it is a particular risk when the weather is warm and humid. Look for flies gathered round your goats, sweaty patches on the flanks or by the tail, itchiness, rubbing, looking generally out of sorts, and on close inspection fly eggs or at a further stage (to be avoided whenever possible), maggots.

Fly eggs and maggots need to be dealt with immediately; once spotted, clip away any hair around the affected area and remove all eggs and maggots and treat with antibacterial or antibiotic spray depending on the wound (if any). Maggot oil with citronella is also soothing and a fly preventative.

Pour-ons available for sheep can be used as a preventative and/or treatment, depending on the product used. There is a myriad of recipes for creating gentle home-made fly prevention treatments (for example cider vinegar with added tea-tree oil and citronella) for spraying on your livestock; however, using these has to be accompanied by close observation for infestation in case more aggressive treatment is required.

BLOAT

Bloat is the accumulation of gases in the rumen, which shows as distention on the left side of the goat's abdomen, and loss of interest in food. It can be caused by eating too much hard feed or grain, or grazing on lush pasture (frothy bloat), or growths in the oesophagus (obstructive bloat). Urgent attention is needed. Drenching with bloat drench or 100–200ml of vegetable oil and massaging the abdomen can help in cases of frothy bloat, and for obstructive bloat a stomach tube fed down to the stomach will release the gas, or the vet may create an opening into the rumen through the skin as appropriate.

ZOONOSES

Zoonoses are diseases that can be transmitted between human and animal, so particular care needs to be taken when treating or dealing with these. They include orf, ringworm and toxoplasmosis.

Orf

Orf is a type of contagious dermatitis that causes lesions and pustules around the nose and mouth (normally of kids), and can be transferred to the does' teats through suckling. It enters through scratches and small wounds caused, for example, by browsing on thistles or near sharp rush. When handling and treating orf wear disposable gloves, and wash your hands thoroughly afterwards as orf is painful and can persist for a long time in humans. Sudocrem (the zinc sulphate cream used for nappy rash in babies, and an item that should be in everyone's livestock first-aid kit for treating minor wounds) can be used on minor sores, and use antibiotic spray to deal with any secondary infection; antibiotics will not kill orf as it is a virus, not a bacteria.

In humans, orf starts as a small, red, itchy or painful lump, normally on the fingers, hands, forearms or face. Other possible symptoms include a high temperature and general tiredness. It usually clears up within three to six weeks. Orf cannot be spread between people.

Ringworm

Ringworm is a fungal infection that causes circular crusty lesions, normally around the head and neck. It can be transferred to humans by handling infected goats or any of the fixtures with which the goat has come into contact. When treating infected goats, or disinfecting areas they have come into contact with, wear gloves, and be careful not to rub your face while doing so. Treatment of the goat with antifungal preparations may shorten the healing time, but ringworm normally clears up in a couple of months.

Toxoplasmosis

Toxoplasmosis is a parasite carried by cats that can infect goats and humans. Cat faeces can contaminate goat feed and bedding, and can cause damage and death to unborn kids, so keep cats away from feed stores.

Although toxoplasmosis is usually harmless, if a woman contracts it for the first time while she is pregnant, or a few months before she conceives, there is a small risk that the infection could cause miscarriage or stillbirth, or – though this is very rare – birth defects or problems after the baby is born. Pregnant women should therefore not be involved in kidding, or handling the afterbirth or aborted kid foetuses, nor should they handle the clothes of anyone who has. They should also not consume unpasteurized goats' milk or any products made from it, and must not touch or handle pregnant does or kids.

QUARANTINE

When bringing home additional goats, a minimum twenty-one day quarantine is recommended to enable you to monitor any ailments that might arise, and twenty-eight days is better. If you have concerns about CLA, at least two months' quarantine is needed for signs of developing abscesses and swollen glands.

The correct quarantine treatments are essential for all in-coming goats to remove resistant worms. Dosing goats and then putting them straight on to clean pasture increases the risk of wormer resistance developing on your holding. Contain new goats on hard standing for their first two days so that worms voided can't contaminate your pasture. Once the goats are wormed take a dung sample and have them checked to ensure the wormer has been successful; if not, worm them again with a different family of wormer. Do visual checks for lice in multiple places over the goat, and also inspect them for footrot.

MEDICINE DATASHEETS

Datasheets for all veterinary medicines (for when you lose the container or paper insert that tells you about withdrawal periods, dosage, route for administration and so on) are available online at www.noahcompendium.co.uk.

CHAPTER 10

RAISING GOATS FOR MEAT

Cuppers Piece, Beaford, November 1983. (Documentary photograph by James Ravilious for the Beaford Archive © Beaford Arts)

Boer does.

There's no doubt that goat meat is a growing market in the UK. The perception that goat is solely of interest to specific cultural groups is changing, and there are a number of butchers trumpeting the availability of goat on their counters to customers who have never tried it before. The West is finally starting to appreciate what Caribbean, African, South American, Middle Eastern, South Asian, Chinese and Muslim cooks and consumers from all over the world have known all along: goat is a fabulous meat. Touted as the healthiest red meat, being low in cholesterol and fat and leaner than poultry, it's not surprising that goat is desirable. Even so, although you can find goat cheeses and milk in nearly every supermarket in the land, you

can't say the same about the meat: it is still very much a niche product in many parts of the country.

For those purely interested in meat for their own table it is a very rewarding process, and it is reassuring to know that the meat is produced in a way over which you have complete control, and that the goat has had a good and well-cared for existence. The responsibility and consequences of rearing livestock for meat hits home every time you take an animal to the abattoir, and rightly so. You should never become indifferent about this, and that stark awareness will make you a better goat keeper.

This book is aimed largely at those new to goat keeping, who intend to keep goats on a fairly small scale; however, this doesn't

OPPOSITE: Boer doe.

mean that you shouldn't contemplate selling your meat beyond the scope of family and friends. Because we are talking of a product that has not yet reached a mass market in the UK, marketing your goat meat is something that requires both time and skill, just as it would for any micro-business in an embryonic market.

GOAT MEAT

Goat meat has a variety of names. The meat from adults and older kids is known as chevon or chèvre or simply goat, while in various parts of the world, adult goat and sheep meat are interchangeably known as mutton. The meat from younger animals is called cabri or chevreau (French for kid), cabrito (little goat in Spanish and Portuguese), capretto (little goat in Italian), or kid. Certain cultures relish dishes made from mature animals, including from entire bucks that produce a gamey, pungent meat, while others prefer the sweeter, more tender meat of the younger animal.

As well as pure Boer or Boer-cross meat, a number of farms rear male kids that were previously seen as an unwanted by-product of the goat dairy sector, thus avoiding waste and taking positive advantage of the growing interest in goat meat. Other meat goats not yet familiar in the UK are the Kalahari Red and the Savanna, very popular in South Africa and increasingly in the USA, which have the same chunky body shape as the Boer, but are separate breeds entirely, and not just different colourways.

Goat Meat Statistics Compared with Other Meats

Per 85g (3oz) cooked meat	Calories	Fat (g)	Saturated fat (g)	Protein (g)	Iron (mg)	Cholesterol (mg)
Goat	122	2.58	0.79	23	3.3	63.3
Beef	245	16	6.8	23	2.9	73.1
Pork	310	24	8.7	21	2.7	73.1
Lamb	235	16	7.3	22	1.4	78.2
Chicken	120	3.5	1.1	21	1.5	76

Sourced from The American Goat Federation, based on the United States Department of Agriculture statistics 2001.

As for the taste of goat, it's often said that when hot it tastes like lamb, and when cold it is more like beef – though of course it tastes deliciously of itself. You can cook it any way that you would cook any red meat, from pot-roasted joints and tender chops, to burgers, stews, tagines and the more familiar goat curries. Because it is close textured like beef but lower in fat, slow rather than fast roasting is best to get the most out of it. Depending on the cut you can cook it slowly using your favourite tagine, korma or rogan josh recipes, or braise it with pulses and

Leg joint ready for roasting.

spices for a rich, falling-apart stew. For fast cooking there are chops, kofta, sausages, burgers, kidneys and meatballs. You can prepare it over the fire as kebabs, butterflied leg or shoulder; you can roast the shoulder, leg, rack or saddle using recipes by the dozen; or bake it as ragu, hotpots and pies.

REARING GOATS FOR MEAT

Is there anything special that you need to do for goats being raised for meat? Like all goats they need a balanced and varied diet

Meat goats with good body conformation: Boer buck and...

.....Kalahari Red.

to keep them fit and healthy, preferably a sustainable, natural and as it happens low-cost mix of browse, pasture and hay. A diet that limits or avoids concentrated grain-based feeds will result in a slower growing animal, but as for all ruminants, the taste and texture of the resulting meat will be far superior, so it's definitely worth the wait. Good quality, sweet-smelling hay should be available for your growing goats at all times, and during the summer months a meat goat will graze well.

A goat being raised for meat should be, well, meaty. Choose goats that are well muscled and have plenty of width and depth to their body, preferably with a good length of loin and a rounded rump. A chunky conformation rather than a scrawny outline is what you're after. If buying does to use for breeding meat animals, a smaller one doesn't necessarily equate to small offspring; just like cows or sheep, an individual animal may give birth to smaller offspring that then grow on very well if the dam has a good supply of milk and the feed offered is appetizing to both doe and kid.

A large doe with a poor milk yield may well produce less favourable offspring in a meat context. Ideally you want a doe that will have and successfully raise a pair of chunky kids each year, rather than one that keeps all her nutrition for herself. This is one of many reasons to keep livestock records.

Slaughter Age and Carcase Weights

The slaughter age of goats depends on the market or markets you are keen to serve, the condition of the individual animal and, particularly if it's solely for home use, your own preference. Meat goat kids are at their peak as regards taste at a year old, so there is no need to rush to finish them early; goat-meat producers in the UK take meat goats to slaughter from six to eighteen months. Different cultures have their own age and

Goat carcase.

gender preferences for goat meat, ranging from milk-fed kids as young as two to three months to mature bucks.

The deadweight carcase of six- to twelve-month-old meat goats raised on pasture will weigh in the region of 14 to 20kg (30 to 45lb) – 32 to 40kg (70 to 100lb) liveweight – or more, and even dairy-cross males reared specifically for the restaurant market and fed ad lib until they reach 55 to 60kg (120 to 130lb) liveweight can achieve as much as 24kg (53lb) deadweight. At six to twelve months you should expect a killing out percentage of around 45 per cent (the weight of the carcase in relation to the liveweight prior to slaughter given as a percentage), so a 40kg (100lb) kid should return an 18kg (40lb) carcase, though butchery options such as boning and rolling will reduce this further.

Whatever the age and weight of the goat, there's no point taking an animal to the abattoir that is in poor shape, so learn how to assess body condition (*see* Chapter 8).

Cull Goats and Older Goat Meat

Every livestock keeper needs to think about any animals that are no longer fit for purpose in their herd. You may have room for a pet or two, but you also need to think about avoiding over-stocking your land and over-taxing your time, energy and wallet with non-productive animals. If you are breeding you are not going to be able to keep everything unless your land and facilities are made of elastic, and at some point old breeding does need replacing with new blood and younger animals. However, culling doesn't necessarily mean that all older goats are removed from the herd, as some of your best mature females may have an admirable, easy kidding record and be in excellent health, allowing them to be bred for a further year or two.

Having a clear rationale as to culling can be very difficult for new livestock keepers, who understandably want to keep all their old pals. With small herd numbers you become hugely attached to your goats. However, if you want your herd to be productive and healthy, you need to use your head as well as your heart. Your cull policy may include dispatching barren does or ones that fail to deliver or rear live kids, infertile bucks, those with persistent foot or other health problems or who have prolapsed during kidding, does with inadequate milk for their kids, that have traits you don't want to reproduce or that exhibit a seriously challenging temperament.

All these animals, including the older does and wethers, can certainly be used for meat (excepting the mature buck, unless you have an appreciative market for his meat), using the longer, slower cooking methods to achieve tenderness; they will have plenty of flavour.

Small-scale livestock keepers are often not sure how to deal with breeding females that have passed their prime. The temptation can be to put them in with the buck 'just one more time', but if a doe is not fit for another kidding this is not kind or wise, and can easily result in dead does and kids. Using her for meat is a far better option. This is undoubtedly her fate anyway if you send her to market, but then she will be shunted hither and yon by strangers on the way to slaughter. The best option is to take her yourself to the abattoir for a quick, less stressful end. Arrange for the carcase to be hung for at least a fortnight, and be sure to mark the returned joints as mature goat before you put them in the freezer, as failing to do so can result in cooking confusion and chewy disasters, rather than wonderful meals later on.

Goat meat.

The meat from older goats tends to darken and has a deeper flavour than kid. Having lived a productive life the tenderness has to be cooked into the meat, so long, slow cooking with lots of liquid to sauce and moisten the meat is essential. The scent and taste of older goat is more intense than kid, and used in stews, tagines and curries, surrounded by vegetables and warming spices, the meat can take plenty of complementary flavourings. But there are also people who love the piquancy of older goat with no spicy disguise. The contrast between kid and older goat is usefully compared to the difference between lamb and mutton, or veal and beef.

Home Slaughter

For the vast majority of goat keepers the slaughter of livestock is best left to the abattoir. Home slaughter is certainly not appropriate for anyone who doesn't have the skills to dispatch an animal without causing it any suffering. But there are sound arguments if you do have the skill (and not a misplaced confidence) for slaughtering at home, particularly if your nearest abattoir is some distance away and you want to eliminate the stress of a long journey on goats unfamiliar with travelling in a trailer.

You don't need a licence to kill animals to eat at home, provided that you own the animal, you kill it on your property, and are killing it for you or your immediate family to consume (all of whom must live on your property). You can't kill animals in accordance with religious rites at home, and are liable to be prosecuted if you don't follow the current legislation.

You will need to know how to restrain, stun and kill the animal humanely and quickly, and must not cause any avoidable pain, distress or suffering, so familiarize yourself with the guidance that is readily available from the Humane Slaughter Association.

You must always stun animals before killing, a process that makes an animal immediately unconscious but does not instantly kill it. Animals must remain unconscious until they're dead, and you must kill the animal using a method such as bleeding, immediately after stunning. There are strict regulations around the disposal of animal waste, which includes skins not being tanned, blood, skull, brains, spinal cord, eyes, spleen, and any intestines you don't intend to consume, and these must be stained blue and disposed of according to Transmissible Spongiform Encephalopathies (TSE) regulations as 'specified risk material'. This is well beyond the capabilities of most, if not all small-scale goat keepers.

Do note that it is not currently legal to get anyone else to slaughter your animal for you on your holding, even if they are a licensed slaughterman. There is continuing interest in revitalizing the currently redundant role of mobile slaughter services, so perhaps this will become an option in the future.

THE ABATTOIR

Taking those first animals off to slaughter is the moment that most new livestock keepers fear. The week before the circled date in the diary you inevitably remember how cute those kids were when you brought them home or helped them being born, and you grow pale at the prospect of turning them into meat. You sternly remind yourself that the main reason you are doing this is to provide fabulous food for the family, and that you no longer want to put up with horsemeat scandals, dubious welfare practices, and ruminants stuffed with soybean meal rather than natural forage.

It's entirely appropriate that you are nervous; anyone taking an animal to the abattoir needs to fully appreciate that they are rearing livestock and ending their lives in order to produce and eat the meat. It's therefore crucial to know what is required so that you focus on what needs to be done in a manner that does not stress your animals on their final journey. The information provided below should help prepare you.

Not all abattoirs take every kind of livestock, but those that take sheep will also take goats. When you call the abattoir to arrange a killing date make sure they know that you are bringing in goats. Be aware that abattoirs don't necessarily kill every day, and those that take more than one species are likely to have specific days when they take sheep and goats.

Legal Requirements

When taking your goats to the abattoir you need to comply with three legal requirements (*see* Chapter 3 for full details): a movement licence, any medicine withdrawal periods, and ear tags or other identifiers.

Movement Licences

In order to move your goats to the abattoir, the place of departure – that's you – is responsible for arranging the movement licence to the abattoir. You can do this either on-line with

ARAMS/The Livestock Information Service, or using a paper version. If you've completed the movement licence on-line you will still need to print out your haulier's copy at home and take it with you on the journey, ready to hand over to the staff at the lairage, the area where livestock is held prior to slaughter. Back home, you will also need to record the 'off' movement in your holding register.

Medicine Withdrawal Periods

Any medication you have given to your goats needs to be included in your medicine records book, complete with the date that the appropriate withdrawal period will have ended. Before you book your abattoir date make sure that the animals being taken will have passed the withdrawal dates for any medication they have been given. The withdrawal date for every medication is given on the medicine container so there should be no confusion, but some medicines have surprisingly long withdrawal periods, so as part of your abattoir planning think about what medications you are using, and which animals are being treated.

The movement licence includes a section titled Food Chain Information (FCI): this requires you to declare that veterinary medicine withdrawal periods have been observed, and that the animals being taken for slaughter show no signs of disease, or have any condition that may affect the safety of the meat derived from them.

Ear Tags or Other Identifiers

Goats must be identified appropriately before being taken to the abattoir. Ear tags are the most commonly used identifier, but there are other options – *see* Chapter 3.

Animal By-Products Licence

If you wish to collect your skins and horns from the abattoir you need to register with

Ear tagged.

the Animal and Plant Health Agency (APHA) by completing and submitting the relevant form, downloadable on-line. Normally permission is granted within a few days of submission. This is currently a one-off application process.

Transport to the Abattoir

You may have brought your goatlings home in the back of a 4×4, but you can't transport the finished animal to the abattoir in the same way: you'll need to buy, hire or borrow a fit-for-purpose livestock trailer. Although you may feel stressed, goats are easy to load into a trailer. Clean straw should be provided in the trailer – a generous scattering rather than a deep mattress – but sawdust should be avoided as it adheres to the animal's coat and may cause problems when the carcase is dressed.

The Layout of the Abattoir

Abattoir layouts vary, in particular in the amount of room you have available for reversing your trailer to the lairage, the area where animals are kept short-term while they await slaughter. Practise and perfect your trailer-reversing skills at home. If possible, find out what the layout is so there are no surprises. The animals are your responsibility while they are in the trailer; once off the trailer ramp they become the responsibility of the abattoir. Don't expect help unloading – although some places will help, others absolutely do not – so take a companion with you if necessary. If you are concerned that the goats will refuse to come out of the trailer, take a small bucket of feed to shake at them – this should get them trotting calmly down the ramp.

Livestock trailers.

PLANNING YOUR TRIP TO THE ABATTOIR

There is a lot to think about and organize when planning your trip to the abattoir; the following checklist should help you achieve the trip without problems.

- Check that the abattoir takes goats.
- If you are using a smaller abattoir you will need to book well in advance – sometimes several weeks – especially in the run-up to Easter and Christmas. Agree both the date and time of drop-off with the abattoir.
- You'll need a livestock trailer to get your animals to the abattoir (you can borrow or hire if necessary).
- Appropriate ear tags need to be in place before you leave your premises.
- Make sure any medication given has passed the withdrawal period so that the meat is fit to enter the food chain, whether it's for your own consumption or not.
- The goats need to be clean – not wet, dirty or muddy – so in bad weather keep them inside on a clean bed of straw for a couple of days beforehand. Having a clean belly is critical to avoid any bacteria from the coat contaminating the meat, so clip the belly area of any long-haired goats (a 5–8cm/2–3in wide strip from brisket to tail).
- Livestock should be empty, which means they should not have had any food for at least twelve hours before you leave your holding; this minimizes the risk of faeces in the intestine contaminating the meat. The goats should still have access to water.
- If your abattoir offers a butchery service – not all do – have ready a clear cutting list describing how you want your goat(s) butchered. Ask the abattoir in advance for their cutting-list options; most will provide simple guidelines.
- If the abattoir doesn't offer a butchery service and the meat is for your own use, you can cut the meat yourself, and just have the animal

slaughtered and the carcase split. If you intend to sell the meat and/or need it butchered, make arrangements for this *before* taking the goat(s) to the abattoir. Either contact your local butcher to check if they will do private butchery and arrange with them which abattoir to use, or ask your abattoir which butchers they deal with, and contact them to arrange collection and butchery of the carcase(s). If a butcher is doing your cutting, talk to them about butchery options; the more deboning they carry out, the more expensive the service will be, and the lighter the weight of the final produce.

- Don't expect help at the abattoir for unloading your goats. The animals remain your responsibility until they are unloaded; the abattoir staff will take responsibility once the goats are off your trailer and to get the goats into the lairage area, where they wait to be slaughtered.
- Have your movement licence completed, and if you do it on-line, remember to print off and take the haulier form with you. The place of departure (that's you) is responsible for producing the licence.
- You can usually clean out the trailer at the abattoir, or you can choose to do this at home. If the latter, you need to complete form FMAW27 committing you to clean it *within 24 hours, or before the vehicle is next used for carrying livestock, whichever is the soonest;* the abattoir will provide the form.
- Do you want the skins or horns? If so, you need to tell the abattoir. Pick them up the next day, and ask for the skins to be salted if possible. When you get them home, add more salt (on the flesh side) and arrange to get them to a tannery. If well salted they will keep almost permanently before they are taken for tanning (see Chapter 14).
- Do you want the offal? If so, pick it up the same or the next day. It may come back with

the oesophagus and lungs, so you'll need to cut away the heart and liver for use, and discard the rest, or make haggis, or boil it up for the dogs if you have any.

- Pick up the meat on the agreed date one or two weeks later, depending on age (this is up to you to arrange, and best agreed when booking the slaughter date).
- You may prefer small on-farm abattoirs that are used to smallholders with a few animals, but large-scale abattoirs are very efficient and need less notice when booking.

Goat carcases at the abattoir.

Vacuum-packed goat meat.

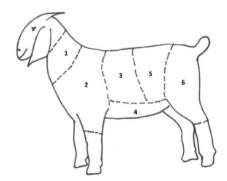

Goat-meat cuts: 1: neck, 2: shoulder, 3: loin, 4: breast, 5: chump, 6: leg.

Finding Abattoirs

Local farmers and smallholders will be able to recommend abattoirs. Very few abattoirs have their own website (nor big notices outside their entrances), but the Food Standards Agency website lists approved butchers, slaughterhouses, cutting and processing plants.

BUTCHERING SERVICES

If the abattoir offers a butchery service and is cutting your meat for you, it's likely that they will offer a simple, standard cut: legs whole or halved, shoulders whole or halved, breast whole or boned and rolled, loin cut into chops or left as joints. If you want the offal, let them know or it will disappear.

A local butcher is likely to offer other cutting options, but note that the more complex your requirements, the more time it will take the butcher and the more they will charge. If the meat is for your own use, think about how you like to cook and eat it, and create your cutting list based on this. You might always cook whole legs and shoulders for Sunday family gatherings, relishing any leftovers to make all sorts of supplementary meals. Or you might prefer small joints that will be demolished at one sitting. Your butcher can also bone and roll the shoulders, cut meat in cubes for casseroles and mince the breast, keep the carcase whole to create a saddle joint or Barnsley chops, or make burgers and sausages.

Admire what's on offer on their counter, and ask what's possible. They can also bag, or vacuum pack and label your cuts, giving you the whole lot back in a cardboard box, or laid out on disposable trays, or in a courier-friendly box ready to send out to your customers.

Suitable packaging and labelling that meets Food Standards Agency requirements is essential if you are selling your meat, and options that exclude plastic and are more environmentally friendly are being developed all the time. It may sound obvious to those of you who know your meat, but if the phone calls I get are anything to go by, it's anything but; for example, you do not get four legs from a goat: a carcase has two legs (the hind legs) and two shoulders (the front legs) - *see* the box for an example of a cutting list.

EXAMPLE CUTTING LIST

	Cutting and other requirements	*Notes*
Number of goats	Two	Date to abattoir Date for collection
Skins	Skins to be salted	Date for collection
Offal	Livers and hearts only (lights not required)	Date for collection
Whole goat	Legs whole Shoulders halved Breast boned and rolled Loin as chops Chump steaks Neck Kidneys	Vac packed and labelled with weights. Chops in bags of two
Half goat	Leg halved Shoulder whole boned and rolled Breast minced Loin as a joint Chump joint Neck Kidney	As above
Half goat	Leg into joint and separate shank Shoulder cubed Breast whole on the bone Loin as chops Chump as steaks Neck	As above

SELLING YOUR MEAT

Regulations

There is a range of regulations that you need to abide by when selling food. Your first step is to contact your local Environmental Health Office, as you are almost certainly going to have to register as a food business - and you should make that contact well before contemplating selling meat to anyone other than local friends and family. An Environmental Health Officer (EHO) will visit you to discuss what your intentions are, and to inspect the premises as appropriate to your proposed venture. You will then have to meet all their requirements before advertising and selling your meat.

Remember that only if the animal has been slaughtered at an approved slaughterhouse is it lawful to place the meat on the market (this includes offering it for sale in your own farm shop or serving it to guests of your bed-and-breakfast enterprise, if you have such things).

There is continuing confusion over what sort of enterprises need to register as a food business. If you sell small quantities (as defined by your local EHO: it's not for you to define what is a small quantity, you must ask them) of primary products – which includes simple cuts of meat but nothing processed, direct to your customer face to face, or to a local retailer who directly supplies the final consumer – then you might not have to register. However, if you sell anything processed – such as sausages, burgers, curried goat – then you must register. And no matter what goat product you sell, if you do what is called 'selling at a distance' you must register: this is defined as anything other than selling face to face, and includes advertising your meat on the internet, whether it be on your own website or via social media, or selling your goods by phone. And if your meat is transported or couriered to your customers, no matter how small the quantities involved, you must register.

In all cases you really need to get in touch with your local EHO so they can determine whether you really are exempt from registering or not. The good news is that registering is both quick and free.

A small goat-meat enterprise that has all their meat cut and packed by a licensed butcher on the butcher's premises, with the keeper (or a courier) simply delivering the produce direct to the customer and never actually touching the raw meat with their hands, is seen as 'low risk'.

Vac-packed goat joint.

In this case you won't need to set up a meat processing room or similar that would need to comply with all the regulations – in effect the butcher has taken on that role.

If you sell direct to the consumer you must put a statement of the weight in with your meat, and what it is (goat meat), so make absolutely sure that weighing scales are calibrated accurately. If you sell cured meat or charcuterie you need to label the presence of additives including any preservatives, and if you sell processed meat such as sausages or burgers you also have to state the percentage of meat in the product.

The go-to source for precise and current information, in addition to your EHO, is the Foods Standards Agency, whose website has all the information required for meeting food hygiene and labelling regulations. Acquaint yourself with the rules before registering as a food business, as this will make the process easier, and you will be able to ask the EHO to clarify any particular areas that concern you. EHOs recommend that anyone starting a food business undertakes food hygiene training to ensure that they understand all the food hygiene risks.

Marketing Advice

The first thing to say is that some people absolutely love the process of marketing and

Air-dried goat meat.

selling their produce to customers, while for others, the prospect conjures up images of a very particular type of hell. If you are in the latter category, don't put yourself through a personal version of purgatory, and simply avoid creating a surplus by limiting the numbers of goats you keep so that they just meet your own needs. There is no requirement to become a grade A sales person just because you have a few goats, particularly if one of the primary reasons you want to keep them is to get away from a commercial cut-and-thrust existence.

There are many ways to sell your goat meat, and some approaches will suit you, and others won't. Choose what makes you happy, and what gives you a buzz, and matches what you want from your life. If spending every Saturday morning at a busy local food or farmers' market doubles as your social life, then you're on to a winner; if attending food festivals and food halls at agricultural shows appeals, then go for that. You might have a local butcher keen to sell goat once in a while, which suits the quantities and frequency of your own production. There will probably be chefs at restaurants and gastro pubs in your region that would be interested – all at the right price, of course.

The most lucrative approach will be to sell direct to the end consumer, but unless you have a very large herd or are a butcher, this will inevitably be seasonal and occasional. There is an ever-growing number of people keen to buy direct from the producer, and they will be happy to wait until the meat is ready. The good news is that these potential customers are mostly happy to buy in quantity – a whole or a half carcase, butchered as appropriate – and understand that they need adequate freezer space to store what they don't cook that day.

To start with, most of your customers will be friends and family, then their friends too, if the product is good and word of mouth is encouraged, until eventually you'll be selling to people you've never met. You can, of course, reach these customers at food markets and festivals, but you don't need to if that's not your preferred marketing option. A good website and an active social media presence announcing when things are available, or sharing when you're reserving meat for future delivery, means you may never have to stand behind a market stall.

Whichever method you use to sell your meat, be sure to tell the story behind the meat as buyers love the personal touch and understanding provenance. Critically, make the prices very easy to find; very few people are going to email or phone you to ask how much your meat is, even if they've been salivating at the pictures and description on your website, and if it's on a market stall the law requires clearly displayed prices.

Whatever your chosen route for selling, you must become knowledgeable about your meat

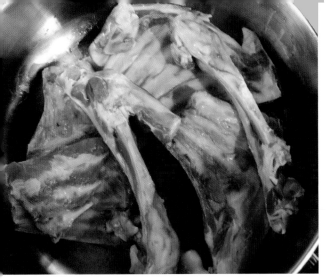

Goat bones for stock.

Cooked goat shoulder.

and how it cooks. And if you're not a good cook yet, make it a priority to become one! Experiment with cuts and different ways of cooking, produce recipe cards for customers, give guidance as to how favourite lamb or beef recipes can be adapted for goat, throwing in some old standards as well as new ideas – a great spice mix, say, or how a marinade can be enhanced with some foraged blackberries. You have to be truly and honestly enthusiastic about your meat if you want to convince people to buy it – and don't under-price it!

Pricing

A critical element of selling your surplus is having a proper understanding of the cost of production. You may decide that including your time is a step too far, and that capital items – such as a goat shed, dairying equipment, hurdles, fencing, feed bins and wheelbarrows – will last you many years and should not be taken into account. That may not be a sustainable model for a business, but may be acceptable if goat keeping is first and foremost your hobby. Even so, there's no shirking when it comes to consumables such as feed, medication, vet bills, slaughter, butchery and packaging: these all need to be included. If it costs you, say, £4.50 per kilo to produce your own goat meat, selling it to your butcher for £2.50 is illogical. It's unsustainable to make things too cheap, and keeping a proper record of your costs is the first step in knowing the

minimum price you can charge and whether your enterprise at least breaks even, including providing yourself with 'free' meat.

If you are selling direct to the consumer, you do have control over your pricing, as long as it's competitive, so it's important to benchmark prices against others selling the same products – and there are no shortcuts to doing your research. You might sensibly choose half-a-dozen or so appropriate competing sources and check against these regularly. However, do heed a word of warning about using established producers and retailers as a definitive guide for arriving at your own prices, as it's not just price similarities that you need to take into consideration. You have to be sure that the quality of the product matches too, and that includes the experience of the whole buying process.

Shopping is not a simple transaction, and purchasers bring their eyes, ears, taste buds, emotions, politics, principles and intelligence to the buying of food, as well as their wallets. Your produce has to look good and be good, it must be presented well, and be exactly as described. Make it as simple as possible for people to buy your goods, and do it in a way that makes sense of what you are producing; for example, don't sell all your goat shanks to one customer if that leaves a desirable cut out of your half and whole goat boxes, because without those shanks the boxes no longer fit that description.

CHAPTER 11

THE DAIRY HERD

Milk and all its derivatives is something so everyday, so common and useful, so core to most diets, that it's quite a surprise that more people aren't producing their own. When urban and suburban gardens increasingly play host to chickens that lay the daily breakfast egg, you'd think that those with a small barn or a patch of land to build on would see a couple of dairy goats as their next livestock choice – but it's not the case. Commercially there are only 54,000 dairy goats in the UK, compared to 2.69 million dairy cows. With seven UK dairy goat breeds to choose from, a real and increasing interest in sustainable living, the fact that goats' milk is easily digestible when compared to cows' milk, and the number of products you can make from it (*see* Chapter 14), the dairy goat deserves a higher profile among smallholders and small-scale farmers.

The need for regular milking and processing, and the perceived tie in terms of time and commitment, are understandable reasons why more smallholders are not dairying, particularly when they are holding

Goat on a bought milking stand.

Old English goat being milked.

down other jobs. Nevertheless, because it requires a closely followed routine, dairying on a small scale becomes increasingly manageable as you and your goats gain experience.

OPPOSITE: **Woman milking goat, sunlit tree with frost, early morning. Millhams, Dolton, December 1981. (Documentary photograph by James Ravilious for the Beaford Archive © Beaford Arts)**

Toggenburgs browsing.

CHOOSING THE RIGHT BREED

The first assessment to make is determining how much milk your household is likely to consume – then you can choose the right breed of goat to meet those requirements. There are many options, and you might like to go with The British Goat Society's advice of two Toggenburgs or Golden Guernseys as being ideal to produce milk for a family with a little surplus in the summer to make cheese and yogurt, with one doe for milking and its companion rearing its kids.

If you raise pigs or calves for meat and want milk to supplement their diets, or intend to make cheese or other dairy products regularly, goats that produce more milk, such as the British Toggenburg, the British Saanen, the Saanen or British Alpine, would be more appropriate. And if the primary driver for keeping goats is the making of yogurt, butter and cheese, the Anglo Nubian with its high quality milk would be a good choice.

It's important to appreciate that not only do daily milk yields vary from breed to breed, from 1 to 9ltr (2 to 15 pints) per goat in summer, but this amount drops dramatically in the winter, to half or less, and also decreases with age. The milkiness

of individual goats also varies within breeds, so before you buy, check with the vendor of your goats on the type of milk yield you might reasonably expect. Early spring to late autumn is the primary goat-milking season.

Milk is normally measured in kilos, but for simplicity you can replace this with the same number in litres – although if you want to be precise, a litre of milk weighs 1.032kg. The richer the milk is in butterfat and protein, the higher the cheese yield and the thicker the yogurt. Contrary to expectation perhaps, a diet that is high in forage, not concentrates, promotes butterfat production. In addition to nutrition, other factors affecting milk solids include age (butterfat declines as a goat ages), the season and the associated quality of the available forage, at what stage the goats are in their lactation, and inherited genetics.

There is considerable variation in milk yield, butterfat and protein statistics, so the statistics given in the table should be seen as indications only, highlighting the average differences between breeds. Individual goats can also vary hugely; as an example, the butterfat of the Anglo Nubians averaged out to arrive at 5.04 per cent in the table below, and ranged from a high of 6.77 per cent and a low of 3.66 per cent.

Butterfat and Protein Statistics

Breed	Average daily milk yield in kilos	Average butterfat %	Average protein %
Anglo Nubian	3.89	5.04	3.55
British Alpine	4.09	4.12	2.97
British Saanen	5.17	3.68	2.8
British Toggenburg	4.54	3.68	2.71
Golden Guernsey	3.16	4.09	2.95
Saanen	4.29	3.81	2.78
Toggenburg	3.61	3.55	2.84

Adapted from The British Goat Society and other sources.

FEEDING THE DAIRY DOE

Saanen and Toggenburg goats at Dunlop Dairy.

Goats need to eat around 5 per cent of their bodyweight daily in dry matter to maintain good milk production. A lactating doe that weighs 70kg (154lb) and produces about 4.5ltr (8 pints) of milk will need to eat around 3.5kg (7.7lb) of dry matter a day, of which the roughage-to-concentrate ratio should be 50:50. Does of the same weight producing nearer to 9ltr (16 pints) per day will need to eat 6–7 per cent of their bodyweight in feed (4–5kg/9–11lb). A doe will lactate (produce milk) for an average of 284 days, with the peak in milk yield at four to six weeks after kidding. For more detail about feeding, *see* Chapter 8.

DAIRYING EQUIPMENT

Dairying equipment can be simple and homely or modern and complex, or a mix of the two. Your basic dairying equipment is likely to include the following:

- milking stand/stanchion
- milk pail(s) (at least one with a lid for carrying milk)

British Toggenburg with its head in the milking stand.

Milk strainer.

Milk churn.

- cheesecloths
- strainer and straining filters
- churn/container
- bottles/jars for storing the milk, with plastic reusable lids
- dairy wipes
- teat dip cup
- strip cup
- dairy cleaners/teat dip/disinfectants/sterilizer solutions
- udder balm/cream.

Milking Stand Design

The milking platform should be around 38-45cm (15-18in) above the floor for ease of milking. Before building one, test out the height at which you'll be comfortable milking when seated in relation to the position of your goat's udder. It's always easier to cut down the stand legs than to add more height. Include a lipped shelf or bowl ring outside the head yoke to keep the feed bowl in place during milking. The stand can also be used

Goat on an upcycled milking stand.

English goat on a milking stand.

Milking on the stand.

when trimming hooves – anything that helps the goat keeper avoid putting strain on their back is to be welcomed.

The Home Milking Parlour

If you are hand milking and don't need an electricity supply you might choose to milk outside in good weather, though that can pose hygiene challenges. However, if that's how you plan to do it, keep a clean container with all the items you need close at hand so they don't get put on the ground until after you've finished using them, and then clean them thoroughly before the next use.

You can create a discrete space in a barn positioned and designed so that the parlour area can be kept really clean, or make a small milking parlour that is used solely for the purpose. The floor of the area you are milking in should be very easy to clean, and must survive being hosed down after every milking; concrete is the simplest option. Milk residue on the floor attracts flies, which is unpleasant for the goat and the milker, so needs to be removed after each milking. The walls and ceilings should also be cleanable, and not attract dust and cobwebs

Although it is clearly possible to milk a goat standing on the ground, most milkers see a raised stand as essential; trying to milk from the floor is really difficult unless you are happy crouching for twenty minutes or more, or don't mind the prospect of getting a bad back. They are simple to make for even the most basic home builder, and are a key part of your dairying kit.

HAND MILKING AND MACHINE MILKING COMPARED

If you milk by hand there is minimal capital outlay and a little less washing involved, as you will be dealing with buckets and simple containers rather than dismantling and cleaning a milking machine. Hand milking is also a lot quieter. Goats mostly have teats of a size that accommodate hand milking (which is not always the case with cows), though milking by hand will take longer than machine milking – but this will improve as you become more practised. It can be harder to maintain scrupulous hygiene with hand milking, with dirt and dust more likely to contaminate the milk in an open pail.

The shelf-life of your milk is your best gauge as to how hygienic your milking process is: good hygiene results in longer-lasting milk.

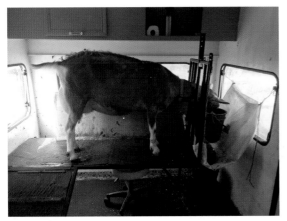

A caravan converted into a milking parlour for a two-goat dairy herd.

Anglo Nubian × Boer goat being milked by machine.

It is also critical to keep a machine clean, and there are some excellent videos on-line on how to use and clean milking machines. If using a milking machine the more natural action using suction/pulse rather than squeeze may be preferred.

Hand milking can have its problems, including testy goats kicking over the bucket while you are milking, so keep a solid grip on the bucket while they learn to settle to your routine. This means starting off by milking one teat at a time, holding the bucket with your other hand. As the goat settles you will be able to move to milking both teats simultaneously. If she hasn't been milked before she should have plenty of handling pre-kidding, should spend time getting used to being on the milking stand, associate being fed her favourite foodstuff with being on the stand, and have her udder touched regularly so that future milking is as stress free as possible both for her and for you.

TECHNIQUE FOR HAND MILKING

- Avoid pulling on the teats when hand milking as this will cause damage.
- Close your thumb and first finger together at the top of the teat, and gently and firmly bring your other fingers towards your palm to squirt out the milk.
- Milk both teats at the same time, alternating the squeezing motion with each hand so that first one teat then the other ejects milk into your bucket.
- Stop milking when the milk stops flowing steadily, and massage the udder to encourage the doe to let down more milk; then continue milking. You may need to repeat this a couple of times.
- Stop milking when no more flows.

Hand milking into a bucket.

Feeding While Milking

It makes the domestic milker's life easier if you give your goats some high value feed that they only get when on the stand. That does not mean expensive feed, but foodstuffs that the goats really enjoy. An example might be dairy nuts mixed into coarse mix, with alfalfa chaff and chopped apple or carrot (remembering that it is illegal to feed to livestock food that has been through a kitchen). For the fidgety goat ensure there is adequate feed to last until their milking is finished.

Goat milking machine.

Commercial dairy goats being milked twice a day will be fed a daily ration of 1.5kg (3.3lb) of 18 per cent protein dairy nuts (almost certainly cattle dairy nuts); these contain the necessary vitamins and minerals including the required copper, in addition to their roughage. Dairy nuts would be given as 0.25kg (0.55lb) feeds while they are being milked (totalling 0.5kg/1lb across their two milkings), the remaining kilo being fed back in the barn alongside their hay.

A Set Routine for Stress-Free Milking

If you watch someone experienced milking it's like watching a carefully choreographed performance. They are quiet and calm, as stress interferes with the release of the hormone oxytocin, which enables the milk to be let down. They also follow a set routine that puts the doe in the right frame of mind for an easy milking, and ensures that none of the steps critical for producing hygienic milk are forgotten. All the necessary equipment and materials should be clean and at hand. Pre-dipping teats with appropriate dairy disinfectant helps to control environmental mastitis and can be applied by dipping with a teat dip cup or spraying.

Start milking one minute after you've cleaned, dipped and dried the teats; this handling will have stimulated milk let-down. It's simple to tell when a hand-milked udder is empty, as milk is no longer flowing. It can take fifteen minutes to half an hour to milk each goat by hand, depending on how cooperative they are and how effective the milker. If machine milking you need to be focused on it to ensure the units aren't kept on too long, which would cause trauma to the teats. It's imperative to learn how to use, clean and adjust a milking machine so as not to damage your goats – the manufacturer will be able to advise.

Milk the youngest goats first, and any with mastitis or a history of mastitis are milked last. The final goats to be milked are any that have had medication for which the withdrawal period has not been reached. Keep any infected milk and any with medicine residues separate, and do not use it for human consumption. It is advisable to wear clean disposable gloves and change these for each doe.

If post-dipping teats to keep contagious mastitis at bay, this is not wiped off but left until the following milking. However, if you live in a very cold climate wipe the dip off after thirty seconds and then dry the teat to avoid them getting frostbite.

You may choose to massage udder cream or salve to soothe the udder after milking to some or all of your goats as needed, keeping the skin soft, avoiding chapped skin and sores. Most udder cream products are basically

Pouring milk into plastic bottles.

moisturizers, they smell pleasant and are also good for the hardworking milker's hands.

Stick to the order you milk your goats in, and the way you do things – they like their routine and that way you won't forget any critical step, either.

HYGIENE

Because milk is potentially a perfect host for bacteria, managing hygiene and temperature is crucial to ensure safe and clean milk and dairy products. Keep your

---

HYGIENE ROUTINE FOR MILKING

The following hygiene routine should be followed whether you are hand or machine milking:

- Keep all your equipment spotlessly clean (lying on a shelf in a dusty open barn won't do).
- The hair on the udder, flank and hind legs can be clipped short and the doe brushed to remove any dust, dung or loose hair before putting her on the milking stand.
- Keep yourself, your clothes and your hands clean. Wear thin nitrile, latex or vinyl disposable gloves. If you have a cut on your hands or arms, clean the wound and cover it with a waterproof dressing before milking, and if you have food poisoning or an infection of any kind get someone else to do the milking.
- Keep your goats and their udders clean using disposable dairy wipes. Avoid using water to clean udders as the dirty liquid will flow on to the teat potentially contaminating the teat opening. If it is necessary to wash the udder use a dairy disinfectant wash, and dry the udder and teats thoroughly using a clean paper or cloth towel before continuing.
- Use a strip cup to catch the first three or four squirts of milk from each teat to check for signs of mastitis (clots or blood) or dirt from the teat. The strip cup has a black strainer that helps you see any abnormal milk. Don't use the age-old process of checking milk for abnormalities by squirting it on to the floor or your hand or boot, as this can spread mastitis from one goat to another.
- If used, pre-dip should be applied to teats after they have been fore-milked, left for thirty seconds and then dry-wiped, or washed and dried. Use an appropriate pre-dip product and not your post-milking teat disinfectant, as their use as a pre-dip may contaminate the milk.
- Milk into a seamless stainless-steel bucket so there is nowhere for milk or bacteria to collect.
- Strip out the last of the milk from the udder into the strip cup to check again for any signs of mastitis. Post-milking teat-dip disinfectant should be applied as soon as milking is complete while the teat canal is still open.
- Filter the milk immediately to remove out any particles of dust, goat hair, skin flakes and so on.
- Chill the milk straightaway and keep it below 3°C (1.5°C in a commercial dairy). This may be a few degrees cooler than your domestic fridge, but the milk will stay fresher for longer at the lower temperature so you may wish to invest in a small fridge specifically for your dairy needs. For small amounts, initial chilling of your milk can be done by standing the filtered milk container in a sink of running cold water.
- Glass is seen as the best storage option for raw milk, and bottles with plastic lids can be thoroughly cleaned in the dishwasher and sterilized as necessary. A small stainless-steel churn is also an option.
- After milking, rinse your stainless-steel bucket with cool water before cleaning it thoroughly with detergent and hot water. Rinsing with hot water initially just hardens the traces of milk on to the bucket, making it more difficult to clean.
- There are various types of dairy sterilizer available (some iodine based, others with hypochlorite) that you can use for cleaning all items too large or inconvenient or inappropriate to sterilize by boiling.

Strip cup.   Teat dip cup.

milking parlour and dairy areas properly clean, free of flies and any strong odours that would be picked up in the milk. The Food Standards Agency recommend that raw milk is pasteurized if it is to be consumed by children under two, or by pregnant women, the elderly, and those with a compromised immune system.

The Keeping Qualities of Raw and Pasteurized Milk

If any goat hair gets into the milk it makes a significant difference to the taste and keeping quality of the milk, so filtering is crucial. Kept properly chilled, clean raw goat milk should last at least a week, although some goat keepers won't keep their milk beyond three days; you will have to experiment. By day four a stronger goat taste starts to develop. Be aware that pasteurizing milk kills off the live bacteria, and that when the milk goes 'off' it is rotten and must be thrown away.

Raw milk sours rather than rots, and there are numerous perfectly acceptable ways of using sour milk as a replacement for baking powder, buttermilk, sour cream or yogurt in recipes, including using as a leavening agent in scones, pancakes, bread and cakes or making cottage or ricotta-type cheeses. Once raw sour milk separates (and smells), it has reached the point of no return, and needs to be dumped.

PASTEURIZATION

There are three main methods of pasteurization:

The Holder process: Heat the milk to 63°C for 30 minutes, and then cool to under 10°C. Stir throughout heating and cooling. This is the method most used for milk for cheesemaking.

The high temperature short time (HTST) process: Heat the milk to 72°C for between 15 and 25 seconds. Once the milk has been heated, cool very quickly to less than 3°C.

Ultra-high-temperature (UHT) pasteurization: Commercially, in UHT pasteurization, milk is pasteurized at 135°C for 1–2sec.

If you want to heat treat your milk and don't want to stand over a double boiler with a thermometer every day, there are small pasteurizers available from a capacity of 15ltr (3gal) upwards that will do the job for you.

Quiet handling of the milk (gentle stirring and slow heating), will minimize the goaty taste of the resulting cheese.

THE SMALL-SCALE DAIRY

Kid-at-Foot Dairying

Keeping calves at foot with their dams and taking some – though not all – of the cow's milk for the household has been a smallholder approach for managing house cows since time immemorial, although it's only entered the commercial dairying scene in the UK in a small way in the last decade. This is an appealing model for goat keepers who don't like the idea of removing the kid from the doe prematurely, who wish to milk just once, and not twice a day, and for those

Kid-at-foot dairying, literally.

who want the option of not having to milk for a day or two occasionally.

The concept of kid-at-foot dairying, or 'ethical dairying' as it is sometimes described, has a number of key features, with variants depending on the preference of the keeper, such as frequency of milking. When a dairy doe kids, she and her kids are left together to bond for at least a week, with the kids receiving all the colostrum and milk. A week after kidding, or a little earlier if the kids struggle to keep up with the mother's milk supply, a small amount of milk is taken. You can start milking around 200ml, increasing daily in 50 to 100ml increments to achieve 1 to 1.5ltr (1.75 to 2.6 pints) per day. Taking more can increase milk production, which in turn increases udder size, which may not be entirely desirable for the domestic milker. A modest udder may be less productive but is less likely to be disabling, as an oversized udder can be for a doe.

When the kids are three weeks old, they are separated from their dams at night. They are usually kept in the same barn, separated only by a gate or barrier, with does kept in one group, their kids in another. In the morning the does are milked – either fully milked out, or an amount left for their kids – then reunited with their kids for the rest of the day.

Kids can be kept with their dams until weaning at eight to ten weeks old, or even later at four or even six months, with the exception of entire bucklings that need to be weaned and separated permanently from females at three months to avoid them breeding with their dams, sisters and other does.

Around six weeks into lactation the doe will produce 2.5 to 3ltr (4.4 to 5.3 pints) per day – or considerably more, depending on breed, feed and milking system.

If you have young twins or triplets suckling equally on both teats, not milking for a day or two shouldn't have negative effects on milk yield or the doe. However, if you have a single kid mostly suckling off one teat, the other side of the udder can become engorged, which is uncomfortable for the doe and can lead to mastitis. If you want to maintain a decent milk yield for the house, don't leave a kid-at-foot dairy doe unmilked for more than a day or two, and as her yield increases, she will need milking daily.

The Home Dairy

The domestic kitchen is perfectly suitable for processing milk into butter, cream, cheese, yogurt, kefir and more for home use. Chapter 14 describes making dairy products in detail, and offers a range of recipes to get you

Cheesemaking in a home kitchen.

started. The equipment you choose should be easy to sterilize and keep clean, and milk should be washed from your kit with cool water immediately after use to remove any milk before it is then cleaned with hot water and your chosen dairy disinfectant. If you use wooden kitchen utensils such as scotch hands or spatulas, clean these thoroughly and then pour boiling water over them.

In addition to having access to a cooker and fridge, your dairying equipment might include the following:

- cream separator
- hand churn or electric mixer
- stainless-steel pans, buckets, double boiler, colanders
- palette knife (as a curd cutter)
- cheese moulds, trays, draining mats
- electronic thermometer
- timer
- cheese press
- yogurt maker or wide-necked vacuum flask
- ice-cream maker
- measuring jugs
- ladle and spoons
- consumables, to include cheesecloths, starter, rennet, cultures.

Butter churn.

When it comes to making cheese or pasteurizing your milk, a good electronic thermometer is essential as correct temperatures are critical.

The Micro Dairy

Just like the term 'smallholding', 'micro dairy' doesn't have an absolute definition, but under ten cows or fifty goats or sheep is a useful approximation. Micro may be small scale, but it's certainly about sales, as that's a dairy size that would produce more milk than even the most determined multi-generation extended family could consume on its own, no matter how much butter, ice cream and cheese was made from the daily output. If you are planning commercial milk production there will need to be enough sales anticipated to cover the capital outlay and ongoing costs. The British Goat Society gauge this at a herd of at least a hundred milking goats, which goes well beyond the term 'micro dairy'. The legal requirements below are all relevant to the sale of milk from a micro dairy as well as those of larger scale enterprises.

THE LEGAL SIDE OF SELLING GOATS' MILK

To sell milk to the public you must be a registered milk-production facility and food business, and must comply with the regulations described here below.

Register your holding: You must register your holding as a milk-production facility with the Food Standards Agency (FSA) if it's to be used to produce milk that you sell to the public, or is to be processed by someone else. You will need to give details of the holding, the number of goats to be milked, the type and time of milk production and the people responsible. The FSA have an Approvals and Registration Team that can give advice.

Raw goats' milk.

The names and address of registered milk-production facilities are published on-line.

Register as a food business: You must also register as a food business with your local authority; Environmental Health will come and inspect.

Standards to be met: There are many standards to be met before you can sell your milk; these relate to animal housing, the milking parlour, milk and feed storage, drainage and waste disposal, isolation areas, vermin and pest control, water quality, animal health, milk quality, packaging, staff cleanliness, milking hygiene routine, the cleaning schedule, and more. The most comprehensive source of information is the FSA's *Milk Producer's Guide*, downloadable from their website.

Testing of milk samples: Milk samples (at least two per month) will need to be tested to ensure the milk complies with health standards: a number of companies offer this service by post.

Labelling for raw milk: Labelling must include the appropriate wording, depending on where you are located; for example in England, the container in which it is sold must be marked or labelled with the words: 'This milk has not been heat-treated and may therefore contain organisms harmful to health.'

External Dairy Hygiene Inspections

All dairy farms selling milk (no matter the size) have external dairy hygiene inspections to ensure that a satisfactory standard of hygiene is maintained and that all legal obligations are being met. The premises, equipment and milk-producing animals are all inspected to ensure that satisfactory hygiene standards are in place. Inspection frequency is every six months for the sale of raw goat drinking milk for sale direct to the final consumer, and every two years for wholesale (for example where milk is sold to artisan cheese producers).

Inspectors will expect to have a range of written documents from you including your Standard Operating Procedure for milking and bottling your milk, which covers each step you take, the amount and dilution of disinfectants used, the temperature of water used at each stage, highlighting daily, weekly and less frequent actions to maintain hygiene. You will also need to keep records on the following:

- The nature and origin of feed fed to the animals.
- Veterinary medicinal products or other treatments administered to the animals, dates of administration and withdrawal periods.
- The occurrence of diseases that may affect the safety of the milk or milk products.
- The results of any analyses carried out on samples taken from animals or other samples taken for diagnostic purposes, which have importance for human health.
- Any relevant reports on checks carried out on animals or products of animal origin.

THE SALE OF RAW MILK AND CREAM

The sale of raw drinking milk (RDM) from goats must comply with the following Food Standards Agency regulations:

- RDM from goats must come from animals that are healthy and belong to a production holding that is brucellosis free.
- RDM must comply with dairy hygiene rules and microbiological standards.
- Compliance with these requirements is monitored at inspections programmed on a risk basis.
- Raw drinking milk from goats has to carry the regulatory health warning.

The sale of raw cream is also subject to strict regulations:

- Raw cream must comply with all the requirements that apply to milk products under dairy hygiene rules and microbiological standards.
- It must be made with milk meeting the herd status criteria – milk may only be sold direct to consumers by the occupier of a registered milk production holding, and RDM must comply with dairy hygiene rules and microbiological standards.
- Raw cream is not required to carry the necessary health warning, but the words 'made with raw milk' must be displayed on the product.
- Compliance with these requirements is monitored through risk-based inspections.

The Commercial Goat Dairy

Commercial goat dairies of five hundred-plus milking goats often sell their milk to a dairy processor, but there are those with half that number of goats making a go of things by selling their milk direct to consumers or to artisan cheesemakers and adding value to their milk by producing their own sought-after products. Saanens are the obvious choice for the commercial dairy, but some use Toggenburg/Saanen crosses (both Saanen does bred by Toggenburg bucks and vice

Making Ailsa Craig soft goat cheese.

Ailsa Craig.

versa). The Anglo Nubian also plays a part in cross-breeding programmes, increasing butterfat content and the length of their legs, the latter making it easier in the dairy for the milker. Payments by the large national milk processors are based on fat and protein levels, so the Anglo Nubian literally gives more value for money. The highest demand for goat milk is from August to December, to produce cheeses aimed at the Christmas market.

Dairies tend to milk at twelve-hour intervals, with equal yields at both daily milkings. Some will adjust this a little to accommodate family life and other commitments, for example milking at 6am and 4pm, with the 4pm yield being the smaller of the two. The aim is to never let the udder get so full that it stops producing milk.

Apart from the need to avoid using wormers wherever possible (*see* below), any dairy selling its produce needs to avoid anything that will contaminate the taste of the milk; as this can only be achieved by regulating what the does eat, herds are kept inside throughout their lactation.

The Milking Goat Association emphasizes the need to buy in healthy stock when setting up a goat dairy, with TB, CLA, CAE and feet problems the main areas of concern. Larger herds often maintain a closed herd policy, using artificial insemination to avoid having to buy in any stock.

DAIRYING AND ANTHELMINTIC USE

Goats are very susceptible to intestinal worms, and unlike other ruminants do not build up resistance. If allowed to graze and browse outside goats are highly likely to require anthelmintic treatment – the use of drugs to kill parasitic worms. This being the case, commercial dairies keep their goats inside throughout their lactation; some allow goats outside in their dry period (managing worm treatments accordingly), and others keep their milking does indoors permanently. Even the very small-scale dairy goat keeper may decide to keep their milking does off pasture during their lactation for the same reason.

At the time of writing there is only one wormer (Eprinex) currently licensed for use in goats in the UK; it is available through vet prescription only and has no milk withdrawal period. Care should be taken that worms don't become resistant, so discuss a plan of action with your vet. Some goat keepers use wormer before kidding, then milk without worming, and at the end of lactation will worm again. If worms become resistant your vet will have to prescribe alternative off-licence wormers that may have a withdrawal period for milk, so base your worming practice on faecal egg counts (FECs) – *see* Chapter 9 – and a herd health plan developed with your vet.

There are some small-scale dairy goat keepers who have adopted another way, with three key elements: FECs showing low or zero worm burdens, mixed or rotational grazing with other species, and access to high-level browse. With ongoing low or nil worm burdens, plus regular mixed or rotation grazing with other species such as horses or cattle, there is minimum worm transfer as cattle, horse and goat worms are different species. The level of parasite contamination on a pasture can certainly be reduced by this type of grazing management. It is not appropriate to rotate or co-graze goats with sheep because for the most part the parasites that infect the two species are the same. The provision of plenty of high-level browse rather than low-level grazing contributes to this method, as goats remove the tops of taller grasses – and with access to plenty of browse, trees and hedges, plus hay fed up off the ground, they are less likely to pick up a worm burden.

A VET'S PERSPECTIVE ON THE USE OF WORMERS IN DAIRY GOATS

Chris Just BVSc MRCVS

The only safe way to avoid your dairy goats acquiring a worm burden is to house them. By all means enrich their environment in as many ways as possible with toys and bringing in browse. They love a branch to strip, but avoid stoned fruit trees as they contain cyanide; some fruit varieties are worse than others, and they are worst of all if the leaves are bruised or wilted and not fully oxidized or dried. Sycamore and ivy in moderation, and ash, elder, willow and hazel are all fine in larger quantities, and as they are fast growing (especially the latter if coppiced) can be part of a holistic plan for a smallholding.

If you are using wormer, SCOPS (www.scops.org.uk 'Sustainable Control of Parasites in Sheep') is the best advice to extrapolate from into goats. Bear in mind the added complexity that Eprinex is (currently) the only UK licensed wormer in goats, so you are obliged to use it unless justified to go off-licence following the cascade rules. (The cascade system is where vets are permitted to use their clinical judgement to treat animals under their care where there is no suitable veterinary medicine authorized in the UK for the specific condition in the animal being treated.) Drug resistance is a valid reason. An off-licence treatment with an alternative wormer when the goat is not milking is the obvious tool to employ, and must be prescribed by a vet, as outlined in the Herd Health Plan with justifications. Working with your vet would involve post-treatment FWEC (faecal worm egg counts) to show efficacy. A proper worm egg-count reduction test would be indicated if resistance is suspected and/or *in vitro* efficacy tests.

DRYING OFF DAIRY DOES

Most goat owners will milk their does for nine to ten months after kidding, but a doe should be dried off (stop producing milk) two to three months before she is due to kid again. This allows her to put energy into the development of her next kids, rather than into milk production, and allows the udder to rest. The doe also has a chance to put on weight, improving body condition lost during the demands of lactation.

Three weeks before your planned drying off date slowly reduce the amount of energy in the diet by removing grain-based feed and alfalfa and switching entirely to hay. This is not about restricting the amount of total feed, but reducing the calorie and nutrient content. After two weeks of the lower calorie diet assess the goat's udder to see how much milk is being produced, and check that the udder is healthy. You can stop milking abruptly to dry off if milk production is now minimal and the udder is sound. If you are concerned about the udder, talk to your vet.

British Alpine goat.

A more gradual approach can be adopted if preferred. For example, if you milk twice a day, reduce this to once a day milking as the doe's yield diminishes through cutting her concentrate rations. Leaving a little milk in the udder after each milking will also contribute to reducing milk yield. You can then milk every other day, then once every three days, before stopping entirely.

There are many goats that can be milked for two seasons without kidding. If you are supporting the rarer native breeds, the Old English can continue lactating for up to eighteen months, a positive for those who wish to lengthen the time between breeding.

MASTITIS IN DAIRY DOES

Mastitis is inflammation of the udder and can be caused by micro-organisms, mostly bacteria, but also viruses or fungi, typically infecting through the teat or via damage to the teat or udder. Mastitis is often contagious, with infection spreading mainly during milking. When a goat lies down its udder comes in contact with the ground, which risks fouling the udder and introducing mastitis. Inside a barn used for housing dairy goats keep the sand, straw, sawdust or other bedding clean of muck, mucking out daily. Ensure bedding is always clean and dry, avoid overcrowding, and in wet weather increase the amount of bedding. The recommended lying area per animal for goats is 1.8sq m (2.1sq yd). To minimize damp, ensure water troughs or buckets are installed away from the bedding area. Keep all hardstanding areas used by goats well swept.

The teat sphincter at the end of the teat that opens to allow milk to be let down contracts about an hour after milking, which naturally helps prevent bacteria from entering the teat, but keeping the goats' environment clean is the human's role. Diagnosis of mastitis is based on bacterial cultures of milk, so talk to your vet if you suspect infection, so that the appropriate treatment can be given. In addition you should observe the following best practice:

- Always check udders before milking, looking for signs of swelling.
- If the teats are clean prior to milking, avoid washing them; if they are dirty, wash and dry them before milking.
- Ensure you pre-dip or post-dip (as works best for you) all teats.
- Treat teats gently, with no rough handling.
- Treat cases promptly when recognized, and keep records so that you can assess any patterns of infection.
- Separate infected does into their own milking group, and milk them last.
- Do not breed from, and cull does with chronic mastitis/those that fail to respond to treatment, to avoid it spreading across the herd.

The following are signs of mastitis:

- Swollen udder (half or whole)
- Udder or teat redness or misshapen udder
- Hot udder
- Pain when the udder is touched
- Abnormal milk (clots, clumps, blood, watery colour), including change in the milk taste or smell
- Drop in milk yield
- Lameness

Note that any trauma to the end of the teat/teat sphincter, including harsh or over-milking, significantly increases the risk of mastitis.

A VET'S PERSPECTIVE ON MASTITIS IN DAIRY GOATS

Chris Just BVSc MRCVS

A vet won't dispense treatment unless they are familiar with the situation. They will want to see any sick goat that is off its feed, or any mastitis with discoloration of the skin. The vet will want to come out to treat the individual, but more importantly to investigate with you why it has happened: prevention is better than cure. Taking clean milk samples and freezing them before any treatment is always useful (get appropriate sample pots from the vet). Cultures can be made from these samples if cases are unresponsive or a lot of cases occur; more than one case per twenty goats per month would definitely ring alarm bells.

A vet would expect a goat keeper to be able to do the following themselves:

- Practise good hygiene to prevent mastitis spreading directly and via the environment (using gloves and teat dips, and isolating infected animals).
- Take and freeze clean milk samples before any treatment.
- Practise good record keeping of the ID of the animal, which side is affected, and the date of any mastitis.
- Administer veterinary medicines (intramammary tubes or systemic injections) after being shown how if a complete beginner.
- If the case is mild/early and such that a self-cure might be expected, to strip out the udder thoroughly (exercising good hygiene at all times), and massage to encourage milk let-down to 'flush out' the udder, and also use udder ointments to help with the massage process.
- Give pain relief/anti-inflammatory medicines: these can often be given immediately if the vet has prescribed them to the farm.
- Never ignore a problem. There are rare but important zoonotic diseases that can cause mastitis, other diseases that can cause lumps in or around an udder, and non-bacterial causes of mastitis (yeast mastitis can be severe and is not uncommon if antibiotics are inappropriately used).

If mastitis recurs after two rounds of treatment a cure is unlikely during lactation, but could clear up if a dry period is feasible. If there are lumps on the udder, or on the lymph nodes above the udder that have been there for more than a week, then the outcome will be poor. Does may be unresponsive to treatment if there is not a bacterial cause, and a culture will be useful to rule things out as much as to find the definite cause, and the vet can also check antibiotic efficacy. Damage to the teat end is associated with chronic mastitis.

Be aware that some mastitis can kill very quickly, especially those where the skin changes colour, or the milk has a bad smell or is very watery or discoloured. In these cases contact a vet urgently.

CHAPTER 12

BREEDING

Millhams, Dolton, June 1984. (Documentary photograph by James Ravilious for the Beaford Archive © Beaford Arts)

Moving on from rearing bought-in livestock to home-producing kids takes your goat keeping to a whole other level of interest, experience, knowledge and complication – but unless you keep goats purely as pets, or stick with buying in youngstock to grow on for meat (which are both perfectly good ways of managing your

goat enterprise), breeding and the subsequent kidding is likely to become part of your goating life. Learning about all aspects of breeding is fascinating, and developing one's husbandry skills is immensely satisfying and rewarding. No matter how exhausted you are at the close of kidding, there is nothing like

OPPOSITE: Golden Guernsey doe and kid.

LaMancha doe and kid.

the joy of witnessing healthy kids hurtling in a mob across the thickening spring grass in an early evening stampede, expressing their joy at being alive.

Taking control of breeding means that you don't risk bringing in other people's problems, whether that's temperament, disease or conformation; this is why many livestock keepers aim to create a closed herd – meaning that no animals are brought into the herd, and no showing or hiring out of stock takes place – with the exception of buying in new males when needed. This can take time, as your breeders have to come from somewhere, but as each year passes your stock will reflect the choices you have made, good and bad.

WORDS OF CAUTION

Having said that, if you are keeping goats purely as pets and have no experience

of lambing, calving or kidding, there are significant risks in taking a doe to a buck 'just to see how it goes', or because kids are just so cute. It's definitely not essential to breed your own stock unless you are dairying, in which case you won't get milk unless you breed.

If you're wanting to add goat meat to the table it's easier to buy in kids, such as males born to dairy herds, which are surplus to their requirements. It means you don't need to pay for, handle, house or feed a buck; it's certainly cheaper not having to feed breeding stock all year round, and you don't end up with surplus kids for which you have not yet built a market. You can buy weaned kids, or bottle-fed kids that are either orphans or come from a litter that is too large for a doe to feed on her own, and take them up to meat weight. Therefore it's perfectly possible to rear your own meat without breeding, so why do it?

The most jaded farmer can become quite emotional about the bringing forth of new life, believing that spring is only fulfilling if there are kids peeping cutely from deep beds of golden straw, and some might suggest that every livestock keeper needs to go through the baptism of the breeding cycle (though I wouldn't concur); but determining whether to tackle breeding or not should be an intensely practical decision, and not based on any romantic notions.

A Time-Consuming Commitment
For the most part, you really need to be around at kidding time round the clock, checking things thoroughly at least every two hours, day and night. This should be the key consideration if you have commitments away from your holding. If you work full time you can plan to take your holidays at kidding time and put the buck with the does for a tightly regulated window of opportunity (or use artificial insemination), to ensure that kidding is confined to a manageable period.

Kidding.

British Toggenburg males.

Far from being a holiday, however, it will be demanding if enjoyable work.

Costs and Returns

There is undoubtedly a significant outlay involved in breeding. If you're good at it you should not be out of pocket, but the learning curve is steep and you may find the returns don't add up for a few years. Costs include feeding breeding stock all year round, buying decent examples of the male of the species, or semen straws, as well as quality does, and creating an indoor kidding area. There's all sorts of kit associated with kidding too: everything from iodine to prolapse harnesses to enough hurdles to create bonding pens, quantities of straw, and emergency medication (*see* Chapter 13). Plus, of course, potential vet's bills at emergency call-out rates.

Mortality

The reality is that kidding is the peak time for goat mortality and life-threatening conditions for both the kids and their mothers. Even a perfect birth can end fatally if, for example, a doe is concentrating on the first kid born and the second slips out and no one is there to clear the membrane bag off its nose. A second's work is the difference between life and death – a quick swipe to clear the mouth and nose of birthing fluids is all that's needed, to show the doe that yes, this one also needs her attention.

Observation will also tell you if there is a malpresentation to deal with, so familiarize yourself with the possible presentations in Chapter 13 so that you know what needs doing in order to achieve a live birth.

Skill Levels and Knowledge

Breeding requires a significant increase in skill levels and knowledge. Having a few kids fattening on your holding is one thing – it can be entirely trauma free and require minimal husbandry, particularly if you have sourced good, healthy stock. But once you start breeding you need to ensure your stock is in optimum condition, is suitable for breeding (no undesirable conformation traits or history of prolapse, for example), and that you are ready for the challenge.

Build a relationship with your vet so that you receive useful updates on developing practice, as expert knowledge moves on all the time. Choose some good training to attend, given by people with solid experience and an ability to share their knowledge clearly (many vets run lambing courses, and the skills involved are the same as for kidding). And be prepared for things to be messy and gory: this inevitable part of the process can be a step too far for some.

SELECTING AND SOURCING GOATS FOR BREEDING

The first thing to say is that not all goats capable of breeding should be bred from. You want to perpetuate the best and iron out the worst of your goats in any breeding programme. If you have goats with poor conformation, unstable temperament or inherent health issues, don't breed from them. Check back to Chapter 6 for desirable traits with regard to testicles, teats, legs, mouth and body conformation.

Boer buck.

If you don't have an entire male of your own you may be able to run your does with a neighbour's buck; alternatively you may have to travel some distance to source the male you're after. For this you'll need access to a suitable livestock trailer and a car hefty enough to pull it. Whether buying, hiring or borrowing, don't just pick any old male to be the sire of your future stock: choose the best that you can find and afford that will enhance your herd, particularly if you are hoping to keep the resulting females for future breeding. Note that owners of stud goats will expect that any does brought to be serviced – mated – will have a certificate to confirm they have tested negative for CAE.

The number of does a male can service (mate with) increases as he matures, and his diet needs to ensure he maintains body condition and energy levels at breeding time. At a year old he should be able to manage up to ten does over the breeding season; by the time he is two this increases to around twenty-five does; and as a mature three-year-old he can cope with as many as fifty does. During the mating season a buck can lose much of his interest in food, so he needs to be in very good body condition beforehand; he will lose quite a substantial amount of weight while he has unbred females with him.

You are aiming for a body-condition score of 3.5–4.0 at the start of tupping for males, and 3–3.5 for females (*see* Chapter 8). Overfed, fat bucks are lazier and tend to have reduced libido and fertility. Check that the buck's scrotum is firm and of good size, that there are no foot problems, and that they are generally fit. If you want to test for fertility you can have it tested by your vet or vet technician. Semen takes six weeks to produce, so getting bucks prepared for the mating season well in advance should help to improve their fertility. Complete any stressful treatments (for example, dosing for worms and foot trimming) to the buck six to eight weeks prior to mating. Once bucks reach six years of age, their fertility, libido and serving capacity can decline, but if you have a small herd this may not be a problem.

Doelings come into season at around six months of age, but it's advisable not to breed them in their first year. Wait until they are more mature and coming into their second autumn at around eighteen months old, giving the young doe a chance to put her energy into her own growth. If a young doe is bred at the first possible opportunity both she and her kid(s) will need a deal of care both at kidding and afterwards; she may require help at kidding with copious amounts of lubrication to ease a tight passage, and plenty of feed to support her own continuing growth as well as the production of milk.

If you don't want young or other does to be bred they must be kept at a distance from the buck; there are many examples of bucks and does breeding successfully through a shared gate or fence. It is particularly recommended that pygmy does, which run a higher risk of needing a caesarean, are not bred until they are at least eighteen months old.

To minimize stress on the does, health management tasks should be carried out at least four weeks before you plan to introduce the buck. Breeding goats should be wormed and fluked if necessary (*see* Chapter 9), and any necessary foot trimming should happen now. 'Teeth, tits and toes' is the colloquial term we use for checking these three key bits of the body before breeding: does should be checked for a good udder (no mastitis), and for their condition - if a doe is too thin she needs to be fed to put on condition before going to the buck, while a fat doe is at risk of pregnancy toxaemia, which puts both her and her kids at risk. Deal with any foot issues at this point, and check their teeth to make sure they are in good order, as this can affect their ability to get the nutrition they need. Only fit, healthy does should be considered

for mating. Problem does identified earlier in the season should be culled for mutton.

ARTIFICIAL INSEMINATION (AI) AND SPONGING

It is becoming easier to find good quality goat semen, and goat AI courses are available too, allowing the keen breeder to bring bloodlines into their herd that they may not otherwise be able to afford or source. A number of vets offer AI services, but it is increasingly common for keepers to do their own goat AI after training. You can also use hormones to synchronize your AI or mating period if you are using a buck (and tighten the subsequent kidding period) through sponging; discuss with your vet if this is a route you wish to

CROSS BREEDING

Anglo Nubian.

If you have dairy does and are looking for chunky offspring to rear for meat, consider a Boer or Anglo Nubian buck. Do not put pygmy goats or small-framed does to large-breed males as serious kidding issues are likely to ensue.

explore, as there is a time-critical protocol to follow. Be aware that AI has a lower conception rate than a natural service.

THE BREEDING CYCLE

It is quite astonishing that male kids become sexually active at just a few weeks of age; this is why they need to be weaned and separated from all females by the time they are six weeks old to avoid unwanted pregnancies of their mother, sisters, or indeed any other doe they have access to. Does come into season as autumn brings in shortening days, which triggers the onset of the females' oestrus. Does will come into season every twenty-one days if not successfully bred, until the spring when the days lengthen once more.

Whether using AI or a buck, the keeper needs to be on the lookout for signs of oestrus when the doe is ready for mating. A buck in good health is always ready for mating at breeding time.

For the most part, does kid once a year, being mated in the autumn and kidding in the spring.

When is a Goat Ready for Mating?

Does will vary in how explicitly they show their heat. In many it is unmistakable, while in others it is more discreet. The heat generally lasts for thirty-six to forty-eight hours, though it can be as short as just a few hours to four or more days; the cycle then repeats every twenty-one days if the doe has not conceived.

- Rapid wagging of the tail (flagging). If you stroke the doe over her back towards the tail this can stimulate the wagging.
- Constant or more frequent bleating.
- Redness and swelling of the vulva, which may also show a clear mucus string.

- Lack of appetite – her mind is on other things.
- General change in behaviour from her norm.

A buck rag can be used to check if a doe is in heat by observing her reaction when it is presented to her. This is nothing more complicated than a piece of cloth that has been wiped thoroughly over a buck when it is in rut in the mating season; at all other times it should be kept in a sealed container as it will stink. Bucks urinate all over themselves at mating time, and their scent glands – which are located at the base of each horn and around the neck and shoulders – become active with the increase in testosterone at breeding time: so these are the areas on which to rub a piece of cloth to create a buck rag. You may find the smell abhorrent, but the does will love it.

THE BREEDING PROCESS – TAKING THE DOE TO THE BUCK

The goat keeper manages the mating season by choosing when they want the does to kid in the spring, and putting the buck in with them approximately 150 days beforehand. If you have your own buck it is common practice to leave the buck with the does for the period of two heat cycles (forty-two to forty-five days), providing a second opportunity for breeding if the first mating hasn't resulted in a pregnancy. However, if you would rather have some barren does than an extended kidding period, leave the buck in for just one cycle.

If you leave the buck with the does you can put raddle (a non-toxic livestock paint) on the buck's brisket, and you can then be sure of which does have been mated. You can use a ram's harness with an attached block of colour crayon; this should be changed

Mating.

Raddle powder.

after fifteen to twenty days to a new colour, so that you can see if a doe has been mated a second time. If you prefer not to attach a harness to your buck, you can use raddle paint: this comes in powder form, to which you add vegetable oil and mix to a paste; then

The Flehmen response.

smear it on to the buck between his front legs and up his chest (wearing your very oldest clothes and gloves as you do so, as it gets everywhere).

The Mating Process

A doe's urine contains pheromones that trumpet to the buck that she is ready to breed, which is why he'll spend his time sniffing her rear end. In turn, the buck urinates all over his own face, beard, front legs and any other bit he can reach; it's part of the reason why he stinks at rutting time. As the doe squats to urinate, the buck puts his face directly into her urine, and curls up his upper lip to test if she's ready – the curling of the lip is known as the Flehmen response.

The buck will stay close to the doe's side and lift a front leg, tapping at her (not a vicious kicking). This can go on for a day or more as the doe keeps walking away, but once she is fully receptive and in standing heat, the buck will mount and mate with the doe. Several matings with a buck will happen within an hour.

There are alternative methods of breeding without keeping the buck running with the does for the breeding season; they can be kept separately except for the actual mating. For dairy goats there is a particularly good reason for this, as the pheromones they produce when a buck is present makes their milk very 'goaty'. Whether using AI, a stud, or your own buck, keeping a diary of a doe's cycle will enable you to plan AI or when to bring together the buck and doe.

GESTATION LENGTH AND CARE OF THE PREGNANT DOE

Goats have a gestation period of approximately 150 days, ranging from 143 to 157 days. Carrying out all health and other 'teeth, tits and toes' checks on your does before mating minimizes the stress caused to her by carrying them out in the early stages of pregnancy when the embryos are most vulnerable.

Scanning

Pregnancy scanning is increasingly an essential tool to manage livestock effectively, firstly for pre-kidding feeding, and then at kidding time, when knowing exactly how many kids each doe is having can save kid and doe lives. We have found scanning to be almost 100 per cent accurate if carried out at the right time. A skilled technician can generally tell whether a doe is pregnant or not thirty days after mating. From 75 to 100 days after mating individual foetuses can be identified so you will know if the doe is carrying singles, twins, triplets or quads. A variation of scanning times from 70 to 100 days is acceptable, but don't leave it any later, because after 100 days it becomes difficult to tell the number of kids expected.

Feeding

Knowing the number of kids expected impacts on how you feed your goats, so make arrangements to separate out those that are barren and those expecting just a single kid: these are unlikely to need any extra feed – good hay will be enough, unless they are in poor condition (thin). In the last six or so weeks of pregnancy the does having multiples will need additional nutrition, as the kids will be developing fast. Keep a close eye on the does' body condition, and manage their feed accordingly. Their normal maintenance rations are appropriate for the majority of their gestation unless a doe is thin, but particular care is needed in the final fifty days to ensure that body condition is maintained, but also that the goat is not becoming overfat: this is something of a juggling act. Hard feed or grain is usually needed to meet the energy needs of pregnant does in their last weeks of pregnancy.

Pregnancy Toxaemia (*aka* Ketosis, Twin Kid Disease)

This disease can occur in late pregnancy in a doe that is having multiple kids and is either too thin or too fat, and is unable to keep up with the nutritional demands being made of her. Indications of pregnancy toxaemia include depression, lack of appetite, minimal dung, recumbency and swollen legs, and the doe's breath may smell of pear drops. Treat with a 50ml dose of propylene glycol syringed into the mouth three times a day for three days, and tempt with high quality feed. Prevent by managing body-condition scores, increasing the energy content of feed in the last six weeks of pregnancy, and ensuring that does are able to get proper exercise.

Hypocalcaemia (Insufficient Calcium)

Another condition that can happen in late pregnancy is when there are low levels of calcium in the blood. It makes sense to treat for both pregnancy toxaemia and hypocalcaemia simultaneously, as the indications are much the same. Signs are collapse, staggering and muscle tremors. Treatment is a subcutaneous injection of liquid calcium (Calciject) over the rib area, and recovery is almost instantaneous,

although follow-up care is needed to ensure that the doe doesn't falter a second time.

Vaccination

Two to four weeks before kidding, does should have their booster vaccination against clostridial diseases (*see* Chapter 9). Depending on the bottle size and that of your herd, it may also be convenient to vaccinate your buck(s) and youngstock at the same time, to avoid waste.

FALSE PREGNANCY IN GOATS

False pregnancy, cloudburst, hydrometra or pseudo pregnancy are all terms for when a goat has all the signs of pregnancy – udder development and a larger than normal abdomen – but is not pregnant, or was but the early embryo died. The term 'cloudburst' relates to the build-up of clear fluid in the uterus that is eventually expelled from the vagina as if she were giving birth. Many does will lactate after this as if they have had a normal pregnancy.

A different phenomenon is that of the maiden milker, a goat with precocious udder syndrome. Talk to a group of goat keepers and they will tell you about their maiden milkers who come into milk spontaneously – does that have not been bred, have had no kids, and still produce milk, sometimes for years! There is absolutely no reason why you shouldn't milk these does: be thankful for the gift.

CHAPTER 13

KIDDING AND CARE OF THE DOE AND KIDS

Calving, lambing, farrowing and kidding – the most joyful and stressful time of a farmer's year. Preparation is crucial for minimizing the risks, and that includes good nutrition for the does in the lead-up to kidding, having the necessary items on hand, and ensuring that you are at your best mentally and physically to deal with very long hours.

It's often said that it's as much work dealing with half-a-dozen pregnant females as it is a herd of hundreds. There's a lot less hanging about and waiting for something to happen if you have larger numbers to attend to, and so with small numbers it's easier to miss signs that assistance is needed. The use of an internet surveillance camera (and these are very affordable) is exceptionally useful because you can check what's happening in the kidding shed from your phone, laptop, tablet or computer.

Does need frequent observation over the kidding period so that you know exactly what's happening and how long it's been going on, and so are in a position to make a good call about whether to intervene or to leave well alone. Mismothering is something all goat keepers work to avoid, so you'll have to make up bonding pens, know which doe gave birth to which kid(s), and have the patience of a saint when dealing with the occasional first-time mother who can be so shocked by their first birth that rather than stick to their kid like glue, they shoot off in the opposite direction.

You can't deal with any of this – as well as the dressing of vulnerable kid navels, ensuring each kid has that first important suckling of colostrum, or any necessary treatments – if you're not on the spot virtually full time.

PREPARING FOR KIDDING

Should you arrange for the does to kid inside or out? This is clearly a personal choice, but I always prefer to have livestock giving birth indoors, and as goats require shelter in any case, adapting their normal hangout as a kidding area should be entirely feasible, as

OPPOSITE: Park Farm, Umberleigh, August 1985. (Documentary photograph by James Ravilious for the Beaford Archive © Beaford Arts)

Kids suckling.

heat lamps if required for hypothermic kids. Exploit the joys of modern technology and install a camera that shows you what is happening from the comfort of your armchair or bed.

For multiple births a distracted doe does not have to be concerned about predators attacking kids when in a shed, and mismothering is easier to control. Barns, polytunnels, pig arks and calf huts can all be used to maximize space for kidding if the existing shelter is inadequate for the purpose.

Get some experience. You may be able to help out a goat keeper at kidding time, but more likely there may be a local sheep farmer who would appreciate an extra pair of hands to clean out bonding pens, fill up hayracks and water buckets, and a multitude of other mundane but critical tasks. Find one that has hundreds if not thousands of sheep, rather than a flock

even an open-sided shelter can be enclosed with hurdles for kidding. Indoors, your does are contained, which means you are not causing them stress by chasing any around that need help, and there are likely to be fewer fatalities. There should be electricity so that you have light and heat available to observe what's happening, and can provide

LEARNING FROM EXPERIENCE

The following are the sort of helpful practices that you might pick up in a busy kidding or lambing shed:

- Use copper sulphate rather than iodine to dress newborn navels; it dries them up in a fraction of the time and so significantly decreases the risk of navel ill.
- When assisting a tight birth and you can't make further progress, flipping the labouring doe on to her other side can shift and loosen things significantly, easing the birth.
- When you can't progress with a posterior (hind legs only) birth, lift one of the kid's legs up towards the dam's spine (the opposite of what instinct tells you), and then the same with the other leg to free things up.
- When a dam starts to give up or has a lazy labour, circling a gloved, lubricated finger just inside the vulva encourages contractions to get going again.
- Two hurdles tied together at angles with a large enough gap between them for the dam's head to go through makes an impromptu adoption crate.
- For water buckets in bonding pens use any colour other than black, because you can't see the poo in black ones!
- Don't position water buckets underneath the hay rack.

of twenty, so that you are guaranteed to be present at all kinds of lambing action. You'll get the chance to observe and possibly help with actual lambing, which has all the same issues and potential presentations as for kidding. Some veterinary practices run lambing courses, as do agricultural colleges – attend as many as you can in your area.

Get plenty of sleep before kidding starts, and stock your shelves, fridge and freezer with nutritious food. Surviving on biscuits and snatching a sandwich from time to time will not give you the energy you need to be on top of things. Eat as well as you can on the lead up to, and over kidding. You might have to become adept at cat-napping, too. Kidding over an extended period is sapping of energy, and to avoid flagging just at the point of the year when you need to be at the top of your game, control the timing and length of the mating process and don't allow entire males to run free with females throughout the breeding season – the results can be exhausting (*see* Chapter 12). Trim your nails short and remove rings other than a smooth band.

Vaccinate your does with their booster against clostridial diseases two to four weeks before kidding (*see* Chapter 9), and if you have fibre or particularly hairy does, trim around the tail, bottom, hind legs and udder a few weeks before kidding so that you have a clear view of udder development and the kidding progress. It will also aid kids in finding the teat quickly and easily after birth and in suckling effectively, and not on grubby and unsatisfying fibre. Make sure the area where kidding will take place has been thoroughly cleaned out and dried beforehand, scattered with hydrated lime or dairy-cow cubicle bedding powder, and bedded down with fresh straw.

It's also time to go shopping. There will be items in the kidding kit that last for many years, and potentially throughout your whole goat-keeping life, and others that need to be refreshed annually. Every year go through the checklist of kidding kit, add anything you'd find helpful (perhaps moving an old armchair into the barn for your own use), and check that any items that have literally or figuratively passed their use-by date are replaced in good time, before kidding gets going.

Draw up a simple kidding record sheet that includes the following information:

- The date that does went to the buck (and a precise breeding date if known), and an expected due date.
- The number of does that went to the buck.
- The number of does scanned pregnant, and the number of kids expected.
- The number of barren does.
- Individual lines for each doe stating: the date and time of each kidding; the bonding pen number; ear-tag number; the age of the doe; the number of kids scanned; the number of kids born live; the sex of the kids; if assistance was needed, and what kind; any treatment or medication administered; if the doe cleansed (placenta passed) successfully; any notes regarding issues (such as a lazy labour), or positives (such as excellent doe kids with the potential to keep as future breeders); the date doe and kids were turned out of the bonding pen.

Pregnant women need to avoid contact with the pregnant does and new mums and kids during kidding time because of the risk of toxoplasmosis (*see* Chapter 9).

KIDDING KIT

Be aware that a lot of the kit required will be sold for lambing, but will do the same job for kidding. Essential kit should include the following:

Saddle hayrack.

- Hurdles for creating bonding pens indoors (for a small herd at least one pen per five does).
- Straw for bedding.
- Hydrated lime or dairy cow cubicle bedding powder to disinfect bonding pens between uses.
- Water buckets for each pen (calf buckets are perfect), plus a water supply for does waiting to kid. Have a bucket of water and paper towels available to wash your hands.
- Feed buckets for each pen.
- Saddle hayracks for kidding pens. Avoid haynets as goats get tangled up in them, and kids strangle themselves in loose loops.
- Marker spray to identify which kids belongs to which doe. It's helpful to use a different colour according to the number of kids born live, so that you know at a glance that any with a red number, for example, should have two kids.
- Notepad and pen or whiteboard for kidding records, and to identify which does/kids need extra care, and of what kind – this is critical when you are doing shifts and need to pass on information to the next person. I use a clipboard with a printout updated daily.

Headcollar.

- Heat lamp for poorly kids (hot water bottles are also very handy).
- Colostrum. It's essential that a kid receives colostrum from its mother in the first six hours of life – if this is not possible, you must feed replacement colostrum by stomach tube. This can be colostrum you've frozen or a powdered type.
- Milk replacer, bottles and teats for feeding milk to any orphan kids. Also jugs and measuring/weighing kit for preparing colostrum and milk.
- Stomach tubes, bottles and syringes.
- Obstetric lubricant and disposable gloves (both short and long-arm versions).
- A carrying bucket (or two or more) for all your equipment.
- Elastrator and rings for castrating bucklings (also a small sharp knife for removing rings if necessary).
- Rope halter or headcollar and lead if you need to restrain a doe (for instance to let her kid suckle).
- Lambing ropes and puller (these are marketed for lambs, but are what you need for kids, too).
- Prolapse harness and spoons.
- Medication: pen and strep antibiotic, propylene glycol (in case of twin kid disease), Calciject 40% CM (in case of hypocalcaemia): *see* Chapter 12.
- Iodine liquid/spray or copper sulphate for navels.

- Syringes and needles.
- Torches/head torch.
- Kid cam – CCTV or a livestock monitoring camera means you can observe the kidding-shed activity from the warmth of your bed, ready to leap into action if necessary.
- Muck fork and wheelbarrow to remove mucky straw.
- Hay and feed.
- Surgical handscrub/hibiscrub – for assisted births.
- Digital thermometer to take a kid's temperature if it is poorly.
- Vet's phone number at hand for emergencies.
- Empty plastic feed sacks for removing afterbirth and general rubbish.
- Penknife – for various tasks, from cutting baler twine to opening packets of this and that.

EARLY SIGNS OF LABOUR

If does are in individual pens prior to kidding, remove their water bucket once labour starts; you don't want newborns to drown by being birthed into them. Every goat will have its own way of doing things, from the time it takes to deliver, to being bothered or not by the presence of a person, but there are key signs to look out for that kidding is imminent:

- Udders start to fill anything up to a month before kidding; others, particularly those of first-timers, may not fill significantly until kidding itself. Just before/during kidding the udder will usually become tight and engorged.
- The pelvic ligaments relax (drop) on each side of the tail, so that the tailhead appears raised. If you feel and observe the tailhead and ligaments at other times of the year the difference will be noticeable.
- The vulva becomes softer, more flaccid and pinker.
- Mucus strings may be seen either hanging from the vulva or flicked on the body (these can be clear, whitish or amber coloured).
- The doe will become less wide and hollower in the flank as the kids drop down lower in the body.

- The doe is likely to make noises you don't hear at other times, communicating with her yet-to-be-born kids.
- She may not eat her feed once contractions start (although others will eat with a kid halfway out!).
- She will become increasingly restless, pawing at the ground and getting up and down repeatedly.

For the most part, does will kid on their own, but as they don't have transparent bodies you need to be alert in case you do need to help.

THE NORMAL KIDDING PROCESS

It's always difficult giving timings as you may miss early signs, and there are always exceptions when things can happen much faster or more slowly; it takes experience to know when to leave things be and when to intervene. Please take the timings below as a general guide only. Those keepers new to kidding are far more likely to want to rush in too quickly and unnecessarily, so sit on your hands and give the doe time to give birth naturally; busy yourself instead by taking notes of what's happening and at what time.

1. The doe will become restless and the cervix will start to dilate. She will focus on a place to give birth (although if in a communal area, this may change). This phase can last between four to eight hours in experienced dams, and six to twelve hours for first-timers. You may not notice early signs, which can make timings somewhat approximate.

2 After plenty of contractions/straining the water bag will emerge, and the doe is likely to get up and down between contractions. The water bag will break, and the front feet and nose of the kid start to show inside a membrane bag. Some does prefer to do all this standing up, most prefer lying down. The feet and nose can appear to pop in and out before making enough progress to be fully delivered – but don't worry: in due course the kid is born. This stage of contractions to birth can take anything from one to four hours. The waterbag may appear anything up to an hour before the kid, but can emerge simultaneously.

3. The doe will lick and clean each kid as it arrives, and they will find their feet with various wobbly starts and falls, and look for the teat to suckle.

4. With multiple births (twins, triplets, quads), one kid can follow the next very quickly, or there may be half an hour or more between births.

5. The placenta will be delivered in due course; this may take several hours or even a day. Do not pull on it as this can cause haemorrhaging. Once the placenta is passed I tend to remove it, to keep the area clean; also the dam will often eat it, which is fine, but there is a small risk of choking. If the placenta is hanging from the doe after a day, let the vet know – they can remove it manually if necessary.

The Stages of Delivery

1. Pushing out the waterbag.

2. Kid on the way (feet are now visible).

3. The diving position, a normal presentation.

4. Head and feet are out.

5. Shoulders emerging.

6. A little further out.

7. First kid has landed.

8. First kid born, another on its way.

9. The dam licks the birth membranes off the first kid.

10. Second kid emerges.

11. Another doe getting ready to mismother.

12. A final helping hand.

13. Bonding immediately.

14. It's twins!

With a normal kidding what help should you give? Clear any membranes and mucus that may be over the kid's nostrils and mouth with a gloved hand so that when it takes its first breath it is able to breathe in air. Then stand back and let the doe get on with her cleaning, bonding and having any further kids. Dip the kids' navels in iodine solution or copper sulphate to stop any bacteria entering.

Give the kid two hours from its birth to work out how to suckle naturally, and only help it on to the teat after that time if necessary. Once it has fed it will curl up and snooze. Each time a kid wakes it will stretch (a good sign that all is well) and head for another feed, and as time passes it will bounce about and explore more and more.

KIDDING PRESENTATIONS

We all like to see the diving position of front feet with nose not far behind, often with the tongue sticking out too, but there are possible alternative presentations, some of which the inexperienced can deal with, and others that require support from the vet or an experienced

Normal presentation.

Hind leg.

goat keeper or shepherd. Being able to identify front and back legs is an important part of knowing what you're dealing with. The ankle and knee bend the same way for the forelegs, but not for the hind legs.

Always expect multiple kids (and allow for this possibility even in does scanned with a single), and remember to check whether the legs you see or feel are from the same kid or not by running your hand down one leg and up the other to see if they are connected. If using a lambing rope for the head, place the loop behind the ears and through the mouth, not round the neck or you will strangle the kid.

There are a range of less helpful presentations, some of which are easy to diagnose (a wriggling tail coming first, or a head only, for example), whereas others require an internal examination with clean examination gloves and plenty of lube (obstetric lubrication gel) to assess what position the kid is in so that you can aid as required. On the subject of lube, it's probably the single most important item in your kidding kit, as it lubricates and eases the path for your hand and the kid. 'An ounce of lubrication is worth a ton of pressure' is the truism to live by here: using plenty of lubrication if you need to assist can make the difference to being able to kid successfully or not.

Make sure your fingernails are short and that you have removed your rings and watch before you enter a doe. You should always wear a new, clean, disposable arm-length

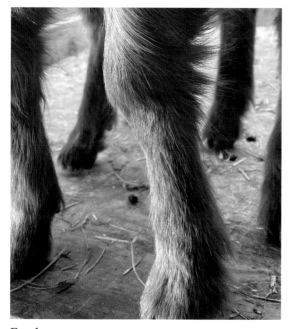

Foreleg.

Disposable gloves and lube.

Lambing ropes.

examination glove. If you find these rather large (they seem to be designed for giants with bananas for fingers), put a short, wrist-length, closer-fitting, disposable glove on top.

First-time mothers can be more susceptible to problems than mature animals that have given birth previously so will need greater vigilance on the part of the keeper; they might, to be frank, be tight, so a squeeze of lube inserted inside the vagina for a doe struggling to give birth where presentation is otherwise all correct can be very helpful. Obesity and lack of exercise during late pregnancy increase the chances of dystocia (kidding difficulties).

If you have done as much as you can and are unable to aid the doe to kid, call your vet or an experienced goat keeper or shepherd; under no circumstances should you get a host of inexperienced people to 'have a go'. A vet can help sort problems if given time, so don't leave it too late to make contact, and they alone can perform a Caesarean if it's needed. For the first-time goat keeper, don't be nervous about calling your vet just because you think you should be able to cope: use their skills and learn from the experience so that you feel better able to manage on your own in future.

Head and One Leg Only (Front Leg Back)

Depending on the size of the kid, if it is small, you can birth this presentation without correcting the position of the backwards leg by bringing forwards the head and protruding leg. If the backwards leg is crooked and locked against the doe's pelvis you will need to cup your hand round the kid's hoof to avoid damaging the doe, straighten the leg and bring it forwards. If the kid is large you will also need to bring the hidden leg forward before you can birth it. If the head is not too far out, push it back first to give you more room to move the leg in the uterus rather than in the confines of the birth canal.

Head and one leg only – a standing birth.

Head and one leg only.

Is this head only? You need to check from all angles.

Head Out Only (Both Front Legs Back)

With both legs back/head out only, there is a real danger that the kid's head will swell as the doe has her contractions, which can be fatal. Do not ever try to pull the kid out by its head alone: if there is room, reach in and draw out a leg. You may be able to birth it as for head and one leg only, or reach in again and draw out the second leg and birth the kid. If there is no room to bring out the leg(s) attach a lambing/ kidding rope around the kid's head behind the ears and through the mouth, and with the help of your trusty lube, push the head back in.

Find and bring out the legs, and then the head using the lambing rope, and deliver the kid.

Elbow Lock

With an elbow lock, put your hand in and hook out the leg(s) one at a time and deliver the kid.

Head Back

With head back you will need to bring the head forwards in order to deliver the kid. Use

Head out only.

Elbow lock.

Head back.

Breech.

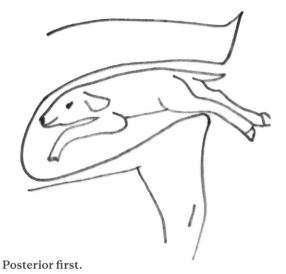

Posterior first.

a lambing aid/rope to stop the head flopping back into its original position.

Breech and Posterior (Coming Backwards)

With a breech (bottom only) or posterior (hind legs only) presentation, speed is needed once your pulling has broken the umbilical cord, so that it is out of the mother and all fluid is cleared from the mouth before it takes its first breath. Do not attempt to turn the kid into the normal presentation.

With a breech you will have to go into the doe to bring out the back legs first and then deliver the kid. With posterior, check the legs are from the same kid, straighten the legs and birth it quickly, pulling downwards.

If the kid gets stuck, lift one leg upwards at a time to unlock. Take particular care in both cases to swiftly clear any mucus from the kid's mouth and nose; use your fingers to remove gunk and hold upside down by the back legs so that gravity further clears any remaining mucus.

More than One Kid Coming At Once

Kids can come together, both facing forwards, both facing backwards, or one forwards and one back. You will need to investigate the situation so that you know whose head and legs belongs to which kid, push one kid back into the doe, deliver first one and then the other.

Mismothering

When kidding in a communal space does can be very active in mothering a newborn that is not their own, particularly when the dam is focusing on delivering another kid. Once the first kid is born and licked by its mother so that she knows it, carry the

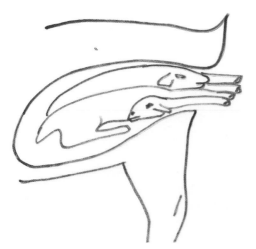

More than one kid coming at once.

Twins, one coming forwards, one coming backwards.

Who's the mother?

kid in front of her nose and lead the pair into a bonding pen, which shuts out the hopeful mismothering auntie and allows the family to bond in peace. This is not misplaced anthropomorphism: if the kid is stolen by another doe she may abandon her own when it is born, or the one she's mismothered; the kids may not receive their colostrum; it can leave you with kids that need to be bottle fed; and you can end up with too many kids on one mother and not enough with another.

Ringwomb

Ringwomb is when the cervix fails to dilate when the doe is in full labour so that the kid cannot be birthed. Do not confuse this with a cervix that has not yet dilated and is in the early stages of labour. True ringwomb is when the waterbag has been presented, the doe has been in labour for some considerable time (around six hours or so) and when you examine her internally the cervix doesn't allow your hand through. You must not force through the cervix: instead use plenty of lube and circle your finger round and round the cervix to encourage it to open; this may need to continue for some time – half an hour or more – continually circling, and the cervix will normally open.

If there is no progress, call the vet; in fact better to call the vet anyway as they can administer a relaxant, and if they turn up as the kid is born, so be it.

The Overdue Doe

There are various schools of thought about overdue does, and whether, after 155 days gestation (where the breeding date is absolutely known), a doe should be induced. The kids grow quickly in their last days, which can make deliveries after an extended pregnancy difficult for both doe and kid. Equally, many does will birth naturally up to a week beyond the expected due date with no intervention. If you have concerns, talk to your vet.

DEALING WITH AN APPARENTLY LIFELESS KID

If you've cleared the mouth of fluid and the kid isn't moving, put a piece of clean straw up its nostril, which should make it sneeze and take its first breath. Check for a heartbeat and stimulate the kid by rubbing it fairly vigorously on the side of its chest; if you see the tongue move and its eye blink, keep going until a breath is taken – you can also tip it upside down, its head hanging down to let gravity remove any further mucus you may have missed. If there is neither tongue nor eye movement, nor a heartbeat, it is unlikely that you will be able to revive the kid.

If you have been inside the doe to assist kidding, then she must be given a dose of penicillin-based antibiotic immediately afterwards, once you have made sure that the kids are fine; your vet will prescribe these for you, and you should have a bottle and syringes/needles as part of your kidding

A lovely live kid.

kit. Far better to have an unused bottle of antibiotics at the end of kidding than not having it immediately to hand if required.

Penicillin is also the antibiotic of choice for use with kids and for does feeding kids, as it doesn't have a detrimental effect on bone growth as can other antibiotics, which is clearly not what you want for growing kids.

After she has attended to her kids, offer the doe a bucket of drinking water – she is likely to drink a calf bucket or two of water fairly quickly post birth as birthing fluids are salty. Make sure she has good quality hay and clean water at all times once she has finished kidding.

COLOSTRUM

Colostrum is the first milk produced by the doe and provides sustenance and antibodies that protect the kid from disease in its earliest days. Kids need colostrum in the first six hours of life, and preferably within the first two hours. Check the doe has milk by drawing it down, which will also remove the waxy cap in the teats. Once the kid is twenty-four-hours old its ability to absorb the antibodies in colostrum disappears, which is why the keeper needs to monitor its intake. This is relatively straightforward for non-dairy herds: the dam is checked that she has plenty of milk once she's given birth, and the kids are checked to make sure they have suckled and are continuing to nurse and are thriving.

If the kid is unable to suckle its dam for whatever reason, colostrum should be fed at 50-75ml per kilo weight of the kid at least three times in the first twenty-four hours of life. As an example, if a kid weighs 5kg (11lb) it should be fed 1.1ltr (2 pints) of colostrum, split into three or four feeds, with the first given within the first hour if possible, and certainly within the first six hours. Fifteen hours after birth colostrum production ceases and the doe produces milk.

If you have does with single kids it's a good idea to harvest some colostrum for future emergencies: milk about 100–150ml colostrum from each doe, put it into a sterile plastic container or plastic ice-cube containers, and freeze so it can be gently reheated for use. Never boil or microwave colostrum as this will destroy the antibodies and protein. For a weak kid or one that will not suck you will have to master the use of a stomach tube, to ensure it gets the necessary nutrients.

Stomach Tubing

In some cases the kid is unable to nurse the doe even with assistance, and stomach tubing is needed to get colostrum into the kid. With the kid's head in a natural position, insert the tube in the side of the kid's mouth, following the roof of the mouth down into the throat. Don't force the tube down, but allow the kid to swallow as the tube goes down the oesophagus; it will go in about 30cm (12in). Although it is difficult to get the tube down the trachea (windpipe), you can check to see if air is coming from the tube by listening or moistening the end of the tube to see if a bubble forms.

Give the colostrum slowly – if using a large syringe that fits snugly into the tube don't use the plunger, but let gravity do the work. After one tube feeding many kids will start to suckle the doe on their own. If not, the kid may need to be tube fed every two to three hours until it will suckle the doe or a teated bottle.

For those who are dairying there are various ways of ensuring that kids get their colostrum and then an adequate milk supply in their first days and weeks. There can occasionally be issues in getting a kid to suck from a bottle if it has been suckling from its dam, so some keepers choose to remove the kids at birth (this may also link to health concerns to avoid the transmission of disease such as CAE),

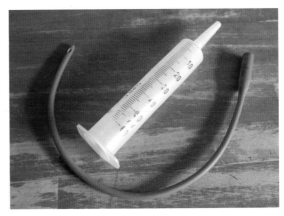

Stomach tube and syringe.

milk the colostrum from the dam and bottle feed it to the kids. Others will leave the kids with the doe but still bottle feed them their first feed of colostrum so that the kids have positive associations with the bottle.

Some choose to leave the kids with the dam for the first day or two so that they get their fill of colostrum naturally, and some will leave the kids with their dam for a few weeks or even longer (*see* Chapter 11 on kid-at-foot dairying) until weaning at eight to ten weeks old, or even as late as four or even six months (with the exception of entire bucklings, which need to be separated from females at six weeks). The choice is the keeper's, and will be arrived at from a mix of concepts: methods picked up from mentors, programmes that have proved to work in the herd, time available and individual philosophies on kid rearing.

It's worth saying here that nothing but colostrum and then milk should be given to a young kid: no bite of your honey sandwich, chocolate bar, breakfast cereal or anything else – please desist.

CARE OF NEWBORN KIDS

Unless kids are removed at birth, for the first couple of days the doe and her kids should be in their own bonding pen. Pen size depends

Meshed hurdle.

somewhat on the size and breed of the doe and the number of kids, but pens made out of 1.2 × 1.8m (4 × 6ft) hurdles should be fit for purpose for most, unless a doe has to be contained longer for observation, in which case a more generous 1.8 × 1.8m (6 × 6ft) pen is desirable. Meshed lambing hurdles are ideal as they stop vigorous kids straying into neighbouring pens or further afield, and solid panels may be needed if kids can vault over the meshed sections; if you cable tie drilled dairy board on to hurdles, this makes a light and washable secure panel.

Pens should be clean, dry and well bedded, and thoroughly cleaned between does; muck out and allow to dry, then scatter with hydrated lime or dairy-cow cubicle bedding powder before putting down a new bed of fresh straw.

If a doe is nervous or disinterested in her kids use a hurdle to partition off a corner of the pen so she can see and lick her kids without trampling on them or butting them until she is calmer and more accepting.

Does and kids should be in their bonding pens for forty-eight hours. Identify each kid a day or two after birth, so that it can be matched with its mother, who is also marked (use a numbering system, spraying the same number on the doe and kids). If they are healthy and the weather is good, allow mother and kids out after forty-eight hours.

Check them several times a day to pick out and treat any sickly or weak kids, and to make sure no kids have been separated from their mothers.

Any heat lamps for hypothermic kids should be used with caution, hung in the corner of the pen at least a metre above the bedding, and where the doe is unable to interfere with the lamp or power cable. Check the temperature after an hour as they take a while to heat up, and use additional heating methods if warmth is needed immediately (such as hot water bottles, heat pads).

The majority of kids are born without any assistance, and within minutes are up on their legs, instinctively seeking the doe's teat. Some are a little slower, and this can depend on breed as well as how easy their birth was. Check that the kid has fed from its mother within the first two hours. If you see a kid asleep in a pen don't just assume that it's fine, but give it a gentle poke – it should stand up and stretch if all is well.

It is normal for newly kidded goats to have a bloodstained discharge that lasts for up to three weeks. To help with hygiene, trim or wash the doe's tail hair if necessary.

Faeces and Constipation

Within the first few hours of its life the kid will pass sticky black faeces (meconium), encouraged by the intake of colostrum, which is a good laxative. After the meconium a kid's faeces are yellow orange and can be very sticky, so keep checking that this fudge-like poo doesn't plug up the kid's anus: if it does, remove it carefully, if necessary using warm water. In about ten days a kid will start passing the more familiar goat droppings.

If a kid strains and does not pass faeces you may need to give it an enema using an old stomach tube and syringe to flush the rectum with 15–20ml of warm soapy water, inserting the tube no further than 5cm (2in). However, do not confuse constipation with hunger or hypothermia – a hunched-up kid may not be straining, but is more likely starving and/or chilled.

HEALTH PROBLEMS AT KIDDING TIME

Vaginal and Uterine Prolapse

A prolapse is when interior organ(s) are pushed outside the body cavity; a doe is most at risk of prolapse in the late stages of pregnancy, when the vagina is pushed through the vulva, appearing as a pink swelling the size of a tennis ball. There are various causes, including multiple kids, being over fat, lameness, so the doe doesn't take enough exercise, and genetics.

A prolapse should be dealt with on the day it emerges. Make sure the protruding area is clean, lubricate a ewe prolapse spoon, and insert it into the vagina. If the goat is a fibre breed you can simply tie the spoon strings

Prolapse spoon.

on each side to the fibre to keep it in place, as you would for a sheep. For short-coated breeds you will need to attach a ewe prolapse harness to keep the spoon in place. A doe will be able to kid past the spoon, which can be removed and discarded after the birth, but the harness will need to be removed once labour starts.

An alternative option is to get the vet to stitch the doe; however, that suture *must* be cut by the keeper before the doe goes into labour or her contractions will cause serious tearing. Keep a particularly close eye on any doe that has prolapsed to ensure she is eating well and acting normally. Careful consideration should be given about retaining the doe (and her offspring) in the herd for future breeding; a doe with anything other than a minor prolapse should be culled from the herd.

A uterine prolapse is a much more serious issue and can happen post birth, immediately or up to a day or so later, the entire uterus becoming inverted and appearing through the cervix. This will require veterinary attention. Keep the doe warm and secure from other goats so the uterus cannot be damaged. Keep the protrusion clean by covering the bedding underneath the doe in a clean towel, clean feed sack or clingfilm, and await the vet's arrival. Have sugar on hand: the vet may want to sprinkle it on the uterus to help it

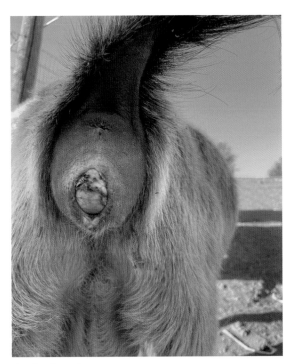

Vaginal prolapse.

shrink in order to reinsert it. A doe may recover well from this and rear her kids successfully, but discuss with the vet whether you should breed from her again.

Kid Checks

Within a few hours of birth carry out a proper examination of the kid:

- Check for swellings on the kid's body, head or limbs, especially around the umbilical cord, which may indicate a hernia.
- Check the anus to make sure there is an opening, and that it's not imperforate, which will prevent it passing faeces (if imperforate this needs to be opened by the vet).
- Check the kid's mouth and lower jaw – if it is severely over- or undershot the kid will have difficulty suckling and may need to be fed by stomach tube. In severe cases the kid may not thrive. The same is true if the kid has a cleft palate.
- Examine the kid's eyes for entropion, where the eyelid is turned in, causing the lashes to rub painfully against the eye. This can often be cured by pinching and rolling out the in-turned lid. If not, it will need a 1ml injection of penicillin horizontally into the eyelid – not a job for the inexperienced, but a simple job for the vet or the keeper once shown how.
- Tucked-under feet or contracted tendons often improve with no treatment, but if they are more severe a splint made with wooden lolly sticks, cotton wool and vetwrap can help straighten the legs and protect the skin.

Hypothermia

Hypothermia is the greatest cause of death of newborns, so if you see a young kid curled up in the corner of the pen don't just assume it's sleeping after a good feed. Is its abdomen full or empty? Will it stand and stretch? Is it warm enough? Hypothermia is having a low body temperature of 37.5° or under. Small kids chill faster than larger ones, and the quicker the doe licks and dries off the kid, the less vulnerable it will be.

Hypothermic kids appear weak, hunched

Normal Temperature for Kids

Normal temperature	Fahrenheit	Centigrade
Kids	101.8-104.5	38.7-40.2

up, the ears and mouth will feel cold, and the kid may not want to suck. If the kid doesn't stand and suck successfully within two hours of birth, you should check its temperature rectally. The age of the kid and its temperature determines your next steps. Don't attempt to bottle feed a cold, weak kid, as there is a danger of it inhaling liquid into its lungs, which will drown it. Proceed as follows:

- If the rectal temperature is between 37.5 and 39°C, milk between 120-240ml colostrum from the doe (depending on the size of the lamb) and feed by stomach tube; repeat every two to four hours until the kid is up and suckling.
- If the kid's temperature is below 37°C, and it is less than five hours old, warm up the kid to 37°C, and when it is able to hold its head up, feed it by stomach tube.
- If the kid is over five hours old do not warm up the kid as its low blood glucose level would cause a hypoglycaemic fit and death. If the kid's temperature is below 37°C, and it is more than five hours old and able to hold its head up, give colostrum by stomach tube, then warm the kid to 37°C or more before further feeding.
- If the kid's temperature is below 37°C, and it is more than five hours old but

unable to hold its head up, it will need an intraperitoneal (into the abdomen) injection of 20 per cent glucose solution. Draw up 12.5ml of 50 per cent sterile glucose solution and equal amounts of boiled water from the kettle, giving 25ml of warm solution; alternatively draw up 15ml of 40 per cent solution and equal amounts of boiled water from the kettle, giving 30ml of warmed solution. Hold the kid by its front legs. Using a sterile 2.5cm 19G needle, inject 2.5cm below 2.5cm to the side of the navel. Direct the needle back towards the kid's tail head. Once administered, warm the kid to 37°C before feeding by stomach tube.

Starvation

Starvation has various possible causes: inadequate intake of colostrum, rejection by the dam, mastitis making it painful for the doe when the kid tries to suckle, teats that are too large or close to the ground, inadequate milk production, joint injury or illness, sore mouth, or a difficult birth. Starvation typically occurs during the first three days of life. A starving kid will stand with its head down, ears drooping, or it will be too weak to stand. The stomach will be empty. Shivering and hypothermia may follow. Ensuring kids receive colostrum and then milk as discussed above is a critical keeper's responsibility.

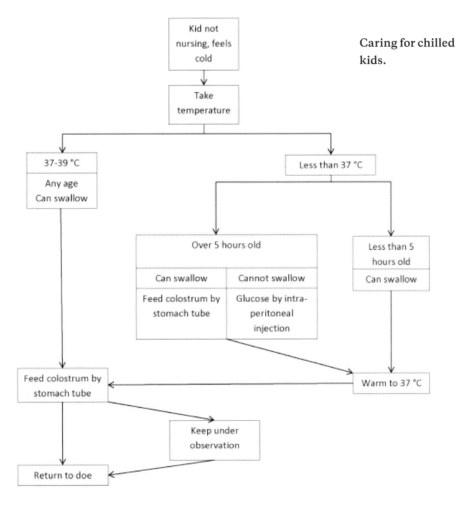

Caring for chilled kids.

Joint or Navel Ill

Joint ill or navel ill is a particular problem when kidding areas have not been well cleaned and disinfected, and the navel has not been effectively dipped in iodine or copper sulphate. Bacterial infection can lead to problems in the joints, the liver and spinal abscesses. Treatment is by antibiotics and anti-inflammatory medication from your vet.

Watery Mouth or Rattle Belly

Watery mouth is associated with lack of hygiene and inadequate ingestion of colostrum, and leads to a form of toxic shock caused by the decomposition of large numbers of bacteria in the kid's gut in youngsters under ten days old and as young as twelve hours. The kid stops feeding and drools, has a cold mouth, and is bloated, caused by gas in its abdomen. The gut will make a 'rattling' sound if the kid is gently shaken. Treat affected kids with antibiotic as advised by your vet, or give an enema to rid the gut of the problematic *E. coli* bacteria – a mild solution of diluted washing-up liquid is commonly used (*see* Constipation above).

Scours (Diarrhoea)

Adequate intake of colostrum coupled with good hygiene is the best protection against scours. Bacterial scours can be treated with antibiotics and fluids to avoid dehydration. One of the causes of scouring in young kids is coccidiosis, a parasite that destroys the gut lining; kids between three to twelve weeks old are at greatest risk (*see* Chapter 9). At the first signs of infection discuss appropriate coccidiostat treatment with your vet. It is usual to treat all kids in the group, as even those with no apparent symptoms may still infect other kids.

Pneumonia

Baby pneumonia shows as a raised temperature, increased respiratory rate, failure to nurse, and death in untreated cases; kids that do not consume adequate colostrum are particularly at risk, although a bacterial infection, draughts and dampness in the kidding shed also contribute. Treat swiftly with penicillin.

ADOPTION (*aka* FOSTERING)

The optimum result is to have two kids for each doe (if she has enough milk), although some will raise three successfully. However, if you have triplets or quads you may want to adopt a kid on to a doe with a single (this is where scanning is a huge advantage). If a doe dies and her kids survive you may find that adoption helps in rearing a healthier kid; if a kid dies, the doe may benefit from having a kid to raise. The aim is to minimize bottle-fed kids, which may not do as well as those that feed from a doe.

Wet Adoption

There are various ways of achieving wet adoption, the aim being to trick the doe into thinking she has had two kids, not just one. You need to be present at the birth of the kid, and be prepared.

Put the kidding doe in a pen. Have a large, clean bucket and fill it no more than 10cm (4in) deep with warm water and about a third of a cup of salt, mixed together. Take the orphan kid and tie its two front legs and two back legs together (not too tight) so that it acts like a newborn, then place it in the bucket. Take the bucket and kid to the kidding doe, and kid her straight into the bucket on to the adoptee. Cover both kids in the juices and take them both out of the bucket. Leave the adoptee's legs tied so it simulates the position of a newborn and allows the other kid to get the good colostrum. The salt further encourages the doe to lick and so mother the adoptee, and makes both kids smell and taste the same. Once the kids have been licked dry and the newborn has had its fill of colostrum, untie the orphan's legs.

If time is short and there's no time for warm water and buckets, kid the doe having a single on to a clean feed sack or a shallow bucket, tie the legs of the adoptee, rub it in the birth juices, and continue as above.

Adoption Spray

Adoption sprays for lambs are available that are also suitable for use for kids. They work by neutralizing the natural odour of lamb and ewe, and help prevent rejection. Spray the kid to be adopted from head to tail, avoiding the eyes, and spray the doe's head and nose (avoiding the eyes) prior to introducing the kid to her.

Dry Adoption

Although not for the faint-hearted, this method of adoption is usually very

Adoption spray.

successful. If a kid dies and is no longer wet from birth (that is, it is not stillborn, but dies a few hours after birth or is a few days old), skin it and put the resulting jacket on a surplus kid (normally the largest and fittest of triplets, robust enough to cope with the transition), and give it to the mum whose kid has died. Make sure the kid's rear end is well covered by the skin as that is the first area the doe will sniff and lick. Do observe the new family until you are sure the doe will not attack the kid. Once successfully adopted, remove the skin after a couple of days – and definitely don't leave it on once it has started to rot and stink.

If a kid is stillborn and is wet, you can use the wet adoption method above by rubbing the adoptee on the dead kid.

HOW TO SKIN A DEAD KID

To skin a dead kid, cut around all four leg joints at the knee/hocks, cut around the neck, and then make an incision under the abdomen from the breastbone towards the tail. Remove the skin as a whole piece starting from the tail end, including the tail, cutting through the bone at the base of the tail so that it stays attached to the skin. Pull the skin off like a tight jumper, turn it the right way, and insert the adoptee through the neck and leg holes.

Adopter Crate

An adopter crate that secures the doe's head and stops her butting an adopted kid away is a useful tool, and safer than using a halter, which might strangle the goat. This system allows the kid to suckle the doe even if she's not keen to adopt at first. It may be seen as the last port of call for (understandably) awkward does, as it is a restraint technique, but it can be very successful for both doe and kid(s).

MONITORING THE DOE

As well as taking good care of the kid, the new mother should also be monitored. Is she eating and drinking well? Is the discharge from her vulva fetid and foul-smelling (this could indicate metritis, infection of the uterus)? Is her milk coming in? Is her udder hard or hot (this could indicate mastitis and treatment would be required)? Has she bonded well with her kids, and is she allowing them to suckle? If all is well, you can carry out any necessary treatments for the doe – such as worming, foot trimming – and then she and her kids can be introduced to other does and kids in the herd, either outside or in a communal crèche area for does with young kids. Having a crèche area is very useful for those family groups you want to get out of bonding pens, but which you still need to monitor closely: kids that are particularly small, or have a minor health issue, or need some sort of extra care, or if the weather is threatening.

CASTRATION

Castration (ringing, banding or wethering) of bucklings must be carried out by a trained competent person, so do ask an experienced shepherd, goat keeper or your vet to show you how it's done. In the UK you can only castrate without an anaesthetic by using a rubber ring and elastrator during the first week of life. Beyond that stage castration must be carried out by a vet. The ring constricts the blood flow, and in three or four weeks the scrotum will have shrivelled up and dropped off. Proceed as follows:

- Put a rubber ring on the elastrator pins and hold the kid by the front legs so that the back legs and scrotum dangle down.
- Open the elastrator and place the ring over the scrotum at its base against the body.

Elastrator and castration rings.

- Close the elastrator but do not remove.
- Make sure both testicles are below the ring before you remove the elastrator (they feel like two firm rods inside the scrotum).
- Release the ring from the elastrator. Check that the nipples are rolled above and free of the ring.
- If you have only caught one testicle in the band, remove the band immediately with a sharp knife and try again later. We keep a small pointed piece of wood and a sharp penknife in the pot of castration rings: the wood is for inserting between the ring and the skin so that you can cut the ring off without damaging the kid.

Don't castrate until the kids are a couple of days old and have bonded well with their dam; castration is undoubtedly painful for most kids for anything from a few minutes up to an hour or more, and you don't want to interfere in any way with colostrum intake, suckling and bonding.

This early castration using an elastrator and rubber ring can restrict the internal diameter of the urethra, which doesn't grow to full size as the wether matures, increasing the risk of obstruction by urinary calculi (*see* Chapter 9). This is a particular risk for wethers intended as long-term pets or buck companions as they mature; the issue is of less concern for those that go for meat within their first year. This being the case, consider the (considerably more expensive) alternative of later surgical castration by the vet – although it may be too much to ask to absolutely guarantee keeping keen-as-mustard entire young males totally separate from all females after they've reached six weeks of age.

DISBUDDING

Disbudding is the cauterizing and destroying of the horn buds before they can grow into horns. In the UK only a vet can disbud kids, and it should be done, if necessary, in the first week of life, ideally at two to three days old. The operation is not without risk, and keeping an entirely horned herd is a valid option, although there are inevitably more opportunities for goats to get themselves caught in fencing. As it is inappropriate to mix horned and hornless goats because of the risk of bullying and subsequent injury, this is an issue to consider right at the beginning of your goat keeping.

It's worth noting that de-horning of older goats is a significant operation, and both

Vet Chris Just with disbudded kids.

disbudding and dehorning are considered mutilations and should not be undertaken purely for cosmetic reasons. Most dairy herds will have their kids disbudded, as horns can cause serious wounds to udders in particular.

MUTILATIONS (ANIMAL AND PLANT HEALTH AGENCY – APHA)

Unless done by a vet, procedures must be carried out by a trained and competent stock keeper over eighteen years old			
Procedure	Age of animal at which procedure may be carried out	Anaesthetic requirement for procedure at specified age	Other conditions
Castration: carried out by means of a rubber ring or other device to constrict the flow of blood to the scrotum	Seven days or under	Not required	
Castration: carried out by means other than a rubber ring or other device to constrict the flow of blood to the scrotum	Under two months	Not required	
	Two months or over	Required	Vet
Vasectomy	Any age	Required	Vet
Dehorning (not including trimming of insensitive tip)	Any age	Required	Vet

Kid with ear tags.

Disbudded dairy kids bottle feeding.

EAR TAGGING

Kids must be ear-tagged by the time they are six months old if housed overnight, and you may choose to do it considerably earlier. When you tag, insert it about a third of the way down the ear, between the two raised lines of cartilage.

BOTTLE-FEEDING AND SUPPLEMENTARY FEEDING OF KIDS

Multiple births of three or more kids are very likely to require supplementary feeding of the kids. The best choice is goats' milk from your own does if there is sufficient, or milk from a local goat herd. If fresh milk is not available, Caprilac is a replacement milk powder made specifically for goats and readily available online, and most ewe-milk replacer powders are suitable for goats, although they may require more water to be added to the mix for kids. Lamlac replacement milk powder should be given at 150g to make up a litre, rather than the 200g (plus 800ml water) that makes up a litre for lambs; for other makes, do ask the manufacturers for the appropriate dilution.

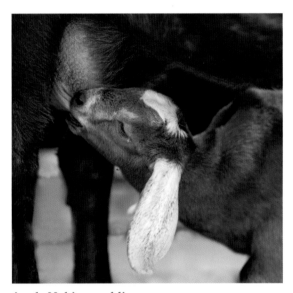

Anglo Nubian suckling.

Start with warm milk feeds using water from the kettle cooled to blood heat. Cold milk becomes more acceptable as the kids grow. Make sure bottles and all other equipment are properly cleaned after each use; human baby bottle sterilizing fluid or tablets are suitable for this. Kids require milk for at least the first three months of their lives, in addition to a gradually increasing amount of solid food. As a guide, this is a typical programme for bottle-fed kids:

Feeding the Bottle-Fed Kid

Age	Amount and frequency of milk feeds
0–1 week	300ml (four times a day)
1–2 weeks	400ml (four times a day)
2–8 weeks	850ml (three times a day)
9–10 weeks	850ml (twice a day
11 weeks	500ml (twice a day)
12 weeks	500ml (once a day)
13 weeks and over	Solid feed and hay only

If you have any orphans or 100 per cent bottle-fed kids, they can be started on concentrated creep feed from two to three weeks of age. Kids should have been eating creep feed for at least ten days before weaning from milk replacer, and be at least 2.5 times their birth weight. Creep feeding is the process of feeding solid foodstuffs to young animals in such a way that adults cannot access it, using vertical bars with narrow gaps (sometimes adjustable to accommodate the growing youngsters). A creep area can be home-made, or a creep feeder or creep gate that excludes the adults can be bought. Make sure creep feed isn't allowed to go stale or mouldy, so only make available what will be eaten in a day (0.4kg/0.8lb per kid should suffice by the time they are weaned). Good quality hay should be available for kids to nibble from a week old, and it won't hurt if they copy their dams and nibble at her hay earlier.

WEANING

For non-dairy breeds weaning can theoretically take place naturally or with human intervention. However, as entire males will need to be weaned from mum and kept away from any females by the time they are six weeks old, it makes sense to wean all kids at the same time so that the mother can be dried off on plain rations that don't stimulate further milk production. For dairy herds, most goat keepers leave the kids with their dam for at least four days. If the goat is producing more milk than is necessary for the kids, the udder can be eased by milking out the surplus. Dairy kids on the bottle should be weaned off milk at three months.

WEIGHING KIDS

It is helpful to weigh kids to monitor their progress and general wellbeing. Weigh on day one for the birth weight, and if you can, weigh daily for the first week to ensure they are gaining weight. After that a weekly weigh-in is helpful, and from a month old, weigh monthly. You can use a digital luggage scale with a hook, attached by a strap to a bucket large enough to hold the kid safely; or create a cloth bag with arm and leg holes to hang from the scales.

Birth weights will vary depending on breed, if the kid is a single or one of a triplet, and from one individual to another, and can range from 2 to 5kg (4.4–11lb) or more. Males tend to weigh more and be larger than females, although there are always exceptions. Weight gains will vary, but look for an increase of about a kilo per week.

DEALING WITH EUTHANASIA AND DEADSTOCK

Although it's a time of great pleasure, kidding is the time when your goats are at most risk. There may be times when kids or does cannot hope to live any sort of quality existence, and humane euthanasia is required. Any does or kids that die or are stillborn will need to be dealt with as fallen stock (*see* Chapter 3).

CHAPTER 14

MAKING THE MOST OF YOUR GOATS

Jo Curzon feeding her goat, August 1979. (Photograph by James Ravilious for the Beaford Archive © Beaford Arts)

THE VERSATILE GOAT

Chapter 10 covers the goat as meat provider, and Chapter 11 the goat as a dairy animal, but the ever-versatile goat has uses beyond a glass of milk and a dish of meat. There are many more edible options, and a

host of non-edible possibilities worthy of consideration. There are flourishing small businesses producing the range of delights explored below, and perhaps your own goat endeavour could create something entirely new, as well as pursuing some of the tried and tested options.

OPPOSITE: Quicke's Goat cheese.

Pack animal trip.

BEYOND MILK

The uses for goat milk are multiple, ranging from butter and cheese, yogurt and ice

Small cheese press, moulds and churns.

cream, kefir and fudge, to an array of skincare products. If you want milk with the highest amount of butterfat resulting in more cream per litre of milk, choose Anglo Nubians (5.04 per cent) or the productive West African (UK) or Nigerian (US) Dwarf goat, which has an impressive 6.1 per cent butterfat content. Other good choices are the Golden Guernsey, Toggenburg or Saanen.

Making Goat Butter

If you haven't tried goats' butter, you're in for a real treat. It's white rather than yellow (unless colouring is added, and why would you?), delicious, and not at all goaty, which should reassure those who prefer a mild sweetness to their dairy products. The first part of the process is to separate the cream from the milk, giving skimmed milk as a by-product. If you intend to use a cream separator do

LEGISLATION FOR SELLING DAIRY PRODUCE, INCLUDING SOAPS

Selling Dairy Produce in the UK:

Your first port of call is the Food Standards Agency for guidance to all the food hygiene legislation and the duty of food businesses to produce food safely and to achieve consistency. The legislation covers the whole food chain from farm to fork relating to the health and cleanliness of the animals, hygiene during milking, and controls on raw drinking milk. Inspections will be carried out on your premises, but there are different approaches across England, Wales, Scotland and Northern Ireland, so similar types of producers in different parts of the country may be subject to different inspection frequencies.

Selling Skincare Products

Any cosmetic product to be used on the skin or hair, in the bath or as decoration – such as lipstick or nail polish for the face or nails – must be safety assessed before it can legally be sold. You must have a valid safety assessment and certification (CPSR – Cosmetic Product Safety Report) that certifies that the product is suitable for use and complies with the current cosmetic regulations. You will need to send your recipe/formulation to a safety assessor, who can provide CPSR. There are a number of assessors who are used to working with small-scale producers and will guide you as to what information to submit alongside your recipe. Good assessors will also offer guidance on other legal requirements, such as:

- labelling
- health and safety for a good manufacturing process
- creating a product information file (PIF) with all the relevant information about the product, its ingredients, manufacture, and any animal-testing information if relevant
- product notification to the appropriate authority.

Goat butter.

check with the manufacturers if it can be adjusted for goats' milk, as the fat globules are smaller than in cows' milk. If you don't have a separator you can stand the milk in jars in the fridge and the cream will rise to the top, and can be skimmed off with a spoon, or use an old-fashioned separator dish.

To get a reasonable quantity of cream may take anything from a few days to a week, depending on the number of goats you're milking. 10ltr (17 pints) of milk should provide 1ltr (1.76 pints) of double cream, and 1ltr of double cream will produce 225g (8oz) of butter. Once you have your double cream, add salt if desired, and if you have strong wrists shake it in a firmly lidded clean jam jar with plenty of air space, for ten to fifteen minutes. This will create a lump of butter plus liquid buttermilk, which is great for making scones or pancakes.

Hand butter churn.

Cream separator.

Ceramic cream separator.

If you intend to make butter frequently, or if you prefer an item of kit, you can use a manual butter churn, or for greatest ease a food processor, simply whisking beyond the whipped cream stage until the butter forms. Rinse the butter in cold water until the water runs clear, then use spatulas or butter hands (also called butter paddles or Scotch hands) to pat it into your preferred shape, removing air bubbles and more of the moisture as you go. Keep the butter in the fridge where it will firm up, or store it in a freezer in useful-sized lumps. More importantly, spread it on some fantastic bread or toast and eat it.

Making Goat Clotted Cream
Take your goat double cream and put it in a saucepan. Create a water bath or double

Scotch hands.

Goat clotted cream.

boiler by placing the saucepan in a slightly larger pan containing hot water, and bring the water to the boil. Simmer for twenty minutes until a golden crust forms on top. To avoid any goatiness be careful not to overcook it. Cool overnight, then skim off the thick, luscious crust of clotted cream and store it in the fridge – or serve it immediately with a fat wedge of your favourite cake. If there's any remaining liquid cream at the bottom of the pan it can be used in your cooking, for example to make scones, or served in coffee.

You can also make clotted cream in the oven by pouring the double cream into a shallow oven-proof baking dish so that the cream is around 4-5cm (1.5-2in) deep. Put it in an oven heated to 80-95°C for twelve hours, and preferably overnight. Take it out of the oven, and when cooled to room temperature put it in the fridge for several hours before skimming the lovely, crusty, thick cream into a dish.

THE NAMING AND LABELLING OF CREAM

The naming and labelling of cream available for sale as stipulated by the UK Cheese and Cream Regulations (1995) is as follows:

Cream type	Definition
Clotted cream	The cream is clotted and contains not less than 55 per cent milk fat.
Double cream	The cream contains not less than 48 per cent milk fat.
Whipping cream	The cream contains not less than 35 per cent milk fat.
Whipped cream	The cream contains not less than 35 per cent milk fat and has been whipped.
Sterilized cream	The cream is sterilized cream and contains not less than 23 per cent milk fat.
Cream or single cream	The cream is not sterilized cream and contains not less than 18 per cent milk fat.
Sterilized half cream	The cream is sterilized cream and contains not less than 12 per cent milk fat.
Half cream	The cream is not sterilized cream and contains not less than 12 per cent milk fat.

Goat Cheeses

Is there a restaurant or gastro pub these days that doesn't have a goats' cheese starter on the menu, or a shop that sells cheese of any kind that doesn't have a mini drum or log of goats' cheese in their chill cabinet? Goats' cheese must be the most mainstream of all goat products, and it comes in many shapes and sizes: hard and soft and semi-soft, from an ash-scattered pyramid, to small barrels with a rind wrinkled like a brain, in squidgy logs, a few blue-veined examples, some smooth and firm in big cheddar-style wheels, or in mouth-sized small balls floating in jars

Goat's cheese.

Glazert soft goat cheese.

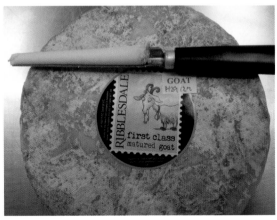

Goatisan cheese.

How To Make a Simple Fresh Soft Goats' Cheese

You'll need some cheese or yogurt starter (C20G starter is available from on-line cheese-making suppliers), a cooking thermometer, butter muslin, and 4ltr (7 pints) of fresh goats' milk left to stand at room temperature for an hour before use. Pour your milk into a stainless-steel saucepan, and heat slowly to 86°C. Stir the milk while it warms, and when up to temperature, take it off the heat and sprinkle ⅛ teaspoon (this equates to a pinch, or 0.625g) of the starter to the milk. Leave for five minutes and then whisk for twenty seconds to disperse the starter evenly. Cover the pan and leave at room temperature for twelve hours.

Put a stainless-steel colander into a large bowl, and line it with damp butter muslin. Ladle the curds from the pan into the colander, and let them drain for two hours, still at room temperature. Add sea salt (about a teaspoon), and stir it into the curds. Pick up the ends of the muslin and tie into a knot, and suspend the curds over the pan (a wooden spoon handle or piece of dowel pushed under the knot works for this). Drain the curds for a further six to twelve hours: the longer you drain them, the firmer the cheese.

And that's it – eat the cheese on oat cakes, or any way you fancy.

of olive oil. Cheeses can be mild and sweet to tongue-tinglingly strong, and artisan goats' cheese making is a thriving mini-industry in the UK, with many more makers across Europe and the rest of the world.

Goat Yogurt

There aren't many fridges without a pot of yogurt sitting on a shelf. Natural yogurts, whether thick or thin, have become an everyday ingredient, eaten plain, spooned on top of cereals, curries, pasta dishes, tagines, used for dips and sauces, and more. Adding nuts and fresh or dried fruit, fruit purées and syrups, turns a previously plain yogurt into an everyday easy-to-create pudding.

As for all dairying, hygiene is critical in yogurt making, and the few items of equipment should be sterilized in boiling water before use. It's a very straightforward process, and all you need is a saucepan, a thermometer, and a vacuum flask with a wide neck, plus a small pot of plain live yogurt as a starter. If you intend to make yogurt regularly you'll be using your own yogurt as the starter after the first batch.

How to Make Goat Yogurt
Heat 1ltr (1.76 pints) of milk to 82°C, and then cool to 43°C. Pour most of the milk into the sterilized vacuum flask. Mix two tablespoons of the live yogurt to the remaining milk, and put the mix into the flask. Screw on the lid and give the flask a shake to mix the contents, and then leave overnight. Spoon the resulting yogurt into a container, and keep it in the fridge, ready to eat. If you want the yogurt thicker, strain it through clean butter muslin.

Goat Ice Cream and Frozen Yogurt

Milk, cheese, butter and yogurt, no matter how fancy and delicious, are still household staples, but ice-cream is a 'special occasion' treat, and there's no limit to the varieties you can make. A scoop to accompany a piece of cake or a ripe peach, or a sundae mix of your favourite ice-cream flavours in a deep glass topped off with goat whipped cream – any of these is a celebratory treat.

Custard Recipe as a Base for Your Ice Cream
There are many good custard recipes, but here's one to get you started on your journey into ice cream. You'll want:

570ml goat double cream or milk, or a mix of both
6 egg yolks
50g (1.77oz) golden caster sugar mixed with 1 level dessertspoon of cornflour
1 dessertspoon pure vanilla extract

Whisk together the egg yolks, sugar and cornflour mixture and the vanilla. Put the cream or cream/milk mix into a pan over a gentle heat and heat to just below simmering point, stirring with a wooden spoon. Whisking constantly, gradually pour the hot cream into the egg mixture. Return the whole lot back to the saucepan and heat gently, whisking until the custard is thick and smooth. When the custard is made, pour it into a shallow freezer-proof container with any added ingredients you fancy.

Once at room temperature, put it in the fridge until chilled, and then transfer the container to the freezer. After an hour, take it out and whisk to disperse the ice crystals (an electric hand whisk is the easiest option). Do this three times with an hour's gap each time, then leave in the freezer until solid and ready to eat.

To make life simple there are plenty of budget (and top-end) ice-cream makers available, but if having another electronic item in your kitchen doesn't appeal, you can make ice cream without one. Use any ice-cream recipe that you like, but the basics involve creating a custard from milk and double cream (both from your goat), eggs or just the yolks as you prefer, sugar, cornflour if you wish, plus whatever flavouring and added ingredients tempt you, including fruit, nuts, chocolate and more.

For frozen yogurt, choose 550g (19.5oz) of fruit from whatever is in season – blackberries, raspberries, strawberries, blueberries, plums, pears, cherries – plus a ripe banana. If necessary stone the fruit and cut into small chunks, then spread on a tray and put into the freezer for a couple of hours until frozen. Spoon a tablespoon of runny honey (for smoothness as well as sweetness) into a food processor with 500g (17.6oz) of goat yogurt, and turn on briefly to combine. Then add the frozen fruit and blitz until smooth (or leave a few visible pieces if you prefer). Eat, or if you have the discipline, store in an airtight container in the freezer.

Dulche de Leche (Cajeta)

Dulche de leche, or sweet milk, is a thick, syrupy caramel sauce for spooning luxuriously over ice cream, bananas, sundaes, pancakes and more. Stir together 1ltr (1.76 pints) of goat milk and 280g (10oz) granulated sugar in a saucepan. Add a cinnamon stick, a quarter teaspoon of baking soda, and a teaspoon of vanilla extract. Bring to the boil, stirring frequently to dissolve the sugar, and then reduce the heat to a simmer. Simmer uncovered for one and a half to two hours, stirring occasionally, until you have reached your desired colour and consistency. Remove the cinnamon stick and pour into heat-proof jars. Store in the fridge.

Kefir grains in milk.

Goat Kefir

Although kefir is an ancient product, it has achieved almost superfood status in recent years as it contains probiotics, the friendly gut bacteria. Kefir is a fermented milk drink, like a thin yogurt with a sour taste and a fizzy consistency made by adding kefir grains, a milk culture that contains bacteria and yeasts, to milk. The grains look rather like tapioca or miniature cauliflower florets. Add 2–5 per cent by weight of kefir grains to goat milk, and store in the dark for twelve to twenty-four hours to ferment at 22–25°C. The more kefir grains that are added, the quicker the fermentation.

Once fermented, strain the grains from the milk; they increase in size during the fermentation and split, creating new grains, all of which are kept to make the next batch and to pass on to other people who also want to make kefir. The grains will multiply as long as they are kept in fresh milk at fermenting temperature; when put in the fridge the cold inhibits the fermentation process.

The kefir milk is acid (and also slightly alcoholic) so must be kept in plastic, glass or stainless steel, and will keep for up to a month. The grains themselves will keep up to a year if washed and dried after use. Kefir can be used to make sourdough and as a substitute for buttermilk in baking. If you don't know someone with kefir grains to spare to start you off, they can be bought online.

Goat Fudge

If you make your own goat butter and have a splash or two of milk going spare, plus a whole heap of sugar and some choice flavourings, you can conjure up something delicious for the sweet-toothed.

Goat Soap

Home-made and artisan soapmaking are becoming increasingly popular pursuits, particularly as a reaction against the plastic bottle containers for the ubiquitous liquid soap, and the desire for using less detergent on what is, after all, our precious, absorbent,

GOAT FUDGE RECIPES

Microwaved Goat Milk Chocolate Fudge Recipe
- 450g (16oz) caster sugar
- 60g (2oz) cocoa
- 100g (3.5oz) goat butter cut into chunks
- 50ml goat milk
- 1 teaspoon vanilla essence

Grease a 20 × 20cm (8in) square cake tin, and line with greaseproof or parchment paper. Combine the sugar and cocoa in a large, microwavable bowl. Make a well in the centre and add the butter and milk, but don't stir it. Microwave on high for two minutes, and add the vanilla. Blend with a stick blender or mixer until smooth. Pour into the greased tin, and put in the fridge until firm. Cut into squares and eat.

Old-Fashioned Fudge Method
This is an old-fashioned fudge method for which you'll need a jam thermometer.
- 100g (3.5oz) goat butter
- 550g (19.5oz) demerara sugar
- 200g (7oz) golden syrup
- 350ml goat double cream
- 1tsp vanilla extract
- ¼tsp sea-salt flakes

Line a 23 × 23cm (9in) square tin with greaseproof paper. Melt the butter, sugar, syrup and cream in a pan, stirring until the sugar has dissolved. Bring to a simmer over a medium heat, stirring occasionally until it reaches 116°C, turning down the heat if it begins to catch. Take the pan off the heat and beat in the vanilla and salt, and keep beating with a wooden spoon until the fudge is thick. Pour the mixture into the tin and leave to set; when cool, put it in the fridge until firm. Cut into pieces and eat (preferably not all at once).

sometimes delicate skin. Goat milk is a favourite choice of soap ingredient for people with sensitive skins.

There can be hazards in soap-making if the processes are not properly followed – very high heats, plus explosion potential if you add water to the lye (sodium hydroxide) powder rather than vice versa – so it's imperative to think about safety before you start making, and to ensure that young children and anyone not involved in the process are kept well out of the way. You will also need good ventilation and protective gear: goggles, mask, rubber gloves and apron, plus distilled white vinegar to neutralize and wipe any lye off your skin in case of spills.

Goat's Milk Soap

Kat Goldin, Gartur Stitch Farm, https://alifeinthemaking.co.uk

Safety tips:

- Never use aluminium around lye as it causes a chemical reaction and can explode. Use enamel, stainless steel, glass or plastic bowls and utensils.
- Have the right safety equipment – rubber gloves, a face mask, goggles and an apron should all be worn, and have white vinegar at hand to neutralize any spills.
- Always add lye to the liquid, never the other way around. You don't want any unnecessary splashes, and this will minimize it.
- Make sure that your work area is clean, ventilated, and that there are no children nearby. This is not a good recipe to let children help with, since lye is caustic until mixed with water and oils.
- Use a recipe that has been tested, or if you are going to change the ingredients at all, run it through a lye calculator to ensure that all of the lye is neutralized in the saponification stage.

Soap-making equipment:

- a large bucket or bowl
- a stick blender
- a metal spoon
- scales
- parchment/wax paper
- a box or container for using as a soap mould (silicon cake moulds are good).

The only difference between this soap and a basic cold process is that the milk is frozen to start with. You want your milk to remain as uncooked as possible, and freezing it gives it more of a chance to stay as close to raw as possible when the lye hits it. Have all your ingredients and materials ready before you begin, so you can just mix everything quickly and easily.

Ingredients:

340g (12oz) coconut oil
425g (15oz) olive oil
370g (13oz) unrefined shea butter
375g (13.2oz) *frozen* goat milk
155g (5.5oz) sodium hydroxide (lye)
29g (1oz) essential oils, optional

The night before you want to make your soap, freeze your milk. This stops the fats from burning. You can freeze it in the bowl you will be working in.

On the day of soap making, start by melting your coconut oil and shea butter. You can do this in the microwave or in a pan. Next, with gloves and eye protection, slowly add the lye to the frozen milk. *Never add the milk to the lye* (this is really important). Stir carefully with a spoon, making sure not to let the liquid come in contact with your body directly. As you stir, this will create a cloudy white mixture that might get warm. Let this mixture cool for about ten minutes.

When you have your melted coconut oil, pour it into a bowl and add the olive oil. Slowly pour in the milk and lye mixture and stir. Quickly rinse out the container used for the water and lye mixture in the sink. Rinse well, and then re-rinse with white vinegar to make sure that all the lye has been neutralized. Use the metal or wooden spoon to stir the lye/water mixture into the oil mixture.

Once evenly mixed, use the stick blender to blend for about 4–5 minutes, or until it is opaque and starting to thicken. If you are going to use essential oils for scent, add them now. Quickly and carefully spoon into moulds. Any container will work, including loaf tins lined with parchment paper or silicon baking moulds. Cover the moulds with parchment paper and set in a cool, dry place, away from children and pets.

After twenty-four hours, using gloves, remove the soap from the moulds and cut into bars. Leave the bars to cure for about four weeks. You can test if they are done by sticking your tongue on them to see if the lye is still active. It will zing you like a battery if they aren't ready.

Goat soap.

Goat Milk Shampoos, Cleansers and Moisturizers

As well as soap, you can use goat milk to create shampoo bars, bath bombs, skin cleansers, lotions and moisturizers. These traditional-style formats of beauty products have made a modern comeback even in high-street shops, with towers of unwrapped, joyously coloured bath bombs, solid moisturizing blocks, shampoo bars and refillable bottles of lotions and cleansers, emphasizing natural ingredients and minimal packaging. Goat-milk lotion is said to relieve a number of itchy dry skin conditions including eczema, psoriasis and dermatitis (with the usual caveat that if you are under a doctor's guidance, do check what you put on your skin with your GP first). The milk is only one of multiple ingredients in these products, which feature a range of natural oils and tellingly avoid the chemical contents that can cause skin and other problems such as petrochemicals, parabens and pthalates.

There are numerous 'how to' videos and recipes for all these products on-line. If you wish to avoid the use of preservatives altogether, you'll need to make small quantities that can be used within a week or so, keeping them away from light and heat and storing them in airtight containers. It's probably more practical to use preservatives that you're happy to put on your skin; there are a number of natural preservatives suitable for cosmetics and skin preparations available.

TAKING MEAT THAT BIT FURTHER

Unlike freezing, preserving meat by curing creates an entirely new product, and you can take your cue from recipes and methods from across the world. And then there are other approaches to making your carcase go that bit further, not by preserving, but by using the bits that at first you might have thought to reserve for the dog.

Offal and Cured Goat Meat

Let's start with haggis, a dish that is loved and hated in equal measure. Traditionally made with sheep's pluck – that's the heart, liver and lungs plus the tongue – boiled and then minced with onion, oatmeal, suet, mace, nutmeg and salt, the mix is spooned into the sheep's stomach (or in a pudding basin covered with muslin) to hold the feast together, and simmered for up to three hours. There's no reason not to do the same with your goat offal. If you use a goat stomach as your haggis container, put it in a strong salt-water bath to clean it, turning it inside out and repeating the process after thirty minutes of soaking with a new lot of salt water.

Your biggest challenge won't be eating what will be a delicious dish, but getting the stomach and tongue back from the abattoir: good luck with that.

Haggis.

GOAT KIDNEYS

Many people wrinkle their nose at kidneys, referring to them as urine strainers and worse, but this really doesn't do them justice: kidneys are delicious. If you've never tried them, do give them a whirl. Use as many goat kidneys as you can get hold of, and supplement them with lamb kidneys if you don't have enough: you'll need at least two per person, and preferably far more. Ingredients:

- Goat kidneys
- Large sliced onion
- Dessertspoon of grainy mustard
- Jellied stock from a recent roasted joint or chicken stock
- Generous gob of dripping, also from your roasting pan
- Half a glass of sherry or marsala

Halve the kidneys lengthways and remove the fatty core (kitchen scissors work best for this). Sizzle the onions in the dripping until translucent and starting to brown. Add the halved kidneys and keep on a highish heat so that they brown too. Flip them over to brown on the other side, and then stir in the mustard. Glug in the alcohol and let that sizzle, then add in the stock. Bring up to a gentle simmer, and cover and cook for fifteen minutes on a gentle heat so as to keep the kidneys tender.

If these are for breakfast or brunch, serve on split hot muffins; if you want them as a starter, stir in a generous gloop of thick plain yogurt, sprinkle with coriander or parsley, and serve on a small mound of carbs: rice, couscous, mashed potato, tagliatelle or ciabatta.

Violino di capra.

Goat salami.

You could mimic goat-type prosciutto, a dry-cured, thinly sliced ham, known as violino di capra: originating from northern Italy, it is made from goat shoulder or leg, preserved in brine and flavoured with garlic, spices and red wine, before smoking and dry ageing; it is served thinly sliced. Alternatively you could do a simpler, salted and air-dried version using the loin, similar to bresaola, which is traditionally made from beef.

Some charcuterie takes months to cure, but biltong, a traditional South African recipe, is ready in a few days, although it keeps for much longer. The meat is cut along the grain in thin strips, rubbed with wine vinegar and covered with a mix of salt, sugar, crushed coriander seeds, pepper, paprika and bicarbonate of soda. After refrigerating for a day, hang up to dry for five days, and then devour or store in an airtight container.

Or you could have a go at goat jerky, a cooked meat, cooked or smoked for several hours. Simply slice your meat into 0.5cm strips, make a marinade of garlic powder, onion powder, salt, pepper and Worcestershire sauce, and marinade the strips of goat overnight. Put the strips on a wire rack in a cool oven (70°C) for three hours or longer until the meat is dried out, then cool completely; store, and eat at will.

Goat Salami

When making goat salami it's advisable to add some pork fat for richness and texture. Mince your goat meat as finely or coarsely as you wish, add seasonings to taste – try a mix from salt, pepper, cayenne, garlic, nutmeg, mace, clove, cinnamon and ginger – add small dices of pork fat, a splash of brandy and a few sprinkles of sugar, and mix well. Fill natural sausage casings (beef bungs) with the mix, and hang from a hook in a well-ventilated space with a maximum temperature of 15°C for four days; then transfer to a cooler place (10°C) to mature for five or six months.

Goat Bacon

Goat bacon is just starting to make an appearance in the UK from artisan makers. It's much leaner than traditional pork bacon, and cures more quickly, as the cut it's made from is smaller. If you make it yourself it's best to use breast or loin from an older goat that has some fat and size to it. Bacon cure mixes contain salt, sugar, and a range of spices, and can be bought or homemade.

Goat bacon.

Rub the cure into the joint of meat, place in a plastic bag and put in the fridge for a couple of days. Cures can have honey or wine, treacle and olive oil, ginger, caraway, juniper, and any number of herbs included, and there are as many recipes as there are bacon curers. After curing the meat can be smoked over woodchips, or simply washed off, dried, and kept in a cool, dry place.

Goat ham (goat *cecina* in Spanish) can also be made from the leg or shoulder, using either a wet spiced brine or dry cure; then the joint is cooked.

FIBRE AND SKINS

Mohair and Cashmere

There are two main types of goat fibre, cashmere and mohair, the latter coming from Angora goats, the former from all other goat breeds and mixes. Cashgora is fibre made from goats that are Angora and cashmere crosses, nigora is from a Nigerian Dwarf buck crossed with Angora does, and pygora from a pygmy goat crossed with an Angora.

Mohair, once processed, produces a thin, hairy yarn that knits into a light, warm, fluffy garment – no self-respecting punk rocker was without a vibrantly coloured or deep black mohair jumper in the 1970s. Angora goats have been selectively bred to produce bright

Basket of mohair.

Angora goat before shearing.

white fibre, and it dyes well, taking on rich, strong colours. Some breeders have cultivated goats with coloured fibre to add interest to their resulting textiles.

Most mohair goats are shorn twice a year, as their coats grow an astonishing 2cm (0.8in) a month. Young goats grow the softest, most desirable fibre; they are shorn

Angora goat after shearing.

Whole raw Angora fleece.

American Cashmere goats.

Mohair yarn and shuttle.

at six months of age, by which time the kid mohair is already 10cm (4in) long. Kids will produce around 1kg (2.2lb) of fibre at each twice-yearly shearing, an adult doe will yield 2 to 4kg (4.4 to 8.8lb), and a buck between 5 and 10kg (11 and 22lb).

Cashmere is synonymous with ultraluxe fabrics, and is made from harvesting the downy undercoat. Certain goats and breeds produce more cashmere than others, with those in cooler climates not surprisingly producing the most. Pashmina is the finest cashmere, and comes from goats reared in Mongolia and the Himalayas. Unlike mohair, yields of cashmere are tiny per animal, which accounts for its value and high cost: around 50 to 200g (1.7 to 7oz) per animal per year, taken in a single shearing, with 20-60 per cent of a goat's whole shorn fleece yielding the desirable cashmere down. As with mohair, the finest cashmere comes from young goats, so if you are interested in producing quality yarns you'll need to keep young herds, as the fibre becomes coarser as the goats get older.

Angora fleece can be hand spun, but if this is not something you wish to do yourself, British Mohair Marketing (BMM), which has close links to the British Angora Goat Society, coordinates the collection of its members' raw mohair, and the grading and sale to

Cashmere yarn.

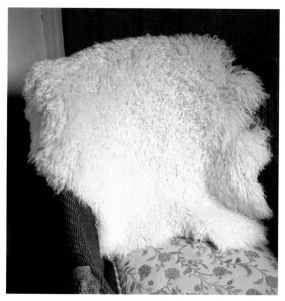

Kid Angora skin.

processors. Cashmere production is primarily an industrial process because any guard hairs must be removed before spinning, a procedure beyond most domestic capabilities, although there are some determined, patient cashmere hand spinners out there. Cashmere yarn retails at about five times the price of best quality lambswool yarn.

Goatskins and Leather

It would be a terrible shame to discard a goatskin when taking a goat to the abattoir for meat. The skins make the most beautiful rugs, from the ringlets of the Angora to the soft shorter pelts of other breeds, with many colours and patterns including mottled, spotted and striped. If good skins are chosen and tanned professionally they can add a useful income stream to a goat enterprise. Skins can be tanned at home, or there are a number of quality tanneries across the UK to whom you can courier your well-salted skins.

Be aware that the skin of any goat that has had even a mild application of purple antiseptic spray will not make a good rug unless you're partial to pink, as it stains

permanently. Be sure that any marker spray you use as part of your husbandry regime is proper stock spray, or it won't wash out in the tanning process, and use it sparingly. Also, pick only quality skins: any tatty, ragged skin

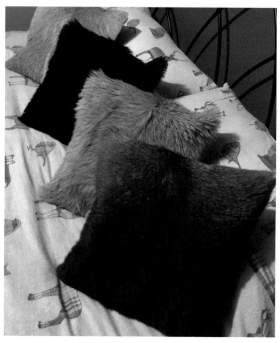

Goatskin cushions.

is not going to be anything other than a tatty, ragged rug.

Emma Allum, who runs the Welsh Organic Tannery, advises that the skin from a billy goat will still smell like a billy goat after the tanning process, so they are not the best skins to use if you are not keen on the smell; also the leather from buck skins is thick and can be very tough.

Unlike sheepskins, goatskins can be tanned from animals slaughtered throughout much of the year, though it is still best to avoid taking a goat to slaughter when they are going through their spring and autumn moults, as the finished rug will be untidy. The winter skins have a much thicker, softer coat and are preferable for rugs and cushions, while the thinner summer ones can be used

GUIDE TO SALTING SKINS READY FOR SENDING TO A TANNERY

Raw skins have the shelf life of offal, so it is vital that skins are salted as soon as possible after slaughter, essentially within hours, or the fleece or hair will slip and the skin rot. The abattoir will not necessarily do this for you (although some will give a skin a first fairly cursory salting if you ask). The guidance below is relevant if you are intending to post or courier your skins to a tannery; if you are in driving distance of a tannery you can do a simple, thorough salting of the skin and transport it while it is still fresh. You will want to contain the skins in some way so that salt and liquids don't contaminate your vehicle or trailer; use plastic barrels or heavy-grade plastic sacks with no holes.

The process for preparing and salting the skins is as follows:

1. Somewhere under cover on a clean surface (plastic pallets or opened feed sacks are ideal), lay the skin flesh side up. The skin/flesh should be white. Any discoloration – orange, pink, yellow, purple or red – means it is 'off', so don't waste your time with it.
2. With a sharp blade, cut off any long frilly bits, the small area at the neck end if it is saturated in blood, and the ears and feet if they are still left on. If skinned in 'sleeves', cut these open so they lie flat.
3. Liberally cover the skin in salt (the flesh side); you cannot over-salt a skin. Take care that the edges are well covered. Your aim is not to be able to see any skin through the salt. Do not put skins on anything metal, as rust stains turn black in tanning.
4. After three days shake off the salt and replace with fresh salt. A skin is 60 per cent water, and you need to draw this out. Leave the skins flat, and do not hang them up to dry as salt falls off a vertical surface. Don't put them in the sun, either, as salt will not penetrate a dry surface and the skins will disintegrate when washed. Skins must have salt on at all times, including when transported.
5. A well-cured (salted) skin will feel firm, but will remain flexible and feel like dry-cured bacon. These skins will take two to three weeks to cure. Do not let them dry out completely.
6. Once the skin is cured, add fresh dry salt (you won't need much, but cover it fully), fold the skin sides to middle, then roll it tightly from the head end down, and place it in a sack. Well-cured skins will keep for months, even years.
7. The skins can now be sent to a tannery.

for handbags and other items needing more intricate working.

The Tanning Process (Welsh Organic Tannery)
The process at a professional tannery involves checking the skin for suitability, removing any marker and trimming away undesirable bits, and tagging it with a unique number so there is full traceability throughout the process. Skins are washed and placed in a pickling tank for twenty-four hours. The next step is fleshing, removing any flesh or fat adhering to the skins, after which they go into a tanning tank for a minimum of a week. The skins are then rinsed, pegged out on a board, and put into a drying room at 27°C for three to five days. Once dry, they're taken off the boards, the leather is buffed, and they are given a final trimming and combing.

Tagged skins.

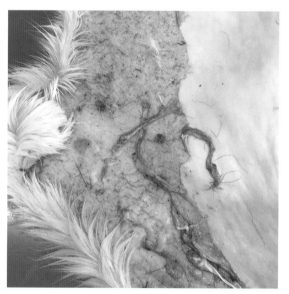

Part-fleshed skin.

Skin in the drying room.

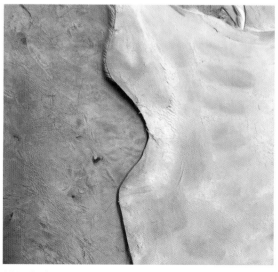

Skin before and after buffing.

Golden Guernsey kid skin.

Goat skin selection.

TANNING YOUR OWN GOATSKIN

There are plenty of DIY recipes available for curing hides, using bark and other vegetable tannins, eggs, oil, cooked brains, alum and more. Ensure that you wear suitable gloves throughout the process, as bacteria can be present in the early days and the salt alum mix isn't pleasant on your own skin (that doesn't want to be cured).

Skinning: If you are home butchering you'll have immediate access to your skin; if you're collecting from the abattoir, ask them to do a preliminary salting and collect it within twenty-four hours of slaughter.

Preparing the skin: Using a sharp knife, scrape away as much fat as possible, being careful not to cut the skin. Apply salt to fresh skins quickly or they start to decompose and the hair starts to slip. Lay the skin in a cool place with the fibre side down, and apply the salt in a generous layer (about 1cm/½in) all over the flesh side; leave for thirty-six to forty-eight hours to allow the salt to draw out as much moisture as possible. Use a fine white salt, such as industrial dried vacuum salt; it's cheaper than buying vast quantities of table salt, and is available from agricultural merchants in 25kg bags. It keeps forever, but make sure you buy the salt before you bring home your first skins, as you'll need it immediately.

Be aware that pools of liquid will drain off the skin, so this is an outside/shed/barn job. If you salt skins on a pallet, make sure it has no iron nails or staples, as this causes discoloration.

Tanning: When you're ready to start tanning, rinse the salt off the skin. In a suitable-sized bucket, mix equal amounts of salt and alum (aluminium potassium sulphate) in warm water, about 25g (0.9oz) of each per litre (1.76pints) of water. Leave the skin in the bucket for about two weeks, stirring daily; you may want to change the liquid half-way through for larger skins. You are looking for the flesh/skin side to whiten.

Drying: Once the skin has whitened, remove it from the bucket and wash thoroughly with warm water (you can add a little detergent if you wish, but rinse it out well). Once rinsed, the skin needs to be dried. Skins tend to shrink and curl, so tack it at the edges on to a piece of ply to stretch it out. Depending on the size and thickness of the skin and the weather, it can take up to a month to dry fully.

Finishing: You can use sandpaper or a similar abrasive material to remove any remaining fat or ugly skin tissue from the inside. Use a brush to comb through the hair, and your skin is ready to use.

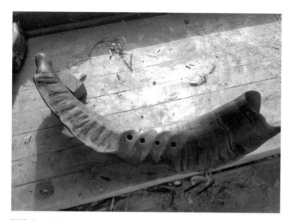

Viking Norwegian horn instrument.

HORNS

Horns and horned skulls have decorated homes for centuries, but goat horn has practical as well as decorative uses. The inner core needs to be removed by immersing the horns in hot water and when softened, scraping out the internal mass - a rather mucky, smelly process. If you have patience you can try burying the horns and letting time and the intervention of invertebrates take their natural course. Horn can be sliced and polished into buttons or toggles, made into spoons, handles for walking sticks, combs and hair slides, used as a drinking horn, as a musical instrument, or to blast a warning signal.

PACK ANIMALS

Able to cross challenging terrain and happy to be with humans, pack goats can be very useful in sharing burdens. Experienced pack goats can carry up to 25 per cent of their own bodyweight, so a sizeable pack wether weighing 80kg (176lb) can manage as much as 20kg (44lb) of baggage, although you would want to start off with smaller loads in training. Goats should be fully mature, at around four years old, before carrying a full load. A goat saddle is

Alpine × Nubian pack goat.

strapped to the goat; this takes soft panniers or rigid boxes on each side, ensuring an even load.

Movement restrictions for livestock in the UK means that trekking beyond one's holding requires a licence from APHA, but goats can be used to carry tools or perhaps

Nan Hassey weighing goat packs before putting them on her goats.

a picnic to the far end of your own holding without any paperwork.

HARNESS GOATS

Goats can be put into harness and used to pull carts, pulling up to a maximum of one and a half times their own weight, so vehicles should be as light as possible. A licence is needed to take any goat off your holding and on to public highways (including bridleways

Boy driving goats in harness.

and green lanes). You can apply to your local Animal and Plant Health Agency for a licence to exercise your goats regularly on a designated route close to your home.

Legal Requirements
There are certain legal requirements for walking goats or using them to drive a cart. In England and Wales, permits can be issued under the relevant Disease Control Orders to take pet sheep and goats for walks. The permit disapplies the six-day standstill on return to the home premises, but keepers of pet sheep and goats need to apply in writing to their local Animal and Plant Health Agency (APHA) office, and must include a description and/or map of the route to be approved. The route will need to be risk assessed and approved by a veterinary officer (VO) at the local APHA office. As part of the risk assessment the VO will need to decide whether a visit is needed. If the VO believes there is a risk with a route, it will not be approved. Reasons for not approving routes include proximity to a livestock market, and risk of contact with other livestock.

If approval is granted, the APHA office should issue the permit in England/Wales or licence in Scotland, with an expiry date of one year in the first instance. The permit will need to be reassessed after the first year, and subsequently at no greater than three-yearly intervals. A copy of the permit/licence will be sent to the relevant local authority to enable monitoring and enforcement as required.

CHAPTER 15

GUIDE TO THE BREEDS – UK AND WORLDWIDE

With over 300 to choose from (and some sources suggest up to 500), an encyclopaedia could be written about the goat breeds of the world, so this more modest guide includes all the UK breeds and a good collection of breeds from across the globe, including a few of the more unusual ones. Breed names can vary according to location, and alternatives are given in brackets where known.

Breed	Information	Image source
Alpine	Medium to large US dairy breed known for its very good milking ability. No set colours or markings (although colour types are named, including pied, sundgau, chamoisee); they have horns, a straight profile and erect ears. Originated in the French Alps, used for commercial and domestic dairy production.	
Altai Mountain	A fibre breed developed in the Soviet Union by cross-breeding the Don goat with local goats for a high wool yield that could withstand the rigours of the Siberian weather.	
American Cashmere	Not a single breed, but a dual-purpose type, often providing both fibre and meat, with a multitude of body shapes and colour variations, selectively bred to produce cashmere in significant amounts. The down and guard hair may be any colour, but the shearable parts of the body (excluding face, stockings and belly) should be of a single colour.	
Anglo Nubian	A distinctive British large dairy breed with long ears and Roman nose, and a short silky coat that comes in many colour variations. Averaging 5 per cent butterfat, their milk is ideal for yogurt and cheese making. Its size and conformation make it a useful meat goat in its own right and as a cross. A heavy, tall goat with males weighing up to 140kg (308lb) and females to 110kg (243lb). Produce an average of 4ltr (7 pints) of milk daily.	

OPPOSITE: **Valais Blackneck.**

Breed	Information	Image source
Angora	Ancient fibre breed of modest size, kept primarily for the production of mohair. Fleece grows 25mm per month, mature animals producing 5–10kg (11–22lb) per year. Not as hardy as other breeds (they do best in dry, arid regions), and extra care needs to be taken regarding risk from external parasites. Seasonal breeders, coming into oestrus in the autumn. Traditionally white, but black, grey, silver and red-brown are possible.	
Appenzell	Swiss white long-haired dairy breed.	
Arapawa Island	Rare New Zealand feral breed. Small and come in a variety of colours, males having widely sweeping horns, the females shorter backward-pointing horns. It is believed that they are a surviving remnant of the Old English breed.	
Argentata dell'Etna (Silver goat of Etna)	Indigenous dual-purpose milk and meat breed from Mount Etna, Sicily. Silver grey, long coat. Their milk is used to make ricotta.	
Aspromonte	Medium sized hardy dual-purpose meat and milk breed from southern Italy, with a long cashmere undercoat. The milk is used for various local cheeses, including ricotta.	
Bagot	Believed to be the oldest British breed, long haired, with distinctive colour pattern of black forequarters and remainder of the body white. Small to medium size, with long curving horns. Primitive breed used predominantly for conservation browsing (the British Goat Society categorize them as non-productive). More tolerant of rain than other breeds. Categorized as 'at risk' by the Rare Breed Survival Trust, with 300–500 breeding females.	
Barbari	Small dual-purpose milk and meat breed found in India and Pakistan. Mostly white with spotted coat.	
Beetal	Commercial large meat and dairy breed, also used for meat and leather. Comes in a variety of colours, with long curled ears. Found throughout the Punjab, the dominant goat in Pakistan.	
Bilberry	Large, stocky, large-horned feral breed believed to have lived as a single herd on Bilberry Rock in Waterford City in Ireland for hundreds of years. Very rare.	

Breed	Information	Image source
Bionda dell'Adamello (Capra Bionda, Mustàscia)	Northern Italian milk and meat breed of ancient origin. Milk used to make mascarpi, a type of ricotta, and the smoked cheese fatuli.	
Black Bengal	Dwarf meat breed of Bangladesh, exceptionally hardy.	
Boer	Originating in South Africa, known as the world's best meat breed. Docile, short-legged, stocky animals that grow quickly and are broad with good muscling. Can breed virtually all year round, making it possible for does to be mated and to kid three times in two years. Mature bucks weigh 120-150kg (265-330lb), mature does 80-100kg (176-220lb). A white goat with red head, neck and ears. Some are entirely red in colouring. Naturally horned, and thick winter coats make them hardier than dairy breeds. Bucks used as a terminal sire on dairy breeds to produce meaty offspring.	
Booted (Stiefelgeiss)	Rare Swiss mountain breed used for meat and grazing management. Various shades of brown coat with black or brown 'boots'; long hairs on their hind end, often a darker colour from the rest of the coat. It has a long mane running the length of the back. Suited to extreme mountainous conditions.	
British Alpine	Black with white Swiss markings, a large active dairy breed developed in the UK. Tall and rangy (does are 83cm (33in) at the withers, bucks 95cm (37in)), with a short fine coat, an impressive animal. The breed is described as highly individual in character, and for enthusiasts who like a challenge. Best kept free range, they are excellent foragers and jumpers. Long lactations, with 4 per cent butterfat. Does weigh around 60kg (132lb), bucks 80kg (176lb). Produce an average of 4ltr (7 pints) of milk daily.	
British Guernsey	Dairy breed with a long coat in all shades of gold. Slightly larger than the Golden Guernsey, not easily distinguished from the parent breed. Obtained by breeding, resulting in a goat that is 7/8 (87.5 per cent) Golden Guernsey with chosen additional characteristics such as increased milk yield or improved conformation, larger and heavier than the original. 3.72 per cent butterfat. Produces an average of 3ltr (5 pints) of milk daily.	
British Primitive	Encompasses what was previously known as the Old English, Scottish, Welsh, Irish, British Landrace or Old British Goat. Descends from goats introduced by the first farmers in the Neolithic period. A small, long coarse-coated goat kept as a multi-purpose animal, a hardy all-weather breed that reared its kids, gave some milk, and was used for its meat, skins, hair and tallow. Colour varies from pure white, light grey and mostly dark brown to a speckled light grey with white patches. Found mostly on hilly mountain areas of the UK.	

Breed	Information	Image source
British Saanen	White dairy goat, developed in the UK and influenced by imported Swiss Saanen goats, but with longer legs. Coat is short and fine. Calm natured, with high yields and long lactations, popular for high production of milk throughout the year and where large groups of goats may be housed together. Foundation stock for some large goat dairy farms. 3.68 per cent butterfat. Produces an average of 5ltr (9 pints) of milk daily.	
British Toggenburg	Brown-and-white dairy goat with Swiss markings, developed in the UK. Slight fringes of long hair on an otherwise short and silky coat. Strong and robust, having good longevity. Compact and hardy, generally slightly smaller than other Alpine breeds. Does are around 75cm (30in) and weigh at least 55kg (120lb), with bucks being slightly larger. Temperament is generally very good and they are easily managed. One of the most popular breeds in the UK, and used in some commercial goat farms where cheese is a main product. 3.68 per cent butterfat. Produce an average of 4.5ltr (8 pints) of milk daily.	
Capra Grigia	Endangered indigenous Swiss mountain breed. Robust multi-use goat (meat, milk and landscape maintenance), with good mobility on challenging terrain. Good fertility with a long lifespan. All shades of grey, from light silver grey to black grey, black boots and strong, outwardly curved horns. Thanks to their hard hooves, a high level of sure-footedness and a preference for bushy and thorny terrain, they are optimally adapted to life in the southern Alps.	
Carpathian	Endangered meat and milk breed from south-east Europe including Romania (where it comes in a variety of colours) and Poland (white). Coarse hair with beards and long, narrow ears, horns are thin and grow in an upward and backward direction. Hair fringe around the eyes, very hardy and well adapted to severe highland conditions, having dense, long hair as well as some underfur.	
Cashmere	Cashmere describes the undercoat or down, not a specific goat breed, and many goats have the genetic make-up that enables them to produce cashmere.	
Chamois Coloured (Gämsfarbige, Gebirgsziegeand Oberhasli)	Found throughout Switzerland, parts of northern Italy and Austria, there are two strains, a horned type from the eastern part of the country, and a hornless type from central Switzerland, sometimes considered a separate breed, the Oberhasli.	
Changthangi (Ladakh Pashmina)	Cashmere breed native to the high plateaux of Jammu and Kashmir, India. Also used as a pack animal and for meat. Generally domesticated and reared by nomadic communities. Usually white.	

Breed	Information	Image source
Corsican	Hardy dairy/multi-purpose breed with a long coat, making up the vast majority of goats on Corsica. Used for milk, cheese, meat, clothing, blankets and rope, their horns are used for knife handles and musical instruments.	
Damascus (*aka* Aleppo, Halep, Baladi, Damascene, Shami, or Chami)	Milk and meat long-haired breed originating in the Middle East, also used for leather. Unusual in that it has a high milk yield and the conformation of a meat breed, so has excellent commercial potential. Some have been overbred to produce an extreme snub Roman nose and overshot jaw.	
Danish Landrace	Medium to large dairy breed originated by crossing local Danish goats with imported German and Swiss Saanen breeds. Various colours including white, black and blue.	
Dutch Landrace	Traditional Dutch dairy breed, also used for meat, fibre and conservation grazing, that came near to extinction. Stocky, medium size, with fairly short legs, mostly with a long rough coat of various colours. Horns are lyre-shaped, scimitar-shaped or twisted, and may reach 100cm (40in) in length.	
Dwarf Dairy	Small, useful dairy goats with many of the breed producing milk with just two kiddings in their lifetime, reducing the need to breed. Descended from West African dwarf goats, known in the USA as Nigerian dwarf goats. Distinct from the pet pygmy in its milking capacity.	
English	A deer-like goat bred to be a hardy multipurpose contributor to the smallholding. Unfussy eater, with a variety of coat colouring, mostly shades of brown or grey with an eel stripe (dark line) along its back. Capable of milking through two years. A downy winter undercoat of cashmere. Categorized as a priority breed by the Rare Breed Survival Trust, with under 100 registered breeding females.	
Erzebirge	Critically endangered German breed, used primarily for milking. Reddish-brown coat with black stripes on the face, back and legs.	
Finnish Landrace (Finngoat, Suomenvuohi)	Dairy breed from western Finland. Originates from native goats crossed with imports, particularly Switzerland. Various colours, most usually grey, pied or white, horned and polled.	

Breed	Information	Image source
Frisa Valtellinese (Frontalasca, Rezzalasca).	Northern Italian meat and milk breed raised throughout the Valtellina valley in Lombardy, bordering Switzerland, from which it gets its name. 'Frisa' comes from its *frisature*, or Swiss markings. Shares common characteristics and origins with the Swiss Grisons Striped.	
Garganica	Italian milk and meat breed. Small head, with long, coarse black or dark chestnut hair. Kids' pelts prized for their curly black coats. Noted for its toughness, suited to difficult habitats.	
Girgentana	Southern Sicilian endangered dairy breed. Twisted spiral horns with long beard and primarily white coat with grey-brown hair around the head and throat.	
Golden Guernsey	Channel Island dairy breed adaptable to free range or stall feeding with an affectionate and docile nature making it a good household goat. Generally smaller than other milking breeds and fine-boned. The coat can be long or short and in all shades of gold with or without small white markings. A moderate milk yield, producing 2.5 litres per day. Milk usually has a high butterfat and protein content and is good for making yogurt or cheese. Categorized as at risk breed by the Rare Breed Survival Trust with 600–1,000 registered breeding females.	
Grisons Striped	Endangered Swiss mountain breed, black and white, with low milk production.	
Hexi Cashmere	Chinese cashmere breed that lives in desert and semidesert regions. 60 per cent of the goats are white.	
Icelandic	Ancient breed believed to be of Norwegian origin, dating back to the settlement of Iceland over 1,100 years ago. Isolated for centuries and rare outside its native land, the breed is highly inbred. Coarse, long guard hair, and high quality cashmere, they are kept mainly as pets.	
Istriana	Critically endangered meat and milk breed from Istria in the north Adriatic encompassing Italy, Croatia and Slovenia. White. Used as the Istrian coat of arms.	

Breed	Information	Image source
Jamnapari (*aka* Jamunapari, Ram Sagol)	Large dairy breed originating from India, also used for meat production. Long eared, long bodied and white, black, yellow, brown or various mixed colours. Ancestor of the American Nubian.	
Kalahari Red	Meat breed very similar in type to the Boer (although not related), and all over red in colour. Originates from South Africa. Copes well in harsh, hot environments.	
Kamori	Indian and Pakistani meat and milk breed. Long ears and neck, with distinctive coloration of dark brown with small dark patches over its entire body. Rare and valuable.	
Kiko	Modern New Zealand meat breed created by crossing local feral goats with imported Anglo-Nubian, Saanen and Toggenburg bucks, now popular in the USA. Hardy, fast-growing on scrub, with good parasite and foot rot resistance. Solid white or cream, although there are some of darker colours including black and multi-coloured.	
Kinder	Modern American dairy and meat breed: a Nubian/pygmy cross. They can be bred throughout the year, a trait inherited from their pygmy ancestors. Multiple colours and markings. Exceptionally high 6.5 per cent butterfat.	
La Mancha (LaMancha)	Distinctive American dairy breed with almost non-existent ear flaps (this does not affect their hearing). Only dairy goat developed in the USA. High milk production with high butterfat content. People-oriented breed. Differentiated according to ear size: gopher ear has maximum length of 2.5cm (1in) but preferably non-existent. Elf ear has maximum length of 5cm (2in). The breed comes in many colour varieties.	
Laoshan	White Chinese dairy breed, resulting from an early twentieth-century cross of local breeds with the Saanen.	
Majorera (Fuerteventura)	Dairy breed from the Canary Islands. Its thick, aromatic high-fat milk is used to produce Majorero cheese, which is similar to the better known Manchego. Hardy breed adapted to arid, semi-arid, and even tropical regions.	
Malabari (Tellicherry)	Indian meat breed from Kerala, also with some milk use. White, black and piebald varieties.	

Breed	Information	Image source
Maltese	High milk-yield dairy breed; white body with long hair, black head and large drooping ears, and without horns. Kidding occurs throughout the year. There are no 100 per cent Maltese goats in Malta now, but they are found in Sardinia.	
Messinese (Nebrodi, Siciliana Comune)	Sicilian primarily dairy breed used to make caprine cheeses. Also used for meat. Comes in various colours. Long haired.	
Myotonic (Fainting, Falling, Stiff-legged, Nervous, Tennessee Wooden Leg)	American meat breed with a hereditary condition (congenital myotonia) that causes it to stiffen or fall over and lie rigid when startled. They remain conscious and recover in a few seconds. Densely muscled with a wide body, they are small and have a large weight range from 27 to 80kg (60 to 176lb) with bucks up to 90kg (198lb). Hair can be short or long, with certain individuals producing a great deal of cashmere during colder months, with coats of any colour or pattern. Meat is high quality – tasty and tender. Good foragers, less agile than other breeds. Breeding polled does to polled bucks of this breed can have a high chance of hermaphroditism.	
Nachi	Known as the dancing goat ('nachi' means 'dance') because of its unique high-stepping gait, rather like a carriage horse. A meat breed from the Punjab. Medium size, black or brown in colour with short rough hair and small twisted horns.	
Nera Verzasca	Milk and meat breed from southern Switzerland. Also found in northern Italy. Black-coated.	
Nicastrese	Southern Italian milk and meat breed, used to make cheeses such as the Giuncata di capra calabra, Cacioricotta, Canestrato and Pecorinio Crotonese. It also has some use as a cashmere breed.	
Nigerian Dwarf	Milk, meat and companion American dwarf derived from the West African Dwarf. Short-coated, coming in a variety of colours. More angular dairy-type frame than the pygmy. Docile, hardy, long-lived.	
Nigora	Small to medium modern American milk and fibre breed created in 1994. It is the result of cross-breeding Nigerian Dwarf bucks with Angora does.	

Breed	Information	Image source
Oberhasli	Polled version of the Chamois Coloured goat. Swiss dairy breed, exported to the USA. Athletic and strong, males are used as pack animals. Brown with light tan, reddish-brown, and black points.	
Old English	Typical cottagers' goat in the nineteenth century, it became less common as the fashion was to breed bigger, higher-yielding types. Similar to the English goat but smaller, with a longer, rougher coat and lower milk yield. Thrifty, suitable for providing a household with milk and a kid for the freezer. Noted for long lactation, typically up to eighteen months and being kidded for milk every other year. Hardy and self-sufficient, able to find its own shelter where it is used in out-of-the-way conservation grazing. Various shades of brown and grey, with dark legs, sometimes with white patches. The outer coat is thick and has a cashmere undercoat, and the does have a beard, trousers and other hairy trimmings. Categorized as a priority breed by the Rare Breed Survival Trust, with under 100 registered breeding females.	
Old Irish	Ireland's indigenous landrace breed, now critically endangered and only found in remote mountain ranges roaming in feral herds.	
Orobica	Northern Italian dairy and meat breed. Impressive twisted horns and long-haired coat in varying colours (grey, beige, black, brown or dappled). Used for raw-milk cheeses such as Valsassina Formagìn, Valtellina Matuscin and Val Brembana Robiola. At the end of their useful life, the meat is cured for the classic violino.	
Peacock (Pfauenziege)	Swiss dairy breed, predominantly white with black boots, the rear half being mostly black.	
Poitou (Poitevine, Poitevin)	Rare dairy breed used for cheese production, from western France. Tall with long, shaggy hair, black-brown with white marks on the head and neck while the underbelly and legs are white.	
Pygmy	Miniatures, genetically dwarfed, kept mainly for enjoyment, interest and companionship. Various types of dwarf goats distributed across Africa; the British Pygmy Goat Club discarded regional names such as Nigerian, Cameroonian, Nilotic, Sudanese, West African in favour of the general term 'pygmy'. Hardy, good-natured, but dislikes the cold. Maximum height at the withers 56cm (22in) for males, less for females. Weight 15-30kg (33-66lb) for does, 18-40kg (40-88lb) for bucks. Short legs and cobby bodies give the impression of perpetual pregnancy. Any colour except completely white. Lifespan ten to fifteen years. Breeders have to be prepared for the possibility of Caesarean births.	

Breed	Information	Image source
Pygora	Fibre and companion breed produced by crossing the white Angora and the pygmy. Colours variously white, black, greys, caramels and browns.	
Pyrenean (Chèvre Pyrénéenne)	Long-haired ancient milk and meat breed from the French and Spanish Pyrenees and the Spanish Cantabrian Mountains.	
Rove	A French breed with long twisted horns, originally a meat breed but now used for dairying. The Rove Brousse cheese is produced exclusively with their milk. Also used to maintain inaccessible areas in need of clearing to minimize the risk of wild fires. Smooth-coated, mostly red or black, but also in a wide range of grey, red, white and tan speckles and markings.	
Rustica di Calabria	Southern Italian milk and meat breed, thought to have been influenced by a medley of other breeds including the Abyssinian, Maltese and Tibetan.	
Saanen	The largest breed of Swiss dairy goat, with bucks 90cm (35in) at the withers and weighing a minimum of 85kg (187lb), does 70-80cm (27-32in), weighing 65kg (143lb). It has white skin and a short white coat. Black spots on the udder and ears are typical of the breed. Well balanced, with a stocky yet elegant appearance. The most productive of dairy goats, unsurprisingly found across the world. Because of its pale skin it doesn't tolerate strong sun, and copes well being kept inside. 3.8 per cent butterfat.It has been exported all over the world, and given rise to many local sub-breeds through cross-breeding with local goats, including the Banat White in Romania, the British Saanen, the French Saanen, the Israeli Saanen, the Russian White, the White Noble in Germany, and the Yugoslav Saanen. Produces an average 4.25ltr (7.5 pints) of milk daily.	
Sable Saanen	A coloured variant of the Saanen dairy goat was recognized as a breed in New Zealand in the 1980s. They come in all colours except white, including silver, roan, chamois, blue, black and red, chocolate, golden and more, and with various patterning from belted to spotted.	
Sahelian/Sahel	Long-legged West African meat and skin breed, best suited to desert and semi-desert conditions.	
Sarda	Milk and meat breed from Sardinia, hardy and well suited to being raised in tough conditions. Originated as a cross between various breeds, especially the Maltese.	

Breed	Information	Image source
Savanna	All-white meat breed, originating from South Africa, similar in all but colouring to the Boer and Kalahari Red, and very hardy.	
Swedish Landrace (Svensk Lantras)	Dairy breed used for cheesemaking. Various colours: solid white or black, variegated brown, black or grey. Closely related to the Norwegian Landrace. Their long coat enables them to withstand cold weather.	
Tauernscheck	Very rare Austrian dairy breed derived from the Austrian Landrace and Pinzgauer goats. Spotted brown and white.	
Toggenburg	Swiss dairy breed and the first of the alpine breeds to reach Britain. Good length and depth, without legginess. Smaller in stature than its British counterpart, it has strong, sound conformation. Its colour ranges from mid-brown to shades of grey or fawn, with white Swiss markings. The hair can be any length, but fringing is usually present to some degree, and the coat is silky in texture. 3.55 per cent butterfat. Produces an average of 3.5ltr (6 pints) of milk daily.	
Valais Blackneck (Walliser Schwarzhalsziege, Gletschergeiss, Col Noir du Valais, Chèvre des Glaciers, Race de Viège, Vallesana, Vallese)	Meat, milk and grazing management breed from Valais, southern Switzerland, and neighbouring northern Italy and Germany. Distinctive colouring, black from the nose to behind the shoulder, and white from there to the tail. The English Bagot is similarly coloured and is possibly descended from the Valais Blackneck.	
Valdostana	Long-horned mountain goat of North Italy, used for milk and meat.	
Verata	Traditional Spanish dual-purpose milk and meat breed, of various colours including black, black-brown, chestnut brown and grey. Long-legged, hardy and adaptable to different climates and management approaches. Able to breed year-round.	
West African Dwarf	African dwarf breed, the ancestor of pygmy and dwarf breeds in Europe and the USA. Typical height 30 to 50cm (12 to 20in), adult males 20 to 25kg (44 to 55lb) and females 18 to 22kg (40 to 48lb). Legs are short and the udder is small. Most have short hair, and colour varies, although dark brown with black points is most common. A useful dairy breed with a high butterfat of 6.1 per cent, and a long lactation between kiddings.	

APPENDIX

GLOSSARY OF GOAT TERMS

abomasum Fourth compartment of the stomach of a ruminant.

abortion Premature loss of a pregnancy.

abscess Localized collection of pus.

acidosis Condition in which the pH of the rumen is abnormally low <5.5, normally due to excess grain being consumed.

adoption *See* fostering.

afterbirth Placenta and foetal membranes expelled from the uterus after kidding.

amino acid One of the building blocks of protein.

anaemiaLower than normal number of red blood cells.

anthelmintic Drug that kills certain types of intestinal worms, also known as a wormer.

antibiotic Drug that inhibits the growth of/destroys micro-organisms/bacteria.

antibodies Proteins produced by the immune system to fight specific bacteria, viruses, or other antigens.

antitoxin Antibody that can neutralize a specific toxin.

ARAMS Animal Reporting and Movement Service is the on-line recording system for movements of sheep, goats and deer in the UK. The Livestock Information Service is taking over this role.

artificial insemination (AI) Placing semen into the uterus by artificial means.

banding (or ringing) Process of applying a rubber ring to the scrotum for castration.

beard Male and female goats can have beards.

blind teat Non-functioning teat, either an additional teat not connected to a milk duct, or one that is non-functional due to mastitis.

bloat Excessive accumulation of gases in the rumen of an animal.

body condition score (BCS) Numeric value that assesses the degree of fatness and condition of an animal's body.

bolus Object placed in the reticulum, containing slow-release medication or electronic identification information.

bottle jaw Oedema or fluid accumulation under the jaw. Often a sign of infection with haemonchosis (*see* below). Also known as Johne's disease.

breech Delivery position in which the kid is presented backwards with its rear legs tucked underneath.

TOP: Woolridge Cross, Dolton, May 1982. (Documentary photograph by James Ravilious for the Beaford Archive © Beaford Arts)

breed Group of animals with similar characteristics distinguishing them from other animals, and which are passed from the parents to the offspring.

broker/broken-mouthed A goat that has lost or broken some of its incisor teeth, usually due to age.

browse Bushy or woody plants consumed by goats.

buck Sexually mature intact/ entire (uncastrated) male goat used for breeding.

buckling An entire sexually immature young male.

buck rag Cloth rubbed on a buck to impregnate it with his scent. The rag is kept in a closed container and used to assist stimulating heat/oestrus in does.

burdizzo Bloodless castration method that involves crushing the blood vessels leading into the testicles.

bursae Fluid-filled sacs that act as a cushion between bones, tendons, joints and muscles.

butting Method of fighting where one animal strikes the head and horns of another.

caprinae The group of even-toed ungulates that includes sheep and goats.

caprine Of, relating to, or characteristic of a goat.

caprine arthritis encephalitis (CAE) Infectious disease in goats that causes arthritis and progressive inflammation in organs or tissue systems such as the joints, bursae, brain, spinal cord, lungs and udder. Currently incurable.

carcass/carcase Dressed body of a slaughtered animal (the intestines, head, feet and skin are removed).

carding Process of using a metal-pronged carding comb or brush either to groom a goat or sheep for showing or to prepare a fleece or fibre for spinning.

caseous lymphadenitis (CL) Chronic bacterial disease characterized by abscess development in the lymph nodes and other tissues. Highly infectious.

cast Animal on its back unable to regain its footing.

castrate Process of removing the testicles (verb); a male that has had its testicles removed (noun).

cellulose Component of plant cell walls that is not digestible by most animals.

cervix Lower section of the uterus that protrudes into the vagina and dilates during labour to allow birth.

chevon French word for young goat, animals that are slaughtered near or shortly after weaning.

cleats (clays, claws, clees) two halves of the goat's hoof.

cleft palate Congenital disorder where the roof of the mouth is split, sometimes accompanied by a cleft lip.

closed herd No new animals are introduced into the herd, animals are not hired out or taken to shows.

clostridial diseases Potentially fatal infections caused by clostridia (soil-borne) bacteria.

cloudburst Pseudo pregnancy where a goat appears to be pregnant and can even lactate. This false pregnancy can produce a cloudy discharge, hence the name.

coccidiostat Chemical agents mixed in feed or drinking water to control coccidiosis in animals.

colostrum First milk a doe gives after birth. Rich in antibodies, it helps protect newborns against disease.

combing Straightening of wool fibres and removal of short fibres and other impurities.

concentrates Hard feed, also known as cake, compound feed, grains etc. High-energy, low-fibre feed that is highly digestible.

conception Fertilization of an egg by a sperm.

conformation Combination of structural correctness and muscling of the animal, including its frame and shape.

corpus luteum A yellow, progesterone-secreting mass of cells formed after a mature egg has been released from an ovarian follicle.

CPH number County parish holding number, which registers land as being for agricultural use.

creep feed Small pellets of high-protein supplementary feed given to young animals.

creep grazing Allowing young animals to forage in areas with restricted access, while older livestock are kept out.

crimp The natural waviness of the fibre.

cross-breed Animal whose parents are of two different breeds.

cross-grazing Using two or more species of animals on the same land, because they graze in different ways and benefit the sward.

crutching *See* 'dagging'.

cryptorchidism Failure of one or both testes to descend.

cud Food that is regurgitated by a ruminant to be chewed again.

cull Animal no longer suitable for breeding, which is sold for meat.

culling Slaughtering an unwanted animal.

dagging Also known as 'crutching': the removal of fibre from around the tail and between the rear legs of a goat.

dam Mother.

DE Digestible Energy.

dehorning Removal of the horns of a mature animal.

dew claws The horny nubs above the foot that give traction when climbing rocky surfaces.

diarrhoea Also known as 'scouring': an unusually loose or fast faecal excretion.

disbudding Removal of horn buds to stop horns developing.

doe Adult, sexually mature female goat.

doeling Young female not yet sexually mature.

drench Orally administered liquid medicine (n); to administer a liquid medicine (v).

dressing or killing out percentage Percentage of the live animal that ends up as carcass.

droving/driving Walking livestock from one location to another.

dry doe Doe that is barren/not carrying kids.

dry matter Foodstuff that remains once water content is removed.

dystocia Difficulty in giving birth or being born.

ear tag Method of identifying animals by using a plastic or metal tag placed in the ear of the animal.

elastrator Tool used to apply rubber rings to the scrotum for castration purposes.

embryo Animal in the early stage of development before birth.

embryo transfer Implantation of embryos or fertilized eggs into a surrogate mother.

epididymis Tiny tube where sperm collect after leaving the testis.

external parasites For example fleas, keds, lice, mites, nose-blot flies and ticks that feed on body tissue such as blood, skin and hair resulting in irritation, blood loss and disease.

faecal egg count (FEC) Process of assessing the level of parasite load in goats based on the number and type of parasite eggs found in the faeces.

faeces Manure or excrement produced by an animal.

fallen stock Dead stock.

false pregnancy Pseudo pregnancy where the doe shows false signs of being pregnant.

FAMACHA © Acronym for Faffa Malan Chart, a method of using the colour of the inner eyelid to determine the level of *haemonchus contortus* (also known as the barber's pole worm) infection in sheep and goats.

fertilizer Natural or synthetic soil improvers that are spread on pasture to improve fertility.

fibre Goat hair, short for many goats, and long in the case of mohair and cashmere types.

finish/condition The amount of fat that covers the body.

first freshener A doe that is kidding/lactating for the first time.

flushing Increasing nutrition in the few weeks before mating to improve fertility, or in the period before birth to increase kid birthweight; sometimes referred to as 'steaming up'.

flushing (eggs/embryo) Removing a fertilized or unfertilized egg from an animal as part of an embryo transfer procedure.

flystrike Where fly eggs have been laid on an animal and which hatch into maggots.

fodder crop Plant grown for animal feed.

food chain information Regulation requirements if you are intending to slaughter animals for human consumption.

footbath Long trough filled with a chemical preparation in which livestock stand for protection from/treatment of hoof conditions.

foot rot Infectious pododermatitis, a painful, bacterial infection affecting sheep, goats and cattle.

forage Edible plant material used as livestock feed.

forequarters Area on the animal's body that includes the withers, front legs, feet, shoulder, chest and brisket area.

fostering (adopting) Encouraging a doe to accept a kid from another female.

freshen When a does gives birth (kids) and starts to produce milk.

gambrel restrainer Restraining device made of plastic placed over the top of the animal's neck, with slots on either side to hold both front legs of the animal.

gestation Length of pregnancy. In most goat breeds, approximately 145-152 days.

goatling Young goat (female)

halal Set of Islamic dietary laws that regulate the preparation of food.

hay Fully dried preserved grass, the main foodstuff for goats.

haylage Part-dried preserved grass.

heat Period when a doe is fertile and receptive to the buck; also known as 'oestrus'.

hectare Metric unit of area equal to 10,000sq m (100 × 100m), or 2.471 acres.

hefting (or heafing) In certain breeds, a natural instinct to keep to a particular area or 'heft' throughout life.

herd number Required in the UK for identifying livestock belonging to an individual herd.

heritability Extent to which a trait is influenced by genetic make-up.

hermaphrodite Sterile animal with the reproductive organs of both sexes.

heterosis Increase in performance (for example fecundity, yield, growth rate) of hybrids compared to that of their pure-bred parents.

hot carcass weight Weight of a dressed carcass immediately after slaughter prior to the shrinkage that occurs in the chiller.

hybrid vigour Increase in performance due to cross-breeding.

hypothermia Condition characterized by low body temperature.

immunity Natural or acquired resistance to specific diseases.

inbreeding Mating or crossing of closely related animals; sometimes referred to as 'line-breeding' when carried out to pass on or strengthen certain desirable traits.

in kid Pregnant.

internal parasites Parasites located in the gastrointestinal system in animals.

intramuscular (IM) injection Given straight into a muscle.

intravenous (IV) injection Given directly into a vein.

Johne's disease (*myco-bacterium paratuber-culosis*) Also known as bottle jaw - bacterial disease causing severe weight loss and diarrhoea. Not currently curable.

joint ill (navel ill; pyoseptica-emia) In newborns, an inflammation of the joints caused by bacteria entering the body, normally via an untreated umbilical cord.

jugular Vein in the neck that carries deoxygenated blood from the head back to the heart.

keds Large, flattened, bloodsucking parasitic flies.

ketone Acidic substance produced when the body uses fat instead of sugar for energy.

ketosis Metabolic disorder where ketones build up in the body.

kid Young goat (n). To give birth to a kid (v). The meat from an animal less than one year old (n).

kidding Giving birth.

kidding percentage Number of kids (including multiple births) successfully reared in a herd compared with the number of does that have been mated.

kosher Food prepared in accordance with Jewish dietary laws.

lactation Production and secretion of milk; the period when the doe produces milk.

lairage Area of holding pens where livestock is held at the abattoir before slaughter.

line-breeding *See also* 'inbreeding': mating of closely related animals within a particular line.

liver fluke Small, leaf-shaped organism that thrives on wet land. Causes liver damage and is fatal if not treated (through a preventative programme of treatment in susceptible herds).

live vaccine Vaccine in which a live virus is weakened through chemical or physical processes to produce an immune response without causing the effects of the disease.

lungworms Roundworms found in the respiratory tract and lung tissue.

lutenizing hormone (LH) Hormone that triggers ovulation and stimulates the *corpus luteum* to secrete progesterone; in males, it stimulates testosterone production.

maiden milker Doe that comes into milk without being bred.

masculinity Secondary male characteristics exhibited in the head, neck, shoulders and chest.

mastitis Uncomfortable and potentially serious inflammation of the mammary glands due to bacterial infection.

micron Measurement unit for fibre diameter; one millionth of a metre.

milker Adult dairy female.

mineral Inorganic group of nutrients, including elements such as calcium, phosphorus and copper.

moiled Hornless; polled.

monorchid Male with only one testis descended into the scrotum.

motility Commonly used to describe active sperm.

movement licence Legal requirement for moving livestock on and off premises.

movement standstill Restrictions on the movement of livestock off premises.

mutton Meat from a goat or sheep aged two years or older.

necropsy Post-mortem examination.

nematode Parasitic roundworm.

oestrogen Female sex hormone produced by the ovaries, which is responsible for the oestrus cycle.

oestrus Heat period, during which females are fertile and receptive to the male.

oestrus cycle Reproductive cycle of the female.

omasum Third part of the ruminant stomach, between the reticulum and the abomasum.

open Female that is not pregnant.

orf Virus that causes contagious ecthyma in sheep and goats; a zoonotic infection – it can be passed to humans.

orphan Orphaned kid, or one rejected by its mother, or from a multiple birth where the doe has inadequate milk to feed all her kids.

ovulation Release of mature eggs from the ovary.

oxytocin Naturally secreted hormone that encourages the contraction of the uterine muscles during labour and milk let-down; a veterinary product used to stimulate contractions and help lactation.

parturition Birthing process.

passive immunity Acquiring protection against infectious disease from another animal – for example, when a newborn consumes antibody-rich colostrum from its mother.

pastern Lower part of the leg, above the hoof.

pasture-fed Entirely grass- and browse-fed livestock, either fresh or preserved.

pasteurization Partial sterilization to make milk safe for consumption and improve keeping quality.

pedigree Family tree showing the ancestry of a registered, pure-bred animal.

pelt Animal skin, complete with fibre.

pH Value indicating the acidity or alkalinity of something (for example rumen, soil).

phenotype Observable physical characteristics of an individual.

pink eye Infectious keratoconjunctivitis; a condition in which the conjunctiva (the membranes lining the eyelids and covering the white part of the eye) become inflamed or infected.

pizzle Penis.

placenta Organ that protects and nourishes the foetus(es) whilst in the uterus.

pneumonia Inflammation of the lungs, caused by a bacterial or viral infection.

polled Without horns.

polyoestrus Able to breed all year round.

pour-on Chemical preparation for the control of internal/external parasites, which is applied to the skin of the goat and is gradually absorbed; an alternative to injectable treatments.

predator Animal that lives by hunting, killing and eating other species.

probiotic Living organism used to manipulate fermentation in the rumen.

progeny Offspring of an animal.

progesterone Female hormone produced in large quantities by the placenta during pregnancy and secreted by the ovaries.

prolapse Interior organ pushed outside the body cavity (for example vaginal, uterine, rectal).

prolific Highly productive in kidding; fecund.

prostaglandin Compound in medications used to induce birth, abortions, or to synchronize oestrus.

pure-bred Not crossed with another breed.

quarantine Confine and keep an animal away from the rest of the herd to prevent the spread of disease.

quarter Half of the udder.

raddle Coloured pigment applied to the male's brisket to mark the females he mates; a harness used to hold a raddle crayon.

reticulum Second chamber of the ruminant digestive tract.

ringwomb Failure of the cervix to dilate sufficiently, which causes delivery problems.

rotational grazing Organized system of moving stock from one grazing unit to another.

roughage High-fibre feed that is low in both digestible nutrients and energy (for example hay, straw, silage).

roundworm Unsegmented parasitic worms with elongated rounded bodies that are pointed at both ends.

rumen First compartment of the stomach of a ruminant animal. It contains bacteria and protozoa, which break down cellulose.

ruminant Animal with a multiple-chambered stomach that is able to digest cellulose.

scab Irritating skin condition caused by the parasitic mange mite *Psoroptes ovis*.

scouring See 'diarrhoea'.

scrapie Fatal, degenerative disease affecting the central nervous system of sheep and goats.

scrotum Pouch of skin containing the male's testicles.

scur(s) Small rudimentary horn.

semen Combination of sperm, seminal fluid and other male reproductive secretions.

sharps Needles, syringes, scalpel blades, and anything else that can puncture the skin.

shearing Removing the fibre using mechanical clippers or hand shears.

silage Fodder prepared by storing and fermenting grass or other forage plants in wrapped bales or in a silo.

sire Father.

skirting Removing the stained, unusable, or less desirable parts of a fleece.

smooth-mouthed (broken-mouthed) Animal that has lost all of its permanent incisors, usually at seven years of age or older.

spinning Working natural fibres into thread or wool.

sponging Oestrus can be induced and synchronized by using progestagen-impregnated sponges.

stanchion/stand Device for restraining a goat by the neck for feeding, milking, hoof trimming or artificial insemination.

standing heat Period in which the doe will stand still and accept the male for breeding.

staple Length of a lock of shorn fibre.

stillborn Kid that is delivered dead.

stocking density/stocking rate Relationship between the number of animals and an area of land.

store Weaned kid not ready for slaughter and which is kept for fattening.

straw Stems of cereals such as wheat, barley or oats that are cut and baled and used for fodder or bedding.

strip cup Cup covered with mesh to draw foremilk for examination to detect abnormalities.

strip-grazing Controlling grazing by confining animals to specific areas of land (often using electric fencing) for short periods of time before moving them on to fresh ground.

stun To render unconscious, for example prior to slaughter.

subcutaneous injection Given under the skin, but not into the muscle; sometimes shortened to 'sub-Q' or 'SQ'.

supplement Feed/minerals designed to provide nutrients deficient in the animal's main diet.

sustainable farming Approach that uses on-farm resources efficiently, reduces demands on the environment, and may help rural communities.

Swiss markings White markings that extend as broad facial stripes from above the eyes to a white muzzle and around the edges and tips of the ears, also on the legs from the knees and hocks downwards, and on the rump beside and below the tail.

tapeworm Ribbon-like parasitic flatworms found in the intestines.

tassels See wattles.

teaser Male that has been vasectomized to prevent reproduction, used to stimulate females for mating.

testosterone Hormone that promotes the development and maintenance of male sex characteristics.

tethering Tying an animal to restrict grazing and movement.

toggles See wattles.

total digestible nutrients (TDN) System used for expressing the energy value of feeds.

twin kid/lamb disease Pregnancy toxaemia, a metabolic disease affecting very underweight or overweight does/ewes carrying multiple kids/lambs.

udder Milk-secreting organ.

ultrasound Procedure in which high-energy soundwaves are used to create images of organs and structures in the body, for example in pregnancy diagnosis.

umbilicus Where the umbilical cord was attached during gestation.

urea Main end product of protein metabolism in animals.

urinary calculi Stones formed within the male urinary tract. Common in goats, it is caused primarily by an imbalance of dietary calcium and phosphorus.

uterus Organ in which the foetuses develop; the womb.

vaccine Injection given to improve resistance to/prevent disease.

vagina Passageway from the cervix to the external organs.

vulva Exterior part of the reproductive tract.

wattles/toggles/tassles Small fleshy appendage attached on or near the throat area of the goat, and which serves no known function.

weaning Process of taking young animals away from their source of milk.

wet adoption Covering a kid that is to be adopted with birthing fluids from the doe.

wether Castrated male.

withdrawal period After treatment with a medical product, the amount of time that must be allowed to elapse before meat or milk is allowed into the human food chain.

wormer Commonly used term for anthelmintic – medication for killing intestinal worms.

yearling Animal between one and two years of age.

yield Amount of milk, meat or fibre produced per goat.

zero grazing System of growing fodder but not allowing livestock to graze it directly; instead, the crop is cut and taken to the animals.

zoonosis Disease or ailment that is zoonotic – one that normally exists in animals, but can be passed to humans.

FURTHER INFORMATION, READING AND COURSES

SOCIETIES AND ASSOCIATIONS

British Goat Society Secretary: Mrs Rachel Fox, PO Box 137, Swanley, Kent BR8 9BW, tel: 01322 611767, email: admin@ britishgoatsociety.com, www. britishgoatsociety.com

Goat Veterinary Society Secretary: Benjamin H Dustan BVSc Cert CHP BSc(Hons) MRCVS, Tarn Farm Vets, Woolbarn, Shap Abbey, Shap, Cumbria, CA10 3NB, tel: 07734 458412, email: gvs. enquiries@gmail.com, www. goatvetsoc.co.uk

Harness Goat Society Email: harnessgoats@gmail.com, www.harnessgoats.co.uk

Milking Goat Association Michaelwood Lodge Farm, Charfield, Wotton-under-Edge, Gloucestershire, GL12 8HA, tel: 01454 436046, email: office@milkinggoat.org.uk, www.milkinggoat.org.uk

Raw Milk Producers Association Website: rawmilkproducers. co.uk/

UK GOAT BREED SOCIETIES

Anglo Nubian: Anglo-Nubian Breed Society, www. anglonubian.co.uk

Angora: British Angora Goat Society, www.angoragoats-mohair.org.uk

Bagot: The Bagot Goat Society, bagotgoats.co.uk

Boer: British Boer Goat Society, www.britishboergoatsociety.co.uk

British: British Goat Society, www.britishgoatsociety.com

British Alpine: British Alpine Breed Society, www.facebook. com/britishalpinebreedsociety

British Guernsey: c/o Golden Guernsey Goat Society, www. goldenguernseygoat.org.uk

British Saanen: c/o British Goat Society, www.britishgoatsociety. com

British Toggenburg: British Toggenburg Society, www. britishtoggenburgs.co.uk

Cashmere: British Cashmere Goat Society, Mrs Pat Thorne Tel: 01525 237308

English: English Goat Breeders Association, www.egba.org.uk

Golden Guernsey: Golden Guernsey Goat Society, www. goldenguernseygoat.org.uk

Old English: Old English Goat Society, oldenglishgoats.org.uk

Pygmy: Pygmy Goat Club, pygmygoatclub.org.uk

Saanen: Saanen Breed Society, www.saanen.co.uk

Toggenburg: Toggenburg Breeders Society, toggenburgbreederssociety. yolasite.com

British Primitive Goats:, www. rarebreedgoats.co.uk

British Dwarf Dairy Goat : British Dwarf Dairy Goat Society, www.dwarfdairygoats.co.uk

TOP: Cuppers Piece, Beaford, June 1983. Documentary photograph by James Ravilious for the Beaford Archive © Beaford Arts

LOCAL GOAT SOCIETIES

Ayrshire Goat Club: Mrs A Dick, Rowanmyle House, Tarbolton, Mauchline, Ayrshire, KA5 5LU, tel: 01292 541981, email: a_m_dick@hotmail.com

Bath & District Goatkeepers Society: Secretary: Miss Gaynor Smith, Pear Tree Cottage, Lower Common, Rangeworthy, Nr Bristol BS37 7QE, tel: 01454-228471 Email: yorgangirls@gmail.com

Beds & Herts Goat Society: Mrs D Padian, Bury Leys Farm, London Lane, Houghton Conquest, Bedfordshire, MK45 3LP., tel: 01234 740365, email: doreen.padian@btinternet.com, http://bhgs.btck.co.uk

Cambridge & District Goat Society: Mrs W Hardy, Lower Hare Park Farm, Six Mile Bottom, Newmarket, Suffolk CB8 0TS, tel: 01638 570241, http://www.goats.co.uk/club/cambridge/

Cheshire Dairy Goat Society: Mrs D Rudkin, 1 Dingle Hollow, Compstall Road, Romiley, Stockport, Cheshire. SK6 4ED, tel: 01614 303805

Cleveland Dairy Goat Society: Mr B.Perry, 24, Station Road, Norton, Stockton on Tees, Cleveland, TS20 1NH, tel: 01642 890621, email: b.perry@ntlworld.com

Cornwall Goatkeepers Association: Mrs L Russell, Highland Meadow, 139 Tresaize Road, Roche PL26 8HQ., tel 01726 891343, email: lindar32@hotmail.co.uk

Derbyshire Dairy Goat Club: Mrs C Woodward, Headhouse Farm, Mapperley, Ilkeston, Derbyshire, DE7 6BX., tel: 0115 9324706, email: christine@headhouse.freeserve.uk

Devon Goat Society: Mrs V Day, Leats Farm, Aylesbeare, Exeter, Devon, EX5 2JQ, tel: 01395 233985, email r.calcraft@btinternet.com

Durham Dairy Goat Society: Mrs J Harbour, Golden Corner Bungalow, Byers Green, Spennymoor, Co. Durham, DL16 7QE., tel: 01388 604284, email: jennifer.harbour@btinternet.com

Essex And Suffolk Goat Club: Secretary: Mrs Hazel Francis, Farm End, Barford Road, Topcroft, Bungay, Suffolk NR35 2BB, tel: 01508 498499, email: h.francis@btinternet.com

Fenland Goatkeepers & Smallholders Club: Mrs C Wilkinson, Three Lays, 3, Lutton Gate, Gedney Hill, Spalding, Lincs, PE12 1BY,

Gloucester & Wiltshire Goat Club: Mrs E Kingstone, 8 Harris Lane, Easton Royal, Pewsey, Wiltshire SN9 5LX, tel: 07854 931680, email: glosandwiltsgoatclub@outlook.com

Grampian Goat Club: Ms Katy Whityby-Last, West Braehead, Cairnie, Huntly, Aberdeenshire AB54 4TU, tel: 01466 760321, Mobile: 07790 196765, email: katy.whitbylast@gmail.com

Guernsey Goat Society: Miss Carole Turner, Le Catillon de Bas, Rue Du Catillon, St Pierre Du Bois, Guernsey GY7 9HG, tel: 01481 265100, email: carolet@guernsey.net

Hampshire Goat Club: Ms Jane Barker, 29 Kings Hill, Beech, Alton, Hampshire GU34 4AW, tel: 01420 562137

Herefordshire Goat Club: Sharon Williams, Bank Lodge, Coldwells Road, Holmer, Hereford, HR1 1LH., tel: 01432 276424

Irish Goat Producers Association: Ms Janet Morrison, Faulkland, Glaslough, Co. Monaghan, Ireland H18 KF25, tel: 00 353 83 8019291, email: irishgoatproducersassociation@gmail.com, Facebook: Irish Goat Producers Association

Isle Of Wight Goat Club: Mr D J S Sprake, Springfield, Town Lane, Chale Green, Ventnor, Isle of Wight, PO38 2JS., tel: 01983 551234

Kent Goat Club: Mrs Rachel Fox, 42 Manse Way, Swanley, Kent, BR8 8DD, tel: 01322 614882, email: rachelfoxuk2002@yahoo.co.uk

Mercian Milk Recording Group: Miss A Freeman, Whitmans Hill Farm, Storridge, Malvern, Worcestershire, WR13 5HF, tel: 01886 880498, email: afwhitmans@aol.com

North Midland Milk Recording Club: Messrs R & M Cooper, 143 Heanor Road, Smalley, Ilkeston, Derbyshire, DE7 6DY., tel: 01773 760206 Email: mlcooper009@gmail.com

North Staffordshire Goat Society: Mrs P Clee, Russells Bank Farm, 78 Upper Way, Upper Longdon, Nr Rugeley,, Staffordshire, WS15 1QD.

North Wales Goat & Smallholders Society: Mrs S D Bartram, Cefn Nen, Groeslon, Caernarfon, Gwynedd, LL54 7UA., email: geifr.dulyn@btinternet.com

Northern England Goat Club & Milk Recording Club: Acting Secretary: Mrs Christine Birkbeck, Whyber, Bolton, Appleby, Cumbria CA16 6AW, tel: 01768 361583, email: birklyn@msn.com

Northern Ireland Goat Club: Ms Pauline Weir, 5 Ballycairn Cottages, Co. Down, Northern Ireland, tel: 02890 827195, email: paulineweir58@gmail.com

Northumbrian Dairy Goat Society: Roger Wilson, Gibshiel, Tarset, Hexham, Northumberland NE48 1RR, email: rogerwilson01@gmail.com

Norwich & District Goat Club: Mrs Lynn Jermy, Half Moon, The Street, Bintree, Dereham, NR20 5AH, tel: 01362 683506, email: lynn.jermy@btinternet.com

Nottinghamshire Goat Club: Mrs V Hardy, 1 Cottage Ashfield School, Sutton Road, Kirkby-In-Ashfield,, Nottinghamshire, NG17 8HR., tel: 01623 555155, email: kinmeaherd@btinternet.com

Pennine & Bingley Goat Club: Mrs G Clough, Shepherds Nook, 1 Daisy Bank, Hebden Bridge, West Yorkshire HX7 8PU, tel: 01422 843 263, email: gillian@prepress.demon.co.uk

Pontefract & District Goat Club: Mr R Parkin, 3 Station Cottages, North Howden, Howden, Nr Goole, East, Yorkshire, DN14 7LD., tel: 01430 431929

Quintet Milk Recording Club: Mr G George, Ardross, South Drove, Martin, Lincoln, Lincolnshire LN4 3RF., tel/Fax: 01526 378215, E-mail: ardross@live.co.uk

Scottish Goatkeepers Federation: Mrs Lisa Sinclair, Millstane,

Meikleour, Perth Ph2 6EH., telephone: 01250 884358, email lisa.sgf@tesco.net, www. scottishgoatkeepersfederation. com

Shropshire Goatkeepers Society: Mrs H Alderson, Strawbarn, 47 Wellington Road, Coalbrookdale, telford,, Shropshire., tel: 01952 433045, email: aldergoat@yahoo.co.uk

Somerset Dairy Goat Club: Mrs S R Summers, Homeacre, Stowey Road, Fivehead, Taunton, Somerset, TA3 6PP., tel: 01460 281418, email: lynne. homeacre@gmail.com

South West Wales Goat Club: Mrs Corinne Stewart, Arfryn, Oakford, Llanarth, Ceredigion. SA47 0RP, telephone: 01545 580976, email: ploughcottage@sky.com, www. southwestwalesgoatclub.co.uk

Surrey Goat Club: Mrs E Short, Withybush Farm, Knowle Lane, Cranleigh, Surrey GU6 8JP, tel: 01483 273641

Sussex County Goat Club: Mrs Erica Willis, Lukes South, Langton Lane, Hurstiepoint, Hassock, West Sussex. BN6 9HA., tel: 01273 833632, email: ian.churchill1@ btopenworld.com

Worcestershire Goat Society: Wendy Grantham, Trinolly, Delly End, Hailey, Oxfordshire OX29 9XD, tel: 01993 868340, email: trinolly.868@btinternet. com

Yorkshire Goat Society: Mr Chris Hagain, 581 Halifax Road, Broad Oak, Hipperholme. Halifax, HX3 8DD, tel: 01422 206244, email: chris.hagain@ btinternet.com

GOVERNMENT AND OTHER HELPFUL ORGANIZATIONS

Goat movements in England: Animal Reporting and Movement Service (ARAMS), tel: 0844 573 0137, email: farmershelpline@arams.co.uk, www.arams.co.uk/

Goat movements in Wales by EIDCymru, website www. eidcymru.org

Goat Movements in Scotland by ScotEID, website www.scoteid. com

Goat Movements in Northern Ireland by the Animal and Public Health Information System (APHIS), website www. daera-ni.gov.uk/aphis-online-support

Goat movements in the Republic of Ireland

Livestock Information Service, website https:// livestockinformation.org.uk

Department for Environment, Food and Rural Affairs (DEFRA) and Animal and Plant Health Agency (APHA)

In England, tel: 03000 200 301

In Wales, tel: 0300 303 8268

In Scotland call the relevant field office:
Ayr, tel: 03000 600703, email: APHA.Scotland@apha.gov.uk
Galashiels, tel: 03000 600711, email: APHA.Scotland@apha. gov.uk
Inverness, tel: 03000 600709, email: APHA.Scotland@apha. gov.uk
Inverurie, tel: 03000 600708, email: APHA.Scotland@apha. gov.uk
Perth, tel: 03000 600704, email: APHA.Scotland@apha. gov.uk

In Northern Ireland Department of Agriculture, Environment and Rural Affairs (DAERA) www.daera-ni.gov.uk/ contact Tel: 0300 200 7843, email: daera.helpline@ daera-ni.gov.uk

Food Standards Agency (FSA)
www.food.gov.uk/
In England:, tel: 0330 332 7149, email: helpline@food.gov.uk
In Wales, email: walesadminteam@food.gov.uk
In Northern Ireland, email: infofsani@food.gov.uk

Food Standards Scotland (FSS) www.foodstandards.gov.sco, tel: 01224 285100, email: enquiries@fss.scot

Farming and Wildlife Advisory Group (FWAG), email: info@ fwag.org.uk, www.fwag.org.uk

Humane Slaughter Association, tel: 01582 831919, email: info@ hsa.org.uk, www.hsa.org.uk

Moredun Research Institute, tel: 0131 445 5111
E: info@moredun.org.uk, www.moredun.org.uk

National Animal Disease Information Service (NADIS), tel: 07771 190823, email:

contact@nadis.org.uk, www.nadis.org.uk/

National Fallen Stock Company, tel: **01335 320014**, email: member@nfsco.co.uk, www.nfsco.co.uk/

Rare Breeds Survival Trust (RBST), tel: 024 7669 6551, email: enquiries@rbst.org.uk, www.rbst.org.uk/

National Milk Laboratories (to test for pathogens), tel: 01902 749920, email: milk@nmrp.com, www. nationalmilklaboratories.co.uk

International Goat Organisation, www.iga-goatworld.com

Goat Aid, www.goataid.com/

Transport certificates Training and testing for the City and Guild Certificate of Competence In The Transport Of Animals By Road is available online at www.hushfarms.co.uk and through some agricultural colleges.

ORGANIC CERTIFICATION

Organic Farmers & Growers CIC, tel: 01939 291800, email: info@ofgorganic.org, www.ofgorganic.org

Organic Food Federation, tel: 01760 720444, email: info@orgfoodfed.com, www.orgfoodfed.com

Soil Association Certification Ltd, www.soilassociation.org, tel: 0117 914 2412, email: prod. cert@soilassociation.org

Biodynamic Association Certification, tel: 01453 766296, email: certification@ biodynamic.org.uk, www.bdcertification.org.uk

Irish Organic Association, tel: (+353) 090 643 3680, email: info@irishoa.ie, www.irishorganicassociation.ie

Organic Trust Limited, tel: 00 353 185 30271, email: organic@iol.ie, www.organic-trust.org

Quality Welsh Food Certification Ltd, tel: 01970 636688, email: info@wlbp. co.uk, www.wlbp.co.uk

OF&G (Scotland) Ltd, tel: 01939 291800, email: certification@ sopa.org.uk, www.ofgorganic. org

EQUIPMENT

Goat Genetics (artificial insemination), email: info@goatgenetics.com, www.goatgenetics.com

Goat Nutrition Ltd, tel: 01233 770780, email: Info@gnltd.co.uk, www.gnltd.co.uk

Frenchall Goats, tel: 01638 750665, email: info@frenchall-goats.co.uk, www.frenchallgoats.co.uk

Homestead Farm Supplies, tel: 01295 713188, www.homesteadfarmsupplies.co.uk

SPR Centre, tel: 01243 542815, www.sprcentre.com

Dairy Spares, tel: 01948 667676, email: info@dairyspares.co.uk, www.dairyspares.co.uk

Hamby Dairy Supply: US company, ships to the UK, email: orders@hambydairysupply.com, www.hambydairysupply.com

Shearwell (ear tags), **tel: 01643 841611,** email: sales@shearwell.co.uk, www.shearwell.co.uk

Dalton Tags (ear tags and pasterns), tel: 01636 700990, email: sales@daltontags.co.uk, www.daltontags.co.uk

TANNERIES

Bradford Hide Company, www.bradford-hide.co.uk/

Devonia, Devon, tel: 01364 643 355, email: c.worth@devoniasheepskinsandtannery.co.uk, www.devoniaproducts.co.uk/

Organic Sheepskins. The only organic tannery in England (Dorset), tel: 01935 891204, email: mark@nevillefarm.co.uk, www.organicsheepskins.co.uk

Institute for Creative Leather Technologies. Tans and processes a wide range of hides and skins in small batches., www.northampton.ac.uk/info/200174/british-school-of-leather-technology

Skyeskyns. Clive and Jessica Hartwell, Isle of Skye, tel: 01470 592237, email: office@skyeskyns.co.uk, www.skyeskyns.co.uk/

Welsh Organic Tannery. The only organic tannery in Wales., tel: 07966 470421, email: info@welshorganictannery.co.uk, www.welshorganictannery.co.uk/

GOAT COURSES

Humble by Nature, tel: 01600 714595, email: info@humblebynature.com, www.humblebynature.com

Just Kidding, tel: 07875 331434, email: info@cotswoldkidmeat.com, cotswoldkidmeat.com/ourcourses/

Goat Meat (Cockerham Boers), tel: 07962812528, email: info@goat-meat.co.uk, www.goat-meat.co.uk/courses.htm

Blackwater Alpacas (Pygmy goat courses), email: blackwateralps@aol.com, www.blackwateralpacas.co.uk

Buttercups, tel: 01622 746420, email: enquiries@buttercups.org.uk, www.buttercups.org.uk/

Happy Valley, www.happyvalleywales.co.uk

Thrift Farm Holdings, tel: 07889 640199, email: sales@thriftfarmholdings.co.uk, www.thriftfarmholdings.co.uk/goat-training-courses/

Devon Valley Anglo Nubian Goats, www.facebook.com/devonvalleyanglonubiangoats

Penborn Goat Farm, tel: 01288 381569, email: penborngoats@btinternet.com, https://www.penborngoats.com/courses.htm

The Blue Cottage (Keeping dairy goats), tel: 01286 882 208, email: thebluecottagesmallholding@gmail.com, https://www.thebluecottagesmallholding.co.uk/dairy-goat-keeping-course

BUTCHERY COURSES

Perrys Field to Fork, tel: 01785 851911, https://perrysfieldtofork.co.uk/product/goat-butchery-course-copy/

CHEESE AND DAIRY PRODUCE COURSES

Fielding Cottage, tel: **01603 880685, email:** sales@fieldingcottage.co.uk, https://www.fieldingcottage.co.uk/cheese/cheese-making-courses/

Gartur Stitch Farm, tel: 07807 339413, email: hello@garturstitchfarm.com, https://alifeinthemaking.co.uk

Specialist Cheesemakers Association, tel: 020 7253 2114, email: info@specialistcheesemakers.co.uk, www.specialistcheesemakers.co.uk/cheese-making-courses.aspx

SOAP-MAKING COURSES

Soap School, tel: 01484 310014, email: sarah@soapschool.com, https://soapschool.com/

BOOKS

Belanger, Jerry and Thomson Bredesen, Sara, *Storey's Guide to Raising Dairy Goats* (Storey, 2011)

Biss, Kathy, *Practical Cheesemaking* (Crowood, 2005)

Harwood, David, *The Veterinary Guide to Goat Health and Welfare* (Crowood, 2019)

Hetherington, Lois, *All About Goats* (Farming Press, 2002)

Mackenzie, David revised and edited by Ruth Goodwin, *Goat Husbandry* (Faber and Faber 1993)

Ross, Patricia, *Goats, A Guide to Management* (Crowood, 1989)

Sayer, Maggie, *Storey's Guide to Raising Meat Goats* (Storey, 2007)

Thear, Katie, *Starting with Goats* (Broad Leys, 2006)

Thear, Katie, *Cheesemaking and dairying* (Broad Leys, 2003)

Whetlor, James, *Goat Cooking and Eating* (Quadrille 2018)

ACKNOWLEDGEMENTS

Writing this book has been a real pleasure, giving me an excuse for contacting people from all over the world. So many people have been generous in giving of their time and sharing their caprine knowledge, experience and photos. Particular thanks go to my husband Andrew Hubbard, and Liz Shankland without whom there would be no book. To Beaford Arts for allowing me to use the stunning photographs taken by my favourite photographer James Ravilious; it's an honour to have his work grace these pages. Thanks to Gert van den Bosch for his many wonderful images and to all of you listed below; the time, photos and advice you gave so freely are much appreciated.

Emma Allum, Welsh Organic Tannery
Neoclis Antoniades, www.antoniadesfarm.com
Erika Bangerter
Kathryn Burrell and Mark Wallace, Beaford Arts
Charles Boundy, Food Standards Agency
Joe Coburn, coburn.com
Elisabeth Dancey
Martina Federer
Gartur Stitch Farm
James Holland and Jenny Venning, Wrixhill
 Dairy, http://www.goatsclottedcream.co.uk/
Chris Just BVSc MRCVS, Veterinary Surgeon
Clare Nichols, Milking Goat Association
Amy Powdrill, Ethical Dairy Company
Jane Ross
Jo Seymour Tavernor, Appletree Herd of Pedigree
 English Goats

Volac International Ltd
Mel Wilson
Avril Wooster

IMAGE CREDITS

Adam Short, Temple Farm, pages 125 (bottom), 209 (second down); Alice Griffiths & Surrey Docks Farm (page 53 (top right); Amy Powdrill, page 134 (top); Andrew O'Shea, pages 56, 114, 154; Anja Arola and Kelley Hines, page 207 (sixth down); Annina Staub, page 204 (third down); Ashley Kennedy, page 207 (fifth down); Barnacre Alpacas, page 37 (top), 202 (top); Becci Helm, page 38 (bottom right); Brian Payne, page 211 (top); Broughgammon Farm, page 192 (top left); Caleb Byerly, page 198 (top left); Carolyn McAllister, pages 6, 60, 74 (right), 94, 101 (bottom), 102 (left), 161 (top and bottom), 176 (top left); Caryl Bohn, page 36 (top), 78; Chasity Riggen, page 208 (third down); Cheryl Cobern Browne, page 209 (third down); Chyril Walker, page 209 (top); Christine McBrearty-Hulse, North American Cashmere Goats Association, pages 193 (bottom left), 194 (top left), 201 (third down), 204 (fifth down); Consorzio Turistico Valchiavenna (www. valchiavenna.com), pages 122, 191 (left); Dalton Tags, page 19 (top, bottom left and bottom right); Danielle Drew, pages 33, 34 (bottom right), 81 (middle); David Meaden-Kendrick, page 205 (second down); Deb Tamblyn, page 76; Debbie

TOP: **Millhams, Dolton, September 1976. Documentary photograph by James Ravilious for the Beaford Archive © Beaford Arts**

Francis, Cwmstwrdy Fibre Farm, pages 52 (top), 67 (top), 75 (top), 192 (top right and bottom right), 193 (top left, top right and bottom right), 194 (top right); Debs Scothern, page 75 (bottom); Denis Brinicombe Group, page 89 (bottom left); Donna McDaniel, page 208 (bottom); Dr Floro De Nardo, pages 202 (fifth down), 208 (sixth down), 210 (fourth down); Dr Katy Whitby-Last, page 129 (left); Dunlop Dairy, pages 127 (left), 137 (left and right), 184 (middle); Emily Julka, page 191 (right); Emma Curtis, page 72 (bottom); English Goat Breeder's Association, pages 28 (top), 29 (top right), 48 (top), 66 (third down), 92, 128 (bottom middle), 205 (sixth down); Farms For City Children, page 53 (bottom); Fiona Gerardin, pages 115, 119 (bottom left), 121, 123 (left); Gallagher, page 39 (top and bottom); Gert van den Bosch, pages 28 (bottom), 34 (top right), 42, 49 (bottom), 50, 69 (bottom), 88 (bottom), 145 (top), 147, 158–160 (all), 162 (bottom), 163 (top right), 165 (bottom left), 166, 176 (bottom right); Goat Nutrition Ltd, pages 89 (top left), 128 (top left and top right), 135; Heidi Fluharty, page 144; Helen Davies, Shearwell Data, pages 67 (middle), 209 (bottom); Homestead Farm Supplies, page 156 (bottom); IAE, pages 29 (bottom), 40, 68 (top), 85, 88 (top left, top right), 90 (right); Ian Foks, page 208 (top); James Ravilious, Beaford Archive, pages 7, 11, 17, 27, 43, 51, 71, 79, 93, 111 (left), 124, 143, 152, 179; Janet MacDonald, page 145 (bottom); Jennifer Venning, Wrixhill Dairy, pages 87 (top), 128 (bottom right), 176 (top right), 183 (bottom); Joanne Sugden, page 59; Joyce Greenslade, page 129 (right), 130 (bottom); Julie Waite, page 44 (top); Katie Venner, page 186; Kelai Hjort, Vita Geten Farm, Sweden, page 211 (second down); Kerbl, page 173; Kirsten Tardiff, Echolight Farm, page 201 (top); Klaus Rudloff, page 211 (fifth down); Klisse Foster, page 210 (sixth down); La Buvette, pages 34 (left), 47, 49 (all drinking options: top left, top right, bottom left, bottom right), 90 (left); Lakeland Farm and Ranch Direct, page 41; Lesley Brabyn, Salmon Creek Ranch, page 207 (fourth down); Levend Landgoed NOVA, page 209 (sixth down); Liz Shankland, pages 13, 48 (bottom), 80 (middle); Liz Turner, page 206 (fourth down); Luigi Guffanti, Formaggi 1876, page 210 (bottom); Lynbreck Croft, page 82; Malan van Heerden, pages 113 (bottom), 207 (second down); Martina Federer, page 10; Matt Austin, pages 178, 181, 184 (top); Megan Riggins, page 169 (bottom); Mel Wilson, page 205 (fifth down); Michael Trotter, pages 72 (top), 202 (third down); Nan and Phil Hassey (www.goatorama.com), pages 180, 198 (top right and bottom right), 199; Nick Parr, pages 63 (right), 65 (bottom left), 204 (top); Philippe Pierangeli, page 205 (top); Premier 1 Supplies, page 125 (top); Prof. Gary F. Bath, FAMACHA System Coordinator, page 106; Rachel Jones, page 128 (bottom left); Ribblesdale Cheese, page 184 (bottom); Richard Scrivener, page 203 (bottom); Rupert Kirby, pages 8, 70; Sally Prydderch, pages 69 (top), 80 (bottom); Salvo Liotta, pages 202 (fourth down), 208 (second down); Schweizerischer Ziegenzuchtverband (Swiss Goat Breeding Association), pages 200, 201 (bottom), 202 (second down), 203 (third down), 204 (sixth down), 206 (fifth down), 208 (fifth down), 209 (fifth down), 210 (fifth down), 211 (third and fourth down); Sledmere Farm Park, pages 2, 35 (left), 142; Smallholder Range, page 84 (top left, top right, bottom left, bottom right); Tereza Fairbairn, pages 112, 126, 127 (right), 130 (top), 131, 136, 189, 204 (second down); Totnes Rare Breeds Farm, page 52 (bottom); Valerie Wood, page 57; Vicki Ducote, page 63 (left); Welsh Organic Tannery, page 194 (bottom right), 196 and 197 (all); Wendy Gacem, page 202 (sixth down); Westgate Laboratories, page 105 (bottom); Wilna Boink, pages 68 (bottom), 205 (fourth down); Woozel Farm, pages 26, 67 (bottom).

Wikipedia/Wikimedia Commons:
Buhari Habibu. page 210 (seventh down); Conquistador, page 206 (bottom); Elena Tartaglione, pages 203 (top), 206 (top); Friedrich Böhringer, page 206 (third down); Heather Lion, page 208 (seventh down); Indusgf, pages 202 (seventh down), 204 (bottom); Joseph Valet, page 203 (fourth down); Klaaschwotzer, page 205 (seventh down); Marianne Madden, page 210 (top); Marsmux, page 202 (eighth down); Menesteo, page 211 (seventh down); Ómar Runólfsson, page 206 (seventh down); Patafisik, page 209 (fourth down), 211 (sixth down); Roland Darré, page 210 (third down); Sami Sieranoja, page 205 (bottom); Saruman, page 210 (second down); USAID, Pakistan, page 208 (fourth down).

Other images and diagrams by Debbie Kingsley.

INDEX